Messages Of Praise
From Darkness

A truly inspiring story! The heartfelt message instils a valuable lesson about not judging the differences in others.

Even through the many difficulties which are encountered along the way, this gripping story highlights the need to be honest and true to one's self.

This is an affirming example which shows that it is possible to overcome adversity and celebrate our differences.

A must read for those who symbolise the letters in which PFLAG represent.

Shelley Argent OAM, National Spokesperson, Parents and Friends of Lesbians And Gays (PFLAG) Australia

This is a raw, courageous and uplifting story that you won't want to put down. Although beyond that, most people, regardless of their own sexual orientation, will identify a little of themselves or someone who they know throughout aspects of this journey.

Similarly, it parallels with the path that many young people are on, even in this day and age, as they work out who they are and what is truly important to them.

This book reiterates the need for our communities, our societies and for the entire world to accept our differences, on our own terms, or risk being surpassed.

We are also reminded along the way that we must be genuine with ourselves and live the life we want, without fear of judgement, before it's too late.

The powerful message that's delivered is simple: The Sky(e) isn't the limit, it's only the beginning!

Roger A. Roberts-Loose, The Global Thinkx2 Initiative

Just like the truth, our own individual LGBTI (Lesbian, Gay,

Bisexual, Trans, Intersex) stories will set us free. One of the biggest challenges we face is being able to share our stories in our own words, in our own way and in our own time.

Skye's journey is an intensely personal narrative with an important reminder of the challenges so many have faced, and continue to face, on the road to simply being themselves.

This captivating journey will resonate with many different people, for many different reasons.

Daniel Witthaus, Author of *Beyond Priscilla, Beyond That's So Gay* & Founder of the National Institute for Challenging Homophobia Education (NICHE)

It's real. It's honest. It's Skye High's own perilous adventure to discovering and becoming herself. It hasn't been an easy road, but Skye's tale is both compelling and hopeful. We need more empowering stories like this.

Matt Akersten, Australian National Editor, SameSame.com.au

From Darkness to Diva

From Darkness
to Diva

Skye High

BOOKS

Winchester, UK
Washington, USA

First published by O-Books, 2015
O-Books is an imprint of John Hunt Publishing Ltd., Laurel House, Station Approach,
Alresford, Hants, SO24 9JH, UK
office1@jhpbooks.net
www.johnhuntpublishing.com

For distributor details and how to order please visit the 'Ordering' section on our website.

Text copyright: Skye High 2014

ISBN: 978 1 78535 015 3
Library of Congress Control Number: 2015931476

A CIP catalogue record for this book is available from the British Library.

Design: Stuart Davies
Cover art: Lauryn Gardini

Printed and bound in the USA by Edwards Brothers Malloy

We operate a distinctive and ethical publishing philosophy in all
areas of our business, from our global network of authors to
production and worldwide distribution.

CONTENTS

'In loving memory of Oskar'

'This book is not only dedicated to those who now celebrate their freedom by surviving a life of adversity. It is also dedicated to those who are yet to discover their own courageous voice, which will one day set them free to celebrate their own survival'

Prologue

Have you ever experienced a moment when you question why your life has taken you on the course it has? I believe many of us have. It's worth taking the time to reflect on circumstances and events which have brought us to where we are in life today, right up to this very minute.

Regardless if your path has been harsh, mediocre or abundantly full of riches and pleasure, I believe most of us think our lives could still be more enriched in some way, if only we'd had the experiences we've gained at this very moment to guide us when we were younger. Yet, as I've become older, I believe that very notion of hindsight is nothing more than a 'happy escape from reality', which allows us to feel more secure about the past and the present.

I understand that on the surface, my story may appear no different to other peoples. Nevertheless, this is a story that can only be described as an empowering adventure which may allow you to break free from your own life and experience that of another. This is my own personal story, which highlights the good, the bad and the completely unexpected.

I will take you on a journey, where you'll soon discover how one person's life can be so dramatically different to another, but perhaps parallel in so many similar ways. Allow yourself to indulge in the dreams, hopes and realities of a boy as he conquers adversity, to one day become more of a man than he thought he *could* be and more of a 'woman' he ever thought he *would* be.

Over the years, I've become a firm believer that life is a very precious and a very powerful creation. I know this from firsthand experience, due to certain circumstances within my own life. Having said that though, not all of those experiences am I proud to admit. However with life experience comes a level of personal development and the ability to actually achieve the goals we set for ourselves. Whilst we may sometimes need to redefine those goals from time to time, they are still a driving force behind obtaining what we want to achieve. I believe this type of individual maturation offers solace from the demons that once troubled us, so we are able to become the people we were born to be.

I guess that then begs the question, *'how do we know who we were born to be?'* Even though that's a question which has been asked since the beginning of time, to be honest, I can't offer a definitive answer. The only response I can provide, through my own experience, is once we undergo our own intimate journey of self-discovery, do we then have the potential to find that answer. Amongst the lessons learned during that time of self-examination, we hope that our own personal beliefs, along with guidance from the universe, will at least steer us in the right direction to become that very person.

I consider the universe as we know it, offers much more than what our physical being allows us to concede. Having said that, I'm not actually sure how the universe was created either, but I'm open minded enough to accept all theories and all possibilities. There are many plausible speculations, even including those stories of Adam and Eve and the Big Bang theory. As this is not a story of how humanity was created, nor do I want to preach my own beliefs, it is worth taking a minute to be thankful for all of the beauty that life has to offer, regardless of what you believe your life purpose is or however you believe the universe was formed.

Personally, I believe that there is definitely a higher power of some kind which conceived and continually maintains this stunning, wondrous, ever-changing evolution called life. I also believe with the creation of life, each of us was born with an individual and unique spirit. Although, there's one thing I've learned about the possession of our precious spirit. That is, when we surrender ourselves to those who could abuse or mistreat us in anyway, we surrender that spirit, along with our own identity which therefore, gives greater power to those who may want to hurt us.

More often than not, when we allow a person to take control of our spirit for the purpose of their own self-serving or malicious advantage, our life becomes nothing more than a mere existence, barely worth living, let alone being able to share it with anyone else. However, on the other side of that theory, if we charge ourselves with the belief that we are validated in life, we are then in control of our own future. It is only when we truly accept ourselves and others in life for their differences, can we then understand and open our own minds to become more enriched by the diversity which is shared in so many different varieties of humankind.

Many years ago a very dear and wise friend once shared a poem with me. It states that people come in to our lives for *a reason, a season or a lifetime*. When I heard her speak the words of that poem I thought they were beautiful, but it wasn't until I essentially sat down one day and replayed those very words over and over in my mind, that they revealed their true meaning. I discovered that it was more than a lovely ensemble of words. I considered this poem to be a mantra for living and for the acceptance of allowing people to share my life for whichever time frame that's relevant.

Without people coming in to our lives we never evolve, we just remain stagnant. Surely there is more to life than standing still whilst letting it pass you by. What's even worse, is living a life pretending to be someone, or something that you believe others want you to be.

Everyone has a unique story to tell and I believe it's important for us all to make the time to not only listen to their experiences, but also share our own insights in return. Sometimes when we bare our souls and share our life stories and our experiences with other people, we have the ability to reach out in ways we may not realize or even believe to be possible. At times, I don't think we fully understand the strong influence we can have when we communicate with other people.

I've discovered that these occurrences usually mean that we have the ability to not only help ourselves to understand our journey's a little more, but in return, also help others to understand the meaning behind their own life and indeed, their own destiny. To genuinely learn through another person's shared wisdom can be a very powerful and uplifting experience. We can greatly benefit from each other's narratives and knowledge, regardless if we are together for a reason, a season or a lifetime.

With those shared personal stories and our own valued experiences we all, sometimes unknowingly, have a unique quality to impress vast and contrasting individual footprints onto this world. You may not relate to me as a drag queen, or even a gay man for that matter. However if you take away that small portion of my life, you'll soon discover that I'm just like someone who's already a part of your life, that you're close to.

First and foremost, I am someone's son, someone's best friend, someone's partner or someone who you may perhaps meet on the street one day, extending his hand to you when you need it the most, without judgment or hatred. I am someone who wants to make a positive difference in this world, to enrich the lives of other people. Every other aspect of my personality and sexuality is just an added bonus to make up the generous and loving person I am.

Without trying to sound cliché, remember, life really is all about the journey, not the destination. I think we all have a responsibility to play a part in making a vital difference along our way, not only for ourselves, but for the integrity of humanity. It's important that we all try to be positive toward our differences, respect the views of others, embrace true love, but most of all, learn how to celebrate own individual diversity and indeed, the diversity of others.

Every single person on this earth is living out their own personal journey. Some people have a happy story to tell, some have an unpleasant one and some can't even share their story because they are barely existing through a life of darkness and misery, being too afraid to be the people they were born to be. I believe that everyone has the right to live a life of freedom and acceptance, without fear of persecution, especially those who are ostracized because of their sexual orientation or diversity. Nobody has the right to treat others poorly, or make them feel as though they're any less of a person, simply because of their own beliefs, or because of a perceived difference.

For me, I believe the essence of being human means that sometime in our lives we're all going to be touched by sadness, enriched by courage and affected by adversity. But even more significantly, we also have the right to celebrate a life enhanced by happiness. This should be a sense of happiness which can bring peace and security to a life, that may otherwise seem hopeless or despairing. I think it's also important to remember that every experience we live through should be kept close to us, but not close enough to hold us back from moving forward and exploring the uncharted territory that life has to offer.

When all is said and done, in life, one of the greatest 'pat our own selves on the back' moment should be when we realize that we still have the capability of laughing at ourselves, even through those bad times. Throughout my experiences, I've learned that only when we can openly laugh at ourselves, can we then genuinely love ourselves, even more. It can be too easy to gratuitously harbor an unwarranted grudge against the entire world because of our dire circumstances, or worse, because of the influence of negative people. It is that type of 'chip on the shoulder' approach to living, which only breeds more contempt, for a life that we should otherwise be living to the fullest.

Life really is the one opportunity where you get to act in the moment and *that* moment is right now. I truly believe the universe will provide all that we need. Sometimes we just have to find the courage and conviction from within, to ask for whatever it is we seek. The power of being impeccable with our words can make even those unlikely dreams, become a reality.

Voices, Which Echo From the Past

Let me take you back to a former image of myself. This is where you'll soon gain a firsthand and up-front insight in to my environment, my experiences and the life changing factors, which have eventually led me to where I am today.

Being the youngest of three children, I was born on January 30th 1971. Whilst growing up, for as far back as I can remember, I was an overweight, short stature, slightly effeminate boy. I grew up in the outer south-eastern suburbs of Melbourne, Australia. I consider my upbringing was middle class, as I never seemed to go without anything and I was always very thankful to receive those things I did.

I believe that my siblings and I were treated fairly and equally. At no time throughout my youth was there an under-lying animosity about one child being loved or favored more than the other. More importantly, I wasn't the product of being in an abusive, dangerous or neglectful home environment. Our home environment was always loving and caring. My parents always did the best they could to protect us and provide every-thing we needed. Even though, like most kids, I'd always push the boundaries and want more, whether that was attention, money or the independence which I craved from a very early age.

Yet, it was rare that my parents ever gave in to my demands, no matter how many different ways I'd ask the same question. Whilst no child likes to hear the word 'no', my parents would also justify why they wouldn't meet my demands. I simply had no other option but to accept their reasoning, without further questioning. Although, that didn't stop me from throwing the occasional tantrum in the hope they'd change their minds.

My father was a self-employed man who volunteered on many various local committees. He was an old fashioned thinker who worked hard to provide for the household. He was also well known and commended for the voluntary work he did within our community. I sometimes think he worked even harder to represent the 'picture perfect' image of our family to those who were on the outside looking in.

Sadly, my father rarely ever spoke of his own upbringing or family. It appeared his own childhood and teenage years were vastly different to mine. Although, with the short snippets of his life that he reluctantly shared, I think some aspects of his life were comparable to that of mine, but in many different ways. To this day his early life remains sketchy and a bit of a mystery, which unfortunately, is how it will remain for the rest of my life.

As for my mother, she was a stay-at-home mom who raised my brother, sister and I. She was a wonderful mother, who was very nurturing and tender. Unlike my dad, she was a progressive thinker. She was also a very talented and gifted artist. She could reproduce any image that was in her mind, either on paper or in a more three dimensional way. Our family home was blanketed with the most beautiful artwork which our mom had proudly created.

As I grew older, I started to wonder why our mom seemed to stay in a marriage that didn't seem to provide her with what she needed or deserved. Although, she seemed content enough with the fact that she was living the life she made for herself. However like me, she had a free spirited nature that could have taken her on any path she desired. Regardless of her circumstances or reasoning, I feel extremely honored that she is the lady I could call my mother.

As for my siblings and I, we were very different from one another whilst growing up. By the time I was old enough to appreciate having a close family unit, my brother, who was twelve years my senior, was looking for his own independence and ready to make a name for himself, which he did later in his life. To date, he is the only sibling to have been married and raise a beautiful daughter, who could carry on our family name later in life should she choose to.

From about the age of three years old, I remember my brother was an outgoing, good looking boy who enjoyed time with friends, going to the beach and living his life. I also remember him taking on a father figure when our dad was busy with work or attending to social commitments. To which I also remained grateful, because of that, he ensured I never missed out on having a male role model to look up to.

My brother was also more grounded than me. He would often think his actions through more carefully before making any decisions, or taking a 'leap of faith'. However, he and I share many similar traits. I still continue to find out just how similar we are, as my life progresses. I always admired him for being the person he was throughout my childhood. I still hold that same admiration for him to this very day.

As for my sister, who is six years my senior, she was also slightly different to me. Growing up I thought she appeared somewhat distant and disconnected toward me. I didn't believe she inherited that 'free spirit' gene from our mother. Many times I would often wonder why she and I never seem to connect on an emotional level. I certainly don't think it was because neither of us tried to relate to one another. I just think that we were always moving in two different directions while growing up. Also given the age difference between her and me, she too was living her life when I had just started to explore my own life and who I was becoming.

My sister was a more introverted person with a soft nature.

She seemed content to live a quieter lifestyle and enjoy spending quality time with our mother. Independence didn't seem as important to her as what it had been for me. Whilst she had a small close circle of friends she would associate with on occasion, it was extremely rare for her to venture out on the social scene. She would rather enjoy her own company within the solitude and surrounds of our family home.

To be honest, I think it was difficult for her having to deal with a much younger brother. One who would crave the most attention and who would, at times, be awfully disrespectful towards her by using cutting words as a weapon to make her feel as though she was an outsider. A lot of water has gone under our bridge, however, I'm very proud to call her my sister. Our blood is, and always will be, thicker than the water under that very bridge.

And then there is me, the youngest member of the family. It's almost as though I need to break myself in to thirds, so people understand the different sides of who I was, to who I became, to who I am today.

For as far back as I can recall, I started this life as a vibrant, happy and outgoing young child. I often liked to please people and ensure they were happy and laughing. Whether that was from telling jokes or just to help them out around the house in some way. I guess I was a bit of an attention seeker. Still, seeking the happiness of others would far outweigh any personal gratification I received from my outrageous antics.

Even at that tender age of three years old when I was in awe of my brother's nurturing kinship, I knew I wanted my very own independence. I wanted the same freedom and concessions as he seemed to have. He didn't appear to answer to anyone. It appeared he could come and go as he pleased. To me, that was very appealing.

There was one difference between him and I though, that was, I could be quiet stubborn and somewhat argumentative at times.

I quickly realized that this was sometimes to my own detriment, especially the older I became. Perhaps I was more of a spoiled brat than I ever realized.

As a family, like most back in those years, we would spend every Christmas holiday away from our home. We would usually spend these holidays at Phillip Island, in the South East region of Victoria. This is a quieter, bay side retreat that is well known for its fishing, surfing and its tourist industries, such as the world famous penguin parade. Back in those days, the serenity of Phillip Island was appealing in a somewhat retrospective way.

We would stay in a caravan park within close proximity to the water, which I loved, because it provided a remoteness which I really enjoyed. There were also often many people from all over Australia holidaying there at the same time of the year, which made it easy for me to blend in and remain somewhat anonymous with the other holiday makers. I also basked in an overwhelming sense of freedom when we were spending time there. That was because I could change my personality to become anyone I wanted to be. My imagination was limitless.

Regardless of which personality I took on, no one there knew of my secret desire to want to break free and experience a different life. Sometimes, for me, the fantasy of being a part of another family was appealing. I wanted to see what the other kids lives were like. I needed to know if I was missing out on anything.

Don't get me wrong, I always felt blessed to have been born in to the family that I was. However my family life was rarely what it seemed to be like, especially the view from the outsiders who were looking in. Growing up with a father who was a public figure, my life could sometimes be more about the perception of a golden family, rather than the reality it actually was.

For the most part, we *were* a happy family, probably not that dissimilar to most. We used to play board games, take road trips to the country and spend our holidays away from home. There wasn't a special occasion that went by which wasn't celebrated either. Our birthdays and Christmas' were always a festive highlight of the year, where presents were in abundance.

More importantly, my parents provided us all with an ongoing feeling of love and protection. Although, I could never understand why there seemed to be an underlying current of discontentment in my life. That made me wonder why my family life seemed so different to others, especially those families that I watched on television programs, such as 'The Brady Bunch'.

If you're unfamiliar with that television program, do some research and you'll soon discover that whilst on the surface they appeared to be a happy family, the issues that you and I faced growing up would always be fixed within a thirty minute time slot, no matter how bad the trouble they found themselves in was. I have to admit though, I often look back now and wonder why I ever wanted my life to be as clean cut as the Brady family. I think it's because perhaps I saw them as the perfect perception of all the things which I thought were missing in my own family life. And I'm not just referring to our lack of housekeeper.

I should also point out that throughout my naive younger years, I did believe the Brady family was in fact, a real family. I often wonder if I'm the only crazy person who ever thought that too.

Whilst I did and still do admire the core family values of the fictional Brady family, I believe the reality of those days have long gone. To be honest, I doubt if those extreme fairytale values ever really existed in the first place. It was a way of life which seemed all too good to be true.

This led me to think, *'Why did my life seem so different?'* I could only assume that maybe because my family wasn't fictitious and my problems couldn't be solved within a thirty minute time slot. The idealistic perception of a happy ending, so to speak, always seemed so appealing though. Perhaps in many ways, the perception of my early childhood was really no different from most others kids, even those on television.

In any case, let me get back to the realities of growing up. Especially growing up with an uncertain difference which I thought no one knew about. If truth be told, I wasn't even sure if I knew what that was myself. Although, I guess I always suspected there was something fundamentally different about me, which alienated me from the other boys I admired.

The Brave Face of Fear

As I mentioned, my earliest memory is when I was about three years old. I recall we lived in a big white double story house with many windows. Each window had a beautiful view of bushland sprawling as far as the eye could see. I also recall how fostering that environment was. Each night my mom would sing lullabies as she tucked me in to bed, before I'd fall asleep and dream of the magical words which she had spoken.

On the acres of land that our house was built upon, we had a variety of farm animals including horses, sheep and chickens. That was in a suburb which could only be classified as the country back in those days. However, that is certainly a far stretch from what it is now, considering the urban sprawl that has taken over. Sadly, that beautiful country scenery has now been dominated by an expansive concrete jungle.

Even at that young age, I remember thinking that one day I was going to grow up to be just like my parents. They seemed to have it all. They had a warm family home, three beautiful children, a close circle of good friends and a perfectly happy marriage. Perhaps back in those days I really was living in the 'Brady' house. Although, I really couldn't compare it to anything else, because I didn't really know anything else. So for the time being, I was happy to accept that we were no different from other families.

We only lived in that picturesque home in the country for almost two years before we moved. That move took me to the house which I called my forever home. I use the term 'forever home' as it was a place which was full of continued happiness and fond memories of my early youth. It was a house I never wanted to leave. Of course, there were the usual Christmas and birthday celebrations, but there was also a warm sense of belonging. At that time, our family seemed more emotionally connected than ever before. Perhaps that was because we knew we were going to spend many years at that house without moving again.

The house we moved into was a modest 1970's brick veneer home, which had only been built a couple of years before we moved in. I had a big bedroom which was next to my parents' room, at the front of the house. There was also a large backyard with lush green grass and a newly built cubby house where I spent many days playing.

It was there, I really thought that life couldn't get any better. However, it never occurred to me that growing from a young boy in to an adolescent would only become more difficult the older I got. I was soon faced with so many new mixed emotions. Yet, I never understood why I was subjected to those unmanageable feelings. Those were vast and varied emotions, some, which were more agonizing than I had ever expected to feel.

In February 1976, shortly after celebrating my fifth birthday, I started primary school. I wasn't nervous to start school, in fact, I could barely contain my excitement for that first day to arrive. The thought of playing with other kids and making friends was something I thought would make me even happier than I had ever been. Unfortunately, it wasn't long before I realized that my school experience was going to be very different from what I had predicted.

In fact, those first few years at primary school were a tremendous struggle. I was isolated and alone. I didn't fit in with the other kids. I thought it was because I was overweight that they didn't want to be my friend. Because of that, my lunchtimes usually consisted of wandering aimlessly around the school grounds, on my own, watching the other kids playing and enjoying themselves. At that point, the idea of making any friends seemed like light years away.

As time went on, my mind became pestered with thoughtless questions that buzzed around my head over and over. I used to sit by myself and contemplate, *What was wrong with me? Was I hated because I was overweight? Why didn't the other boys want to play with me?* All I wanted, was to be so badly accepted by those other kids. The harder I tried, the less inclined they were to even acknowledge my existence. They would just giggle among themselves whenever they saw me coming. I was embarrassed and wanted to hide away from the entire world.

At one point, I fooled myself by thinking I related well with some of the girls throughout those early years. That was only because I would often barge in, uninvited, and play hopscotch and elastics with them. I secretly knew they never wanted me to play with them, but I continued to live in hope that they would befriend me. That wasn't the case though. Yet, I could still never understand why I didn't fit in with the other boys. They too would only stare and point at me as they ran off in their groups to play at lunch breaks.

I never knew what I had done to those boys to make me practically invisible to them. The only time that I had been noticed by them, was when I was the center of their ridicule. The more I was ignored by them, the more questions I had running through my head. Why didn't they pick me for their football teams? Was it because I was slightly more effeminate than them? I didn't want to be an outsider. I only wanted to play their games and join in with their fun. Yet, that never happened. I knew I needed to find answers to those elusive questions before they might include me in their fun and games.

As hard as I tried to think about what those answers were, the more I was left totally bewildered. Instead of being accepted by those kids, I found myself in a lonely place of solitude, whereby it was easier to have pretend friends. At least those pretend friends couldn't ignore me or make fun of me. At lunchtimes, my pretend friends and I would sequester ourselves away from everyone while we enjoyed playing our own made up games. At that time, self-delusion was better than the truth of reality.

As far as my younger academic school years were concerned, I was probably no different to many other children. My report card always highlighted that I was easily distracted and liked to talk too much about things that weren't a part of the school's curriculum. I thought that by being disruptive it would mean I'd be taken out of class, away from an environment which was filled with the other kids who made me feel so segregated. I would rather have been alone, as opposed to feeling alone with other kids surrounding me.

Nevertheless, I still managed to progress through my school years without having to repeat any of my year levels. I did actually like school. I enjoyed subjects such as art and drama. They allowed me to be creative and explore my immeasurable imagination. I also liked to learn of different cultures and countries which I never thought I'd be able to go to. I would often day dream about traveling to many other countries, as they seemed to be a mystical world, which was far away from my very own.

Several years later, when I was about nine years old, I was still struggling to find the acceptance I was craving. More than ever, I still so desperately wanted to be playing with those other kids. It was at that time, I thought by offering my lunch, pocket money or other material items it would mean they would like me. Although, I didn't realize those kids were happy to take my things, but still offer nothing to me in return.

I became so needy and desperate to be liked by anyone. I was unaware that I had only been used for whatever it was I was giving away. It didn't take long before I became even more disillusioned with my own choices. It would be shortly after that, I also noticed my trust in people had diminished to a critical point. It seemed as though there was not one person who I could confide in or talk to. I thought everyone was just going to take advantage of me. The realization that those kids were simply abusing my good nature for their own gain, had begun to quickly sink in.

Those same questions from my younger years kept circulating through my mind, much more than ever before. I continued to blame myself for the selfish behavior of those other kids. I wanted to know where I had gone wrong with simply trying to find a friend. I couldn't help but keep asking myself, 'Was I destined to be friendless forever?'

I vividly recall the day that I stopped giving away my toys, posters and pocket money to those kids. Those were the same kids which I still so badly wanted to be friends with, even after they continuously bullied and belittled me. Before I knew it, all of my toys had gone. All of the presents that I had received from Christmas' and my birthdays were all gone. I was left with nothing except the empty feeling of sadness and rejection. I had nothing more to give, either mentally or materially. I was alone, frightened and extremely unhappy.

Unfortunately for me, as I was no longer providing them with material items, that gave them an *actual* reason to really dislike me. For them, that was their opportunity to be crueler than ever before. When I finally found the courage to stop handing over any more of my worldly possessions, those kids teased and tormented me every day, until I broke down and again, only to give in to their demands. I then found myself giving them whatever items I could find around my house to stop them from being hateful toward me. Of course, they never did stop being mean though. They just wanted more and more until I once again had nothing left to give.

For any person who has been the victim of playground

bullying, for whatever reason, you can genuinely understand how lonely and frightening it is to go to school every single day. I lived in hope that at least one of those kids would be away from school on any given day. I didn't want to confront another beating or become the victim of yet another degrading attack. I endured those bullying attacks hour after hour, day after day. I never knew if those vile tirades were ever going to come to an end.

I prayed for those kids to go away and leave me alone. However, I knew the reality was that they would continue to be waiting for me around the playground and on the streets after school hours. Although I only live a two minute walk from my school, there was no pardon from the barrage of daily abuse. It was almost as though those kids lived for their daily ten minutes of glory, just to make my life hell on earth.

One terrifying beating after school became the same as the next. No matter how many different routes I had tried to get home, there was never a safe passage from the school grounds to my house. I was isolated by fear and humiliated by disgrace. I became increasingly ashamed of myself. I had no idea why that was happening to me. I knew I never deserved, or asked for their mistreatment. However, I allowed it to happen. All I wanted was refuge.

I no longer had any control of my feelings. I literally surrendered my soul to those very kids. All I really wanted was to be included in their fun games. Sadly, because no one wanted to like me, I became the abandoned boy who only provided senseless entertainment, for simply wanting to find a friend. My outgoing personality further diminished to a point that I didn't know who I was any more. Every day I struggled through an extreme self-loathing cloud of confusion. I hated the way I was treated, but I hated myself even more.

Even as I tried to perform everyday menial tasks, such as taking a shower, I became panic stricken. I had become nothing more than a human shell, which used to house a somewhat smart and funny child. The person I once was, was now becoming a very distant memory. My new best friends quickly became fear, humiliation and resentment.

My once spontaneous spirit was slowly dying. I thought it was only going to be a matter of time before my physical body died with it. No longer did I live in a world of color. I became accustomed to a monochromatic way of life. I would go to bed every night and cry until my tears would run dry, night after night.

The bright future I once thought I was going to have, was quickly becoming desolate. I couldn't even make plans for the following day, let alone see any of my childhood dreams become a reality. Even at that young age, I literally struggled to find the will to survive. The days became longer as I stumbled to find the answers I needed to change that gruesome situation. The nights then became shorter due to the crippling emotional anxiety which kept me awake night after night.

All that mattered was finding a way to cover up the hurt, sadness and anxiety which I had been made to feel by those people who had only wanted to destroy me. My only instinct for survival throughout those horrendous bullying attacks, was to pretend that my life was actually good. I realized I must lie to everyone around me. I had to put on a brave face, whilst I continued living in fear. That in itself was much easier for me to do, rather than letting anyone else know how I was actually feeling.

I became so consumed by the sadness, guilt and embarrassment which had completely taken over every aspect of who I was. Because of that, I hadn't been able to bring myself to share the story of my pain or talk to anyone about what was happening to me. I simply couldn't find the words to express how I felt. I would emotionally shut down at the very thought of opening up and sharing any part of what was taking place. The thought of letting others know of my anguish had become just as devastating as the actual events I was living. It seemed so much easier to not say anything, rather than convey to anyone how I felt. At that time, I didn't know who I could trust to reassure me that I deserved better than what was happening to me.

I also certainly didn't want to be judged by my parents or other people in authority. Especially if they were only going to misunderstand my grief as 'kids just being kids'. Careless statements such as that were a prevalent way of dealing with those types of situations back then. Therefore, I could see no value in disclosure, nor could I see any resolution in sight. My life remained suspended in limbo, within the depths of despair and darkness.

Over time, I began to think that maybe the kids at school were right about me. Maybe *'that fat kid'* did deserve to be all alone. Throughout my entire primary school years I was more overweight than most. You know the type, the heavier set boy who would always be in the center of the yearly class photographs.

Day after day, there wasn't a lunch break that went by when I wouldn't hear snide comments passed around the school grounds from the other kids. Comments which implied I was going to eat out the entire contents of the school canteen for lunch had become popular. The hostility of their words were extremely hurtful to hear.

I always wondered if I was ridiculed and beaten up because the only difference between me and the other kids was my weight. Then I began to think that maybe the other kids saw something in me that I really hadn't given much thought to at that point, but seemed so much more obvious to them.

I believe it's challenging for most kids growing into their identity, regardless of their sexual orientation. After the bullying attacks started, finding my own identity was particularly difficult because of the hatred I became accustomed to. I was not properly armed to deal with the pressures of peer approval. I had been mentally conditioned by the other children from a young age to believe that my life would amount to nothing, just because I was overweight. They took advantage of that and as such, thought that bullying was an acceptable way of dealing with people who seemed different to them.

During those early years, there was no education on bullying, nor was there a network of people equipped to deal with such issues. There was certainly never a class at school which would teach or prepare me to deal with that extreme victimization. Due to my aggravated humiliation, it certainly wasn't a conversation that I could have ever have had with my parents either. Sadly, I was forced to hold my ruptured emotions inside me and pray they would go away.

If what I had gone through was only going to be brushed off as 'kids being kids' or 'part of the growing up phase' by people in authority, I thought that there would be no chance or hope to change my circumstances. It had actually become easier for me to say nothing and let the pain of what I was going through slowly eat away at me, with every second that went by. Besides, I never had the physical strength or 'know how' to defend myself against those constant bully attacks. Even if I did know how to defend myself, I doubt I could have ever confronted anyone in a physical manner, due to the fear of their retribution. I didn't want to add to the dread which had essentially impaired my life already. I barely even mustered enough inner strength to fight with my own conscience.

In times of distress, I continued to do what I had become accustomed doing. I found comfort and retreat in food. Although that didn't help with my weight issues, food had become my own private salvation. A deliverance, a feeling that I could rescue myself and put a stop to what happening to me, through over-eating.

With the slightest inkling of hope, I prayed the future would lead me to a turning point that would set me free from the internal devastation which had completely taken over me. Deep down, I still never felt as though I deserved the treatment I endured, nor did I ever feel as though I provoked those attacks. I just needed an intervention between how others perceived me and the reality of the person who I was, which was slowly slipping away. Those were perceptions which made the reality of my life two very different worlds.

It wasn't until halfway through grade five when I was about ten years old, the ringleader of the bullies, or 'ringleader' as he shall be known from this point forward, asked me if he could come to my house after school. At first I was very apprehensive, as I didn't know what his motives were. I couldn't understand why all of a sudden he wanted to befriend me. It was then, those insidious internal questions started again. I thought, *'What could he possibly want to take away from me now?'*

That boy was the instigator of the many beatings which I had endured before, during and after school. He was the catalyst who took great delight in encouraging the other kids to continue their tirade of abuse toward me. It was mainly because of him, that I was at the lowest point in my life. I knew he was to blame, but I was too weak and powerless to stop him.

In those brief moments when he insisted he wanted to come to my house, he spoke in a manner which had played on my vulnerability. His words were perfectly articulated which seemed sincere. For a moment, I thought that I had misjudged him for being an evil predator. As he looked in to my eyes, I could see a reflection of his own insecurity staring back at me. With that innocent look and his kind words, it wasn't long before he convinced me that he just wanted to come to my house and talk.

My heart skipped a beat. I saw that opportunity as a glimmer of hope. Finally, I thought that was going to be the perfect way to find a solution to end the relentless tormenting which I had tolerated for many years. I believed that was the golden moment that I had waited to experience. Without further hesitation, I hastily agreed to let him come to my house that very afternoon, once school had finished.

For the first time in a very long time, I thought the secret life of pain I was experiencing was about to come to an end, once and for all. I became excited by the notion that maybe I could at last become that outgoing little boy once again. I then started to again feel a human emotion surge through my body. That was uncompromising to the feeling of nothingness, which I had become so accustomed to.

I still remember hearing his rapid knock on the front door of my home. When I opened the door, there stood that young boy who had bullied and demoralized me, with a look of sheer innocence in his eyes. That gaze had almost been the same look as he had given me earlier that day when he asked about coming to my house. It was also a very stark contrast to the boy who had violently bullied me and knocked in to me around the school corridors, whilst threatening to beat me if I didn't give him my lunch money.

Of course I was still apprehensive about letting him inside my house. Although, my fears had slightly subsided by the fact that he appeared sincere about his motives. Once inside my house, we went straight into my bedroom. He then quickly closed the door behind him. At that time, I didn't mention there was no one else at home, in fear of what may have happened if he knew I had nobody around to protect me.

Trembling, as my heart was beating incredibly fast. With a flood of emotions, my mind was going in to overdrive. I didn't know what he was going to say, let alone what he was planning to do to me. Somehow, I remained hopeful that there was going to be a positive change in store. I wanted to believe that he needed redemption. I thought he was going to apologize for the years of heartache that he'd exposed me to. I hoped that was going to be the moment I could start rebuilding all that was taken away from my life.

With every second that passed, I remained quiet and frightened. At least I knew what his agenda was while we were on the school grounds. My mind continued with a whirlwind of ambiguous questions, such as, *'What does this boy really want from me?'* and *'Was this really going to be the reprieve I'd always wanted?'* Although I wanted to believe his intentions were good, I was still very dubious. I only hoped he wasn't going to physically attack me in my own home, especially in my bedroom. My bedroom was a private place, which I could always rely on to protect me from the harsh and unforgiving world outside.

With him standing directly in front of me, I sat pensively on the edge of my bed. There were still no words spoken. There was only the sound of my shallow breathing, which echoed throughout my entire bedroom. In between the short pauses I gasped for breath, we were surrounded by an awkward silence. All of a sudden, he told me to close my eyes and not open them until he told me to. I found that disconcerting and became more frightened. In a moment of severe panic, I scrambled to ask him to leave my house. Just as I had finished the sentence, he whispered, *'Sshhh it's alright, please close your eyes.'* Whilst startled, I could again see that same innocent look in his eyes as earlier. In a weak moment of uncertainty, with trepidation, I did as he asked.

Virtually paralyzed with fear, a few seconds had passed until he muttered the words, *'You can open your eyes now.'* I cautiously opened my eyes, not sure what I was expecting to see. To my amazement there was that boy, who made it his life's mission to make my life a misery, standing in front of me with his shorts down around his ankles. As he glared back at me, he continued touching and rubbing himself *all* over. He had a demonic look of lust in his eyes, which I had never seen from anyone before.

I gasped for whatever air I could consume. I couldn't believe what I was witnessing. I became more confused than ever.

Although, in the silence of that moment, I remember that I admired every inch of his delicious body. His body was certainly more toned and defined than mine.

I quietly sat in awe, as I continued to watch his performance. He wasn't shy about showing off his body, that was for sure. In fact, it appeared as though he felt no embarrassment at all. He could also see by the look in my eyes that I didn't want him to stop. I was curious to know what was going to happen next. In that moment, I quietly wondered, 'Why was he doing this and what was he expecting from me?'

At that time in life, I was extremely naive about sex education and indeed, why one boy would want to expose himself in front of another. That being said, I knew I liked what I was seeing. Although, I was trembling with fear on the inside as I didn't know what to expect, or what was going to occur. In that very second, after a few minutes of showing himself off, he pulled up his shorts as if nothing had happened. I was at a loss for words.

As I tried to work out what had just happened, with a contentious tone in his voice, he told me if I said anything to anyone, he would beat me worse than ever before. I sat on my bed, shaking, scared and shocked by his words. Before I could say anything, he turned and quickly walked out of my house. I was left with nothing, but confusion and a sense of disbelief for what had just taken place.

In the hours which followed that extraordinary event, I tried helplessly to understand what it all meant. Why had that boy confused me by sending mixed messages? One minute he despised me, then the next, he was showing intimacy. I began to wonder what I had done to encourage him. By all accounts, it was obvious he took great pleasure in doing what he did, but what did he hope to gain by doing that?

It was apparent that I was no closer to finding the resolution I sought. Before he arrived at my house on that day, I truly thought that I was finally going to find a friend. The excitement I felt about possibly putting those years of malice bullying behind me, was now further out of my reach. In a reflective mood, I couldn't help but think that perhaps that incident was only going to make matters worse from then on.

Through my own disarray of thoughts, I also wondered what was going through his mind. That was a kid who was the ringleader to a collective of bullies. He and his friends had gone out of their way to take my possessions, degrade me and literally make me afraid to leave my own home. The more I thought about it, the less it all made sense. I was still no closer to finding an explanation for what happened. There were only endless circles of teasing questions, which relentlessly tortured my mind.

Whilst I was alone later that night, I wondered why I lingered over the thought of what I saw, more so than what he actually did. I thought perhaps I should have found his actions more distressing. However, that wasn't an issue. There was no doubt in my mind that I was attracted to his firm physique. That attraction seemed perfectly natural, which didn't perturb me at all. If anything, it aroused feelings inside me I had never known before. It was only his actions as a bully which I didn't understand.

The next day at school, the ringleader and his friends approached me in the playground. Not knowing how to react, I tried to turn away and hide. Before I could take a step back, the ringleader slowly walked up to me and whispered in my ear. In a vicious tone he said, *'I'll tell everyone what you did yesterday if you don't start buying me presents every day.'* Hearing those words, I was taken aback and rocked to the core. Not only was I more ashamed of myself, I was more confused and scared of him than I had been before.

My mind was once again churning with an abundance of unanswered questions. Why was he blackmailing me? It wasn't *me* who did anything in my bedroom. However, I was too scared not to comply with what he wanted. I knew what he and his friends could be capable of doing to me. I then realized he had taken away the final glimmer of hope that the abuse and bullying would stop, now or at any time in the future.

As far as I could see, the situation I was in could only become worse. If I didn't start providing him the gifts he demanded as the pay off for my own safety, my life could have been changed forever. I had no option but to give in to his demands. The last thing I ever wanted was to continue living a life of fear, which I had never asked for in the first place.

On the days after school that my mom and I went to the shops, I had to ask her to buy me items such as key rings and tiny plastic figurines which I could hand over as payment to that boy. I claimed they were for a different 'friend's' birthdays. There was an endless list of items which that boy had demanded I hand over. Still, I had to betray those I loved, in order to secure my safety, or so I was led to believe.

On those days mom and I didn't go to the shops, I was forced to go through my bedroom, or in some cases, my brothers' bedroom, to find things that looked new enough to deliver to that boy so he didn't tell anyone about what *he* had done. It never seemed right that I was in that position. Although, I believed my hands were tied. I thought I had to do whatever was necessary to stop that boy from ruining the little creditability I had.

It never once occurred to me that I could have challenged him about what did actually happened in my bedroom on that day. I became too frightened of what others might say, but more importantly, what my parents would have said if they were to ever find out. What would my dad have said, given he was such a prominent figure within our community. I couldn't bring that type of dishonor to my family, then expect them to help me. I had nowhere to turn. That was a secret which I had to live with, alone.

I couldn't understand how the ringleader had deceitfully portrayed me as the one who instigated what had taken place in my bedroom. By now, I really believed that somehow I must have asked for it to happen, but had no recall of doing so. It didn't seem long before I had become brainwashed by that boy and his own devious thoughts. Once again, he had the power to make me think that I had manifested that entire scenario.

After that initial time the ringleader had come to my house, foolishly, there would be numerous other times after that I would let him come over also. It became standard that he played out that same scenario every time. The more he visited, the more I became curious about what motivated him to drop his pants in front of me, time and time again.

For a long time afterward, I questioned myself as to why I continued to allow him to blackmail me. At that time though, I still couldn't find the answers to all of my questions. However, I realized I allowed that situation to continue because I truly enjoyed sharing those secret moments with him. I never thought there was anything perverse or unnatural about what was taking place. I saw it as sharing a unique bond. Unfortunately, it was only the vile aftermath of his reaction that always followed, which I found immoral and didn't enjoy.

Each time he came to my house, the more he would slowly linger while touching himself. In some instances, he became very stimulated which seemed to arouse him even more. The more excited he became with me watching, the braver he became about showing himself off. Although, he wasn't the only one who had been aroused by his actions. It was evident that I too, shared the same physical arousal as him.

One thing was for sure, I had never asked him to stop coming to my house. In a curious way, I admired him. He was a good looking boy with sandy blond hair, puppy dog brown eyes and a cheeky little smile. He was also popular with almost everyone at school, especially the girls. Apart from the dark side of his personality, which I became accustomed to, he made me feel wanted in a way that was 'dysfunctionally normal'.

Excluding his physical attributes, I often wondered why I felt such a deep emotional attraction to him. I never knew the terminology for being same sex attracted, but knew I liked looking at other boys for some reason. I often admired the other boys at school without giving it a second thought. I was attracted to their masculine mannerisms and their firm bodies. Compared to the other boys, the ringleader made me feel different when I looked at him. My physical and emotional desire for him was much stronger and deeper.

He also knew I was a captive audience. There were many times where I wasn't able to hide my own arousal from him, which continued to secretly spur him on even more. He knew I didn't want him to stop doing what he did. The more I'd see of him, the more I'd want him. I did however become intrigued to know if he was only doing that with me, or if there were other boys he'd been showing himself off to also. That was a question which I will never know the answer to, even to this day.

At no time did the ringleader and I ever speak about why we did what we did. It was just an unspoken pleasure that we both obviously enjoyed. To this day, I wonder if he was fighting some kind of internal battle with his sexual orientation. I often wonder if he now thinks back to that age of innocence and has any regrets about the events which took place in my bedroom all of those years ago. My hope is that he's being true to himself now, whatever path in life he may be on.

Sadly, the ringleader's visits to my house came to a standstill several months after they'd started. I never had the courage to ask him what I wanted to know, which was, *'Why did he choose me to explore with?'* Although he didn't visit my house any more, I continued to fantasize about him and what could have been for many years after. In many ways, I couldn't find a comparison between him and any other boy for some time after. He seemed to be a complete package, which was a one and only.

Whilst his visits stopped, sadly, the blackmail continued for the duration of my primary school years. Yet, it wasn't as frequent as it had started out. Although, the tormenting and degradation relentlessly continued. It wasn't long before the entire student body joined in on what was a unified crusade of hate. The name calling became more prolific, but I was still unaware of the meanings behind *what* those kids were calling me anyway. I just knew by the tone in their voices that they weren't terms of endearment.

I continued to put on a brave face for everyone who surrounded me at school and at home. I became aware that I wasn't going to be able to erase the years of punishment which I received from my peers. It also became apparent that I had remained affected by missing out on all the simple pleasures that primary school years should have offered. There was never an invitation to other kid's birthday parties, nor was I able to celebrate my own special birthday day with friends, games and ice cream cake.

Instead, I had become the recluse who still played alone in the playground and ate lunch with my pretend friends. I would sit by myself and simply count down the minutes until the bell would ring before it was time to go back in to the classroom. I would then go home after school with a smile on my face and tell my parents the stories of what a wonderful day I'd had. That behavior became an art form which I had perfected over the years.

The solitude of that school year continued, with no change. I became excited as the final weeks of primary school years turned in to the final days. The constant years of bullying which I thought I could no longer take, were finally drawing to a close. I was ultimately ready to embark on what I thought was going to be a brand new chapter in my life, secondary school. I was relieved by the prospect of starting a new school, as I believed I was going to reinvent myself.

I believed that was my chance to become a new person. The end of that school year seemed like the perfect opportunity to try to let go of the angst, frustration and sadness which I had accumulated throughout my primary school years.

I thought I may get the break I needed, to finally be at peace with myself. I hoped there was going to be no more torment, which continued to entrap me. I wanted to become a popular boy at school, one who *could* make his dreams come true. At that time, I was ready to take on the challenges of becoming a teenager, in a brand new environment.

Bright Beginnings & Emotional Endings

There are times in our lives when we believe that our situations cannot become any worse. I believe we can also at times, become too emotionally invested in what other people think of us. This means that we continue to manifest potentially dangerous scenarios in our own minds to the point of completely withdrawing from life.

Throughout my earlier primary school years, that very sentiment was the toxic state of mind which I had allowed to take over my life. I was engulfed by a debilitating mindset which led me in to an emotionally disabled place of total darkness and absolute solitude.

Not only had the constant physical bullying been happening on a daily basis, I had also been called names that I didn't even know existed, let alone knew what they had meant. I became vulnerable, confused and felt very isolated. I was emotionally exhausted by having to keep up my double life. I was merely living behind a facade of happiness. I was actually completely withdrawn and devoid of any kind of happiness or sense of reality.

I perpetually found myself descending into a state of mind whereby it was easier to keep up that lonely fantasy of happiness. I still believed that was easier than taking the steps to confide in anyone. Let me tell you here and now, I was wrong. That was not the case at all. By withholding my thoughts and feelings, I had become nothing more than an emotional time bomb, just waiting to unexpectedly detonate.

During the summer vacation before my first year of high school I didn't socialize with anyone. Instead I stayed at home, read books and watched television in anticipation for the new year to begin. I constantly worried about what the coming years would be like as I entered that new phase of my life. I never wanted to go back to that emotionally empty place where I had been. I still knew I deserved better, but I found it very difficult to sincerely convince myself of that.

I had withdrawn so much because of the events from the previous years. I was totally oblivious to how physically, mentally and emotionally damaged I had actually become. I didn't realize just how exhausting the internal constant torment of leading a double life was. It had taken such a negative and explosive toll on my life, especially at such a young age. I tried as hard as I could to go through the day to day motions of being just like any other happy child. I believed the act which I portrayed was the very key to my own survival.

More often than not, I did fantasize about being one of the popular kids at high school. I truly believed I *was* going to be that new person which I always dreamed of being. I was excited to start high school, as it was going to be my brand new beginning. I hoped I was finally going to be accepted by my peers. I had to try and leave the baggage from the past where it belonged and focus on where I was heading. That alone, was much easier said, than done. However, I needed to find a way to make that happen, if I was ever going to start living the life I deserved.

Through weeks of restlessness, the first day of my high school experience had arrived. It was a day of both excitement and apprehension. When I arrived at the school grounds I was greeted by many new and unfamiliar faces. I felt somewhat at ease knowing that those kids knew nothing of my past. Nevertheless, I naturally remained on guard. As my anxiety levels started to rise, I knew I had to take in one very long and very deep breath and relax. I had to believe that day *was* in fact, going to be the start of a brand new life for me. That day had to be the beginning of the end. I had to find the courage to make that day, my day of triumph.

It wasn't until the very first class orientation that my courage was already being put to the test. I walked in to the home room and looked around, only to see some of the same faces of those kids that I'd shared my primary school years with, staring straight back at me. That brave new attitude which I instilled myself with had just been crushed within that very instant. My heart sank deep into my soul. I wasn't sure what to expect from that moment forward.

The lump in my throat which had instantly formed, felt like a large golf ball, that restricted me from breathing. There I was, being emotionally transported back to the same weak disposition as I was in not even six weeks earlier. I was again confronted by a classroom full of kids, who before long started whispering amongst themselves. At that time, I didn't know what to do. Of course, my natural instinct was run and hide, but I wanted to try to fight through that feeling and show that I wasn't afraid.

I stumbled my way through the classroom to find myself a chair. It wasn't long before even the kids who I *didn't* know began pointing and discreetly laughing at me. By the time I sat down, they too started calling me the same vile names as I'd heard in primary school. Even one of the boys who I didn't know, made the hurtful comment, *'Watch that faggot turn the chair upside down and sit on it.'* It was then, the entire class broke out in to a chorus of raucous laughter. That was the catalyst which encouraged the class to continue making derogatory comments and contemptible accusations about the person they thought I was.

On the verge of tears, I sat quietly with my head down in the hope that they would stop their rant. I tried as hard as I could to hold back those tears, which were rapidly filling my eyes. I didn't want to cry in front of those kids. That would have only spurred them on even more. It wasn't until a teacher entered the room that the outburst of abuse suddenly came to a halt. I thought that was my moment of rescue. Sadly, although the teacher heard most of the names which was flying around the room, he looked at me with a distasteful glance. He assumed I was the one who instigated that verbal assault which had just taken place. It became evident that he wasn't willing to help me put a stop to the childish antics which had left me distressed either.

As I slouched, sitting semi-upright in my chair, I felt nothing but defeated. My hopes of becoming a new person were soon put to rest. That same cloud of darkness which seemed to cover me throughout my primary school years had managed to follow me. There seemed to be no way of escaping who I was, or what the other kids thought I was. Even that teacher refused to make eye contact with me. When he did glance in my direction, his eyes were still filled with a look of revulsion. All I could do was wonder what the future would bring. As I closed myself off from what was happening in the classroom, the only thought which consumed my mind was, *'Would I even have any kind of future to look forward to?'*

That one single thought then started me thinking yet again. Was I going to be the victim for many more years to come? Could I find the inner strength and fight off these bullies? More importantly, how was I going to make any friends, given that it felt like the entire school was once again fighting against me?

On the verge of wanting to give in to the blissful temptation of ending my life, I barely tolerated the first class of that new school year. I was already emotionally destroyed and it wasn't even halfway through the first day. It was shortly after arriving to my second class which reaffirmed that things were definitely not going to be different from what they had been before.

It was there that I noticed the ringleader from my primary

school walk into the classroom. Our eyes met. We exchanged a slightly longer than usual glance before he proceeded to deliberately sit at the desk in front of mine. To be honest, I never expected my day to get worse than that first class, yet, I couldn't have been more wrong.

My entire body was convulsing. My heart started beating at a panicked and extreme rate. My breathing became constrained and shallow. I thought I was going to collapse. From that moment on, all that I could think about was how I was once again going to be subjected to the same kind of bullying, both in and out of school from that boy. He clearly had no remorse or guilt for what had taken place previously. At that time, it still didn't occur to me that I could have regained the power by standing up to him.

That was a time of very mixed emotions for me. I was afraid that he was going to continue his hate campaign against me. Although at the same time, a small part of me wanted him to come to my house again and relive those moments we once shared. My feelings for him were extremely conflicted. I didn't want to cause any trouble at this school. If anything, I wanted the very thing that I tried to avoid during primary school years, which was to be left alone.

I knew I outwardly hated him for what he had done to me, but I was still unknowingly and secretly very attracted to him. I could never understand how my feelings of hate and desire could be so different, but so similar. All I knew was, he still had a power over me unlike anyone else could have. I was consumed by the thoughts of how desperately I wanted him to come to my house again, but without him displaying those horrid feelings of anger which he had toward me after our time together. I knew those thoughts were damaging, but I needed to once again feel that same sense of gratification, which made my soul feel alive.

As the days went on, my circumstances only became worse. It wasn't long before some of the more senior boys at school joined the ringleader's bandwagon. The bullying and degradation had once again started, with more ferocity than I perhaps would have ever expected. They started tormenting me and calling me the same names I'd endured for many years prior.

At that school, those boys took their homophobic remarks to a new level. They would often be evocative and explicit about what they wanted me to do to them, regardless of who was listening around them. If truth be told, I doubted they would have actually gone through with the sexual acts they said they wanted me to do anyway. I knew it was just a trap to lure me to a secluded place so they could punish me for being who they thought I was. I believe they desperately needed to feel the rush of their own masculinity, to ensure they weren't similar to me, in any way.

There wasn't a day at school which went by that I didn't hear the same words echo through the corridors or school ground. Those same disparaging words of, *'Hey fat boy, come suck my dick, you fag!'* and *'Keep your backs to the wall, boys'* had been so deeply engrained in to mind. After hearing those words over and over, I came to the crude realization that I felt an unusual kind of immunity towards hearing them.

Besides, it wasn't so much the actual words that were used towards me which caused the most pain. It was more the pushing, elbowing and tripping me over in the school corridors that I resented. Some of the name calling I could cope with because I still didn't really understand the meanings of some of the terminology back then anyway. Their words were only meaningless sentences that of course, I'd heard before. Although at that time, I'd never heard them spoken with such an extreme hostility behind them.

It was because of the way they articulated those savage hateful words that I felt such an extreme sense of physical intimidation by those boys, who clearly wanted to see me dead. Every single day I would be the victim of their bullying and mind games. They appeared to have no fear or conscience for their actions. To them, they were self-created heroes who believed they needed to protect the school from anyone who appeared different to what *they* deemed, their own sense of normal.

It didn't take long for me to realize that no one from that school was going to protect me from whatever may happen. Day after day I spent hiding away from being exposed to another unwarranted onslaught. I was also a little surprised to learn that even some of the teachers turned a blind eye when I sought protection. That was evident from that teacher who offered me no solace from the initial attack in his classroom. As far as I concerned, there was no asylum in sight. I remained afraid and anxiously on edge.

There was one pivotal aspect of that time which I had found the most difficult to deal with. That was, going home every day and explaining to my parents how I got bruises on my body. Albeit, those bruises were in places that weren't always clearly visible to other people. Those kids were smart, well, so I thought anyway. I would lie to my parents daily about the untoward circumstances that I had been suffering at school, on any given day. I continued to make excuse after excuse about how I'd hurt myself by falling over or accidently walking in to a door.

I now realize that in the process of protecting myself, I was inadvertently protecting those boys who hated me. Back then though, I couldn't bear for anyone to know what was starting to happening to me again. I thought it was best to make up stories, no matter how unbelievable they sounded. I'm not sure if my parents actually believed those stories, but my tales seemed to go unquestioned. I learned that I was able to make even the most extreme excuse sound plausible. Anything was better than exposing the harsh reality of the truth.

Days, weeks and months went by. Each of them seemed to be longer than the last. It didn't take long before I felt as though I was back to those early years of primary school. I was detached, humiliated and frightened. I quickly become confused and broken down by those unpleasant daily events. I truly believed that my life, at that point, had amounted to absolutely nothing. I also actually believed there would be no future for me. Whilst dealing with unstoppable thoughts of ending my life which circulated through my mind, in the short term, I knew I would continue walking a dark, lonely road ahead. Yet, in the long term, I believed I would probably harm myself which could eventually lead to my untimely death anyway.

My already fragile spirit had again been crushed into many tiny pieces. My confidence had become non-existent. It seemed as though all of my childhood years had been stolen away from me. I permitted my life to be snatched away by people who wanted, or needed, to feel more superior than me. They wanted to gain a false sense of respect from those who admired them. Unfortunately, I was nothing more than a pawn in their game of life. Their shining trophy was ultimately going to be my applauded demise.

There were very few places around the school grounds for me to hide away from those frightening constant taunts. Even when I thought I had found the perfect place to hide, it was always exposed. I would often spend much of my lunch break in the library. Not because I liked reading *that* much, but because it was a place of solitude which had a sense of safety surrounding it. The library became my very own secret hideaway where I knew I wasn't going to be assaulted or humiliated.

In many ways, being in the library reminded me of our family vacations to Phillip Island. The similarities were such that I could get lost in the seemingly endless aisles amongst the books and become somewhat anonymous. I was able to read wonderful stories and dream of going to other places that were far away. I had found an escape from what was happening to me through the eyes of other people. It didn't matter that my escape wasn't real, as I was happy to take whatever short lived getaway I could. Because of that, I was able to forget what was waiting for me outside the library doors which I felt had protected me.

It was in the library during my lunch break one afternoon, that I met a boy who was also in the same year as me. He had come from a different primary school previously. I had only seen him around the school grounds a few times, as he was scurrying from one class to the next. On that day, during our lunch break, he was again by himself. He was sitting quietly eating his lunch with his head buried deep within a book. I was curious to know what his story was, as I had never seen him with any friends of his own. I wondered if he also used the library as a diversion from his own reality.

I walked over to the table that he was sitting at and asked him if I could sit with him. He was a slim, very quiet, softly spoken boy, who like me, didn't encourage too much eye contact. He looked up and I immediately noticed that same withdrawn look in his eyes, to that of my own. I was a little taken back by that look of sadness. I wondered if I had projected that same look of loss and despair in my eyes when people looked at me. I wondered if he'd experienced the same type of bullying that I was going through also.

He spoke with a composed subdued tone, although his voice was husky and deep. He told me that I could sit at the table with him and eat my lunch, but I wasn't to talk to him. His snappy reaction surprised me, although, I was just happy enough just to sit at a table with another person. After a few minutes of sitting in silence, my curiosity was getting the better of me. I found it near impossible to not say anything at all. I needed to know something about him, so I broke his one rule and found the courage to introduce myself.

I was unsure of the reaction I was going to receive, given he told me not to talk to him. I cowered away very quickly in case he was like those other boys. He looked up from his book and gave me a half smile then introduced himself too, but then swiftly buried his head back in the book he was reading. In that moment, I was happy to at least be acknowledged by someone else. Although, at that point I wasn't sure if he had heard the stories about me from the other kids. So, I retreated slightly.

I decided that whether he'd heard the rumors about me or not, I didn't care. At least he let me sit at the same table as him and had the decency to tell me his name. Strangely enough though, it was in that same moment I felt as though I had a bond with that boy. There was certainly nothing sexual about that connection. It was all based on a real life human feeling that perhaps, just maybe, that boy may have been looking for a friend too.

Our conversation during that lunch break was extremely stilted. Neither of us really had much to talk about. Although, I think we both gained enough of an insight through our unspoken words to want to know more about one another. I sensed he wanted to ask questions, but wasn't sure how to establish that relationship. Because of that, I felt as though something had, or was currently happening in his life which made him closed off to the world. I didn't want to ask any questions though. I was just happy in that moment, to actually be sitting at a table with another person who wasn't making me feel as though I owed him something. It was a small, but exceedingly powerful delight.

After our first meeting in the library, every day when the lunch bell rang I would go straight back there with the hope of seeing my new friend again. There were even some days where he would get to the library after me and walk straight up to the table I was at and sit down. That confirmed he must have liked my company. Although I had never really had a friend before, I looked forward to that boy becoming the one person I could share with, laugh with and experience new things with. There was so much that I'd missed out on during my school years, I hoped that our friendship was going to be the start of regaining my lost youth.

It didn't seem to matter to me that we didn't speak much from the beginning. For me, it was about sitting next to someone that didn't want to hurt or use me. We both shared a common interest and that one interest was that he and I liked the company of another person. Shortly after the first time we met, we began to speak of many different things, although there were still boundaries. Those limits included the sharing of our own individual torments which we both had to live through. Those painful collective events were never openly discussed. Although, it didn't seem relevant at the time anyway.

One lunch time, on a brisk walk to the library to see my friend, I was abruptly confronted by the ringleader. He jumped out of a bush in front of me and asked if I wanted to play a game in the school gym. I was startled by his approach and took a few steps back from him to catch my breath. I wasn't sure what type of 'game' he wanted to play, however I only imagined that he wanted to do something sinister. In my mind, I was taken back to being that very young, insecure boy who could only think that the worst was going to happen.

I was scared of what he wanted to do with me. Since starting that new school, he'd previously wanted nothing to do with me, except to make me feel as though I was utterly worthless. I began to internally question his motives, *'Why did he now want to play games with me?'* As much as I still desired him, I knew I had to try to break free from his spell. As difficult as it was, I told him I wasn't interested in playing his game and asked him to leave me alone. Just as I turned to walk off, in a raised voice with a vindictive tone he said, *'You don't want me to tell everyone what happened in your bedroom, do you?'*

I froze instantly. I became motionless by the fear which had crippled my body from hearing those words.

As bad as the bullying and teasing had become at that school already, I knew it could have become a lot worse. That boy knew many of the senior kids and could have made it his mission to bring me down, further than I had ever been before. I turned back, only to see the smug look of satisfaction on his face. Once again, he knew that he held a power over me. He was like a magician and I was merely his assistant. That power he had over me was used like magic, without regard to my feelings.

With a heavy deflated sigh, I knew I had to go along with whatever he wanted. Besides, even after all of the pain he caused me, I knew deep down that I could never really put a stop to that bizarre attraction I had toward him. Before I could meet him at the gym, I told him I needed a few minutes, to which he agreed. I wanted to meet my friend in the library and make an excuse as to why I couldn't have lunch with him that day. I never wanted to lie to my friend, but given the circumstances, it was a chance I had to take. I only hoped that he would never find out the truth, as I believed that would have destroyed our new friendship.

Luck must have been on my side. As it turned out, he was away sick that day. It was then I decided to go straight to the school hall to see what the ringleader wanted. Just as I walked in to the gym, the ringleader walked out of the locker room. He gently grabbed my hand. At that stage, I was still unsure of what type of 'game' we were about to play. Although I asked him to explain, the only information he told me was that the game involved me having to hide with him. His answer didn't make any sense. I was confused by his lack of clarity. I also thought it was strange that he wanted to play with me, since his other friends were there too. I then became more skeptical of what was about to happen next.

It really was no secret to him, that he was an addiction for me. I would surrender myself and go along with any whim he desired. I knew the disgusting way he had treated me was wrong. But somehow, I was able to overlook that. No matter how much I tried to fool myself that I wasn't interested in him, I still fantasized about what we used to do in my bedroom. For him, the situation was win-win. He got what he wanted and he knew I wouldn't say anything about it.

Like most high school gyms, at the rear there was a large stage with many curtains which would be used for school productions when the gym was turned into an auditorium. As we walked up on the stage together, I heard his friends in the background, selecting their teams for whatever game was about to be played. At that time, I could feel the blood rushing from my face from fearful anticipation. Suddenly, before anyone could see us together, he quickly grabbed me and wrapped me up in the stage curtain with him. I was slightly disorientated by the quickness of his moves that I didn't have time to think about what could have happened.

As he wrapped us with that thick, heavy black curtain, he placed his hand over my mouth so I couldn't make a noise. I was overcome by curious anticipation, but I also remained nervous about his motives. Before I knew it, we were firmly wrapped up together. Our bodies were pressed firmly against one another. I could feel his warn breath panting on the side of my neck. He then whispered in the same innocent tone as he used in my bedroom, 'It's alright, the lights will go out soon.' I didn't know what he meant by that. I became overwhelmed with a range of emotions. He held me closer as he tightened his grip around my lower back. I was now even more securely restrained between him and that curtain. I was unable to move at all, even if I had wanted to.

What seemed like hours in those curtains, was just a few minutes. Just as he said moments earlier, sure enough, the lights on the stage did go out. There I was, in complete darkness wrapped up in a curtain with a boy who was unpredictable to say the very least. Although I couldn't see him, I could only feel his firm body pressing harder against mine. Not only was I perspiring from being smothered, I felt exceedingly vulnerable. However, my entire body enjoyed an overwhelming sense of physical stimulation. I didn't know what was about to happen next, but at the same time, I didn't care. My desire for that closeness slightly overshadowed my fears. In my mind, I only hoped I was right about what was going to occur.

I could still hear the murmur of his friends' voices in the background as they started playing their game. Suddenly, in the darkness, I felt the ringleaders hand slide down my stomach towards my belly button. He grabbed my hand and placed it between his legs. He then slowly began kissing my neck, all the way up to my lips. It became obvious that he wanted more than what we once did while we were alone in my bedroom.

I caressed his hard smooth body, as our lips passionately locked together. Whatever trepidation I felt moments earlier had now quickly diminished. He was groaning quietly. He then took my hand and placed it inside his pants. I remember thinking how wonderful that sensation felt, but I still didn't know if what I was doing was right. It must have been though, because neither of us wanted it to stop. From deep within my soul, I knew I wanted that moment to continue. Any confusion I may have had earlier about my attraction to boys, simply disappeared. There was nothing sinister or dirty about what was taking place. Everything that was happening in that moment felt so unbelievably right.

I became so consumed with living in that very moment, nothing else mattered. I was overcome with new feelings, both mental and physical which I couldn't express, nor did I want to. I wanted that magical moment to continue, for as long as we could spend together. There was a passion which was ignited that wasn't felt between us before. I wanted him to feel as close to me, as I felt to him. Although we were both young, that was an exploration which I needed to occur more often. I somehow managed to forgot about the pain he caused previously. At that point in time, there was nothing but lust and pure adrenaline running through my veins.

After what had seemed like many more hours in those curtains together, which in reality was only about twenty minutes, he forcefully moved my hand away, then quickly pulled up his pants. That sharpness seemed to be his style. I realized he hadn't changed. He still enjoyed playing those mind games with me. Standing there confused by his mixed messages, he said he wanted more, but not at that time. He then went on to say that he would let me know another time and place. Just before his hasty departure, he once again aggressively enforced the point that if I told anyone, he would do more than beat me, he would in fact, kill me.

There I was again, left alone. He left me feeling both baffled and exhilarated over what had happened. I knew that he didn't want anyone to know what had been going on between us, but why did he feel it necessary to threaten to kill me? Why had he continued to make me feel as though I was worthless after he had taken what he wanted from me? It was becoming apparent that he was unable to accept what we were doing. Perhaps he was actually more scared of whom he was and the feelings he felt towards another boy, more so than how scared of him I was.

At that time, I couldn't really answer those questions. Although, as I look back now from that happy escape from reality, I know exactly why. He not only enjoyed what we were doing, but he also enjoyed having the power and control which I allowed him to have over me. He knew I had a craving for him, but to him, I was nothing more than his dirty little sexual secret.

After leaving the gym, it was back to the unforgiving realities of the school ground. Back to the older kids who were still relentlessly calling me 'faggot' and 'pillow biter' as I made my way from one class to the next. I didn't know when that bullying was going to stop, or even if it was ever going to. One thing that I had become aware of though, it was becoming easier for me to digest those vile names once I had realized that there may have been some truth to what those kids were saying about me. Perhaps I was slowly coming to terms with my own identity faster than those other boys around the school ground were, but I certainly wasn't going to admit that to anyone. I continued to wonder if those boys who bullied me and spoke down to me secretly felt the same way that I did.

I considered it was possible that they too saw me as an image of what they wanted to be, but couldn't act on their feelings for one reason or another. As unfortunate as it was to admit, that very thought got me through many days which were intolerable. At least in times of distress, I still had my friend from the library. He always provided me with the normality that I needed to escape the negative thoughts which I allowed to devour my mind. Over the coming months he and I bonded quickly in many other ways.

More often than not we would hide out together, listen to music, go to the shops on late night shopping nights and even had sleepovers at each other's houses. But no matter how close we became, there were still those limits within our friendship which were never crossed. The physical or emotional pain that we had both been exposed to was still not openly discussed at that time. My friend was also totally unaware of what the ringleader and I had done previously. Although, what he did know, was there must have been some truth to what the other kids were saying about me. He would often hear the barrage of names I'd be called on a daily basis. He would simply tell me to ignore the other kids and stay strong. He believed that if I could ignore their abuse, they would give up and leave me alone. I only wish I could have believed that to be true.

It was almost as though he had the ability to block out those voices which constantly hindered me. Throughout our entire time at school, his conviction toward me never wavered. He encouraged me to let go of the hatred other people wanted to bury me in, even when there seemed no way out of those painful experiences. He was worldly with his words. Whilst he too was the youngest child in his family, he had an older brother and two older sisters. I believe their experiences in life made my friend wiser to understanding the differences in other people. If nothing else, I hoped that was a quality which I could inherit from our friendship.

Even though he had been the victim of bullying when he was much younger, which I found out much later in our friendship, the reasons for his bullying were different reasons to mine. It appeared he had became more mature and knowledgeable because of that experience. I aspired to one day have his level of confidence too. I guess I misjudged him from our initial meeting. I soon realized his spirit wasn't as damaged as mine. He simply withdrew from those at school because he enjoyed his own company too much. It was easier for him to be alone, rather than invest time in friendships which could be meaningless and provide nothing more than a superficial sense of security.

I recall one day while we were having lunch, he finally managed to find the 'right' words to ask me if what the other kids at school say about me was true. I paused for a few seconds and wondered what his reaction would be if I immediately said, 'Yes.' With a solemn tone in my voice, I explained to him that I still didn't really understand the meaning of what some of the words those kids used, but if he meant was I attracted to other boys, the only answer I could give at that time was, 'Yes, I think so, but I'm not really sure.'

In that same breath I was also very quick to deny that I was exclusively gay. I highlighted that I had not only had thoughts of boys in a sexual way, but I also admired women in the same way. I knew that I had again broken his number one golden rule of friendship by lying to him, but I didn't want to risk losing the only person who I could call a friend. It was then our conversation came to an abrupt end. We continued to sit together with nothing but silence between us.

He knew I lied to him. He knew that I wasn't actually heterosexual. However, he respected me enough to pretend to believe that I was at least bisexual. There were many times through our early friendship that he would reassure me that there was nothing to be ashamed of, if I was in fact, gay. I appreciated his words more than he realized, but at that time, I wasn't in the right state of mind to admit that to anyone. Although he was straight and very accepting, I was wary and extremely scared.

As the school year continued I felt the pressure of who I was becoming more than ever before. I was growing in to my own personality and indeed thinking more about my hidden attraction for other boys. I would often sit and question myself about how the other kids knew I might be gay, even before I really knew myself. I pondered how the 'gaydar' of 'straight' men could be so accurate. Was it blindingly obvious to everyone around me that I was gay? If so, I wondered how that could be possible.

I was then back on that carousel of endless thinking. I not only tried to analyze, but rationalize my own thoughts. I needed to reach a black and white conclusion of who I thought I was. Alas, I was only able to reach the same indecisive conclusion of perhaps knowing I was gay, but not ready to 100% accept it. However, I continued to think that if I was undeniably gay, and it was only *if*, was being gay really as disgusting and unnatural as other people thought it was?

There seemed to be more people determined to prove to me that the gay lifestyle was against everything in which humanity stood for. With their ideals being pushed upon me, I began to think that maybe I was the one who was wrong to think that being gay was 'normal'. I again needed answers to questions, which were now begging to be resolved.

The only resources I had available to me at that time were very limited. In an age before the Internet, I could only rely on books from the library, or discreetly browse gay lifestyle magazines from the book store. Apart from those gay magazines, I was starting to believe there *were* more negatives than I could find positives surrounding that shaded gay lifestyle. However, I wasn't going to give up on finding the answers I needed. I had an unquenchable thirst to know more about that elusive lifestyle, which seemed to be cloaked by obscurity and depravity.

By all accounts from my peers and my parents, homosexuals seem to live in the shadows and prey on young boys in toilet blocks and recreational parks. Sadly, even in this day and age, I'm astonished there are still people who believe the inept misconception that all gay men are indeed, pedophiles. However, both of those thoughts and misconceptions were a world away from what I actually thought and how I felt. Whilst I never shared that same belief of others, I became more intrigued than ever about that supposed ominous gay lifestyle. I needed to know if there was, in fact, a secret society of gays that I could one day become a part of.

As far as I was concerned, being gay certainly didn't seem 'wrong', 'perverse' or 'unnatural' from my perspective. Although I was still quite young, I knew I was old enough to know that I was different from other boys. It also quickly became apparent that I wasn't actually thinking of girls in the same way as I did when I looked at boys. I had feelings erupt inside me when I, not so innocently, continued to admire other boys at school. Those were feelings which provided me with a sense of both personal and sexual satisfaction.

As a number of years passed, I was still no closer to escaping the daily hell that continued to be my life. I was now fourteen years old and just started year nine at high school. It was then that my friend and I befriended another kid. That kid was quite similar to me in a lot of ways. He was slightly effeminate, taller and also had a solid build. His father worked in the military, so they would often get assigned to new cities without much notice. His dad was a disciplined and regimented man, whilst his mother was of a similar nature to her son. She had a kind, softness to her that she would only share with a rare few.

It wasn't long before I was quickly embraced by his parents, almost as though I was a member of their family. It was then I realized that there were people in life who could be accepting of other people's differences. His family accepted me without judgment. They could see I shared similar traits to their son, but never once questioned our personal identities. To be honest, at that time I still wasn't 100% sure of whom I was actually growing into, but I could finally see a slight beacon of hope to be accepted, which was more promising than the trials of the playground.

That time had also become a pivotal point in my life. I had finally found the credence which I had been seeking for many years earlier. I had people in my life who I could at last call true friends. The three of us had become very close. We spent just about every waking moment together. If we weren't together, we'd be on the telephone talking. Although, our after school hours and weekends were usually spent at each other's houses listening to 'Culture Club' records, whilst dancing around the living room pretending to be 'Boy George'. We shared a unique kindred bond, unlike any other that I had ever known before.

Whilst the bullying at school never stopped towards me, my friends and I shared a common and united front which made it seem easier for me to deal with the daily teasing and torment. They were both very supportive of who I was becoming and held no judgment toward a way of life I slowly found myself beginning to understand more of.

Unfortunately, it wasn't long before my reign of self-acceptance was to be taken away, almost as quickly as I found it. There was one particular day at school which I thought was going be the day that would end any chance of me ever living a happy life again. There was about to be an unexpected turn of events which no one should ever have to endure. My strength, courage and convictions were all put to the biggest test of my life.

My two friends had left to go on a school camp. I was once again back to avoiding anyone as I made my way through the school grounds. On one particular insignificant day, I was alone walking through the school corridor when I noticed three of the senior students walking towards me. As they got closer, I could see a look of extreme hatred in their eyes. There was no mistake, they were looking directly at me. I looked around for a quick escape, but there was nowhere to run. The closer they got, the more immobilized by fear I became. There was no doubt in my mind that they saw that moment as the perfect opportunity to prove their so called masculinity. Those boys were on a rampage of destruction and they were coming for me.

As they approached, they split up on either side of me. I thought for a brief second I was saved. However, that wasn't to be. One of the boys elbowed me in the stomach with such incredible force as he walked by. The other boy tripped me to the ground, while I was doubled over, crippled from the pain of the first blow. The third boy, who was standing directly over me, kicked me in the stomach repeatedly while I lay helpless on the floor. With every ferocious kick, I felt his hatred towards me ripple through my entire body. They continued to take turns, kicking me harder. I was unable to move. My life literally flashed before my eyes. I didn't think I was ever going to see my loved ones again. I thought my life was coming to an unexpected end. All I could do was lay still and quiet as they continued to torture my bloodied body.

It wasn't long after that there was a circle of other kids surrounding to watch the spectacle that was. Those other kids shouted out their approval for those bullies to continue. They were all taking pleasure in that macabre sight they were witnessing. They stood united, chanting their words of encouragement to 'bash the fag', with every blow those boys served to my lifeless body. I continue to lay on the floor with blood splattered, torn clothing. There was not one person who came to my rescue or who wanted to see that depraved entertainment come to an end. Of course, there were also no teachers around either.

That beating was much more severe than any of the others I had ever received beforehand. Those boys took great pleasure in mindlessly attacking me to promote their own sense of sexuality. The beating seemed to go on and on until *they* were satisfied that every fiber of my existence had been demolished.

Once they finished taking away my dignity, they casually walked off as though nothing had happened. It was obvious that according to the other kids, those boys were the 'heroes' they claimed to be. As those bullies walked down the corridor, I could hear them continuing to laugh and chant hate inspired comments such as, *'The cocksucker finally got what he deserved'* and *'That dirty fag fights like a girl.'* They collectively patted themselves on the back for doing what *they* thought needed to happen. They considered their efforts to be a job well done. Those other kids who surrounded and watched that grotesque attack spat on me while I lay helpless on the floor, before they too, casually walked off, laughing and cheering.

Never in my entire life had I experienced such extreme physical pain or emotional defeat. Crying from that immense pain, I somehow managed to pick my lifeless, semi-conscious body up from the floor and staggered in to the nearest bathroom to clean myself up. Still, there were no teachers to be found anywhere.

Once I reached the bathroom, I remember catching a glimpse of myself in the mirror as I walked passed on my way to the toilet cubicle. The only reflection I could see looking back at me, was one of a person who I didn't even recognize. The alarming realization of what had taken place had just sunk in. In a bewildered and dazed state of mind, I had no other choice but to leave school immediately that day. I wasn't sure where I was going to go, I just knew that I had to get away and hide from the world.

I never had the courage or strength to report that bashing to anyone at that school. I quietly suffered alone with the shame of what had happened. Besides, I didn't believe the teachers or school principal would have acted in my best interests anyway. I never thought they would seek justice or requital on my behalf for that barbaric behavior.

It wasn't until much later that afternoon when I returned home from school, the questions from my parents were relentless. Once again, I found myself lying to the only people who could have possibly helped me. I remember giving them an unconvincing story about how I was hurt while playing football with the senior kids. The words of truth seemed so difficult to find. Where would I have even started with the truth? How far would I have to go back in to my childhood to make them understand what had been happening to me?

Even after that brutal beating, I continued to find it easier to live amongst my own lies. In my mind, I'd rather be dishonest than have to admit to my parents that I was the son who they may not have wanted. At that time, I wasn't prepared to compromise losing my family. It seemed better to lose my own self-respect first. My decimated spirit had already left my body, never to return. I didn't want the same prospect to happen to my family life too.

I couldn't help but think of many different things that night. I began questioning myself over the events which not only led up to, but subsequently had taken place. Why didn't anyone stand up and just say stop, while I was being attacked? Was the ultimate goal to really bash me to death and just leave me there? Did any of the teachers actually witness what took place, but pretend not to? I couldn't find the answers. I was only left with more questions. It seemed as though I was once again back on that cruel spinning wheel of unwarranted emotions. One that would never stop spinning. All the while getting faster and becoming more out of control.

In the days that followed that attack, I didn't return to school out of sheer terror for what was going to happen to me. I tried to convince my parents I needed more time off school due to still feeling sore and bruised after receiving that 'football game' injury. Regrettably, my plights for understanding didn't work.

My parents thought it best that I return to school so I didn't miss any more of my studies. My only option was to pretend that I had gone to school every day. However, I spent the following days, alone, hiding out at a secret park nearby my house.

My friends returned from camp the day after the bashing. Not even they were aware of why I wasn't at school. Although I'm sure they heard the rumors that would have filled the school grounds about what had really taken place. When they finally asked me about what had happened, I found myself lying to them too. I felt as though I had no choice but to play down that entire ugly situation. Besides, I was mortified to have to relive that horrific incident again. Although, it was obvious they never believed my version of events, but they didn't probe too much. They were just thankful that I was on the mend, from whatever actually took place on that horrendous afternoon.

Even weeks after that vicious assault, I couldn't deal with the emotional devastation I had been left with. Over and over I kept reliving that moment when those boys were walking toward me. I can still feel their resentment and explosive anger that they had toward me. The more I thought about what had taken place, the more I was letting go of my life and withdrawing into my own world. It seemed so much easier to believe I was worthless, rather than to go on fighting what I considered to be a losing battle. Perhaps I should have given in to the temptation of ending my life. After all, that's what those sadistic boys had wanted in the first place.

It wasn't until about a week later, when I finally returned to school after hiding out in that secret park. I continued to think long and hard about finding a person who I could trust to talk to. I thought it would be in my best interest to openly talk through my feelings with someone who might be able to offer a small glimpse of salvation. With much deliberation, I managed to muster up enough courage to seek the help I so desperately needed. I decided that I would go and speak to the school

Chaplain.

Although I didn't attend a religious school, I wanted to talk to a person I thought would show the most compassion and understanding for what happened on the day I was beaten and indeed, my sexual identity. I needed to know how to gain the harmonious balance between who I was becoming, along with how to seek true acceptance from other people in my life. Coincidentally, that would be the very first time I ever admitted to *anyone* that I was actually gay.

On the day I decided to bare my soul, I entered the Chaplain's room to find him sitting next to the window. His demeanor seemed pensive, as he was holding a bible close to his chest. He encouraged me to come in and talk to him about whatever was on my mind. He expressed there would be no judgment and that our conversation would remain within his confidence. Hearing those words made me feel a little more at ease. I wasn't sure where to start the conversation, so I thought my early childhood would be best place to begin.

He appeared to listen patiently and attentively. As I nervously stumbled through my words, I tried to make him understand what life was like for me growing up. I declared that I needed his acceptance and understanding towards my situation. I explained all aspects of my life, including my attraction to the same sex. Unfortunately once I mentioned that I was gay, he became somewhat uncomfortable and fidgety. It was then that he took a firmer grip on his bible, which he was now clutching with both hands. It became apparent that he was not particularly well equipped to deal with all of the issues I was facing.

All I needed him to do was wave a magic wand which would take away all of my internal emotional pain and turmoil, or at the very least, tell me that everything was going to be alright. Regrettably, that wasn't going to happen. Once the Chaplain regained his composure, with a stern look on his face, he told me that my homosexuality was a phase that I was going through. He then suggested I see a psychiatric counselor who could take the 'thoughts of perversion' out of my mind. He proceeded to tell me that although I was a sinner in his eyes, he would try and keep an eye out for me while I was at school to ensure I wasn't in harms way.

I was absolutely shocked by his reaction. Due to the tremendous anger I felt, along with the embarrassment of sharing the inner most intimate details of my life, I stormed out of his office. I left feeling upset and dejected. I thought *he* of all people would have shown some compassion for a boy who was reaching out. I kept hearing those repugnant words, 'thoughts of perversion' ringing through my ears for many hours after.

The realization that perhaps my parents and the other kids were actually right about how disgusting being gay was, was starting to take on more depth. I started to think that maybe I actually was destined to loiter around toilet blocks and prey on other young boys. I contemplated, *'Was I in fact, a filthy sinner who didn't deserve the love of anyone?'* I continued to wrestle with my own beliefs and that of my peers.

The only answer I kept coming back to was, no. I wasn't going to believe the unsympathetic words of vitriol which others had spoken. Through whatever inner strength I had, I quickly reaffirmed to myself that I wasn't going to live that lonely, perverted life that other people associated with being gay. I knew I wasn't going to become a predator and regardless what some people thought, I knew I only wanted to express myself in a way that my sexual preference didn't define who I was. More than anything, I wanted to prove to them that I wasn't disgusting. I then began to doubt if the perception other people had of the gay lifestyle was even accurate or realistic. I knew that my sexuality was always just going to be an added bonus to who I was going to become in the future. It was not something I was going to be ashamed of.

Unfortunately though, as that school year continued, so did

the threats, verbal abuse and extremely demeaning behavior. I thought by engaging with several other teachers and people in authority at that school about what I was going through and indeed the day I was physically attacked, I might have found the positive outcome which I was searching for. That wasn't the case at all. My courageous attempts fell on closed minds and deaf ears. Due to not finding the recognition I needed, I struggled with the knowledge that I was right back where I started. I was alone and afraid.

It became evident by the lack of interest shown by the teachers, that there wasn't going to be any action or punishment given to that group of boys who could have cost me my life. It also became blatantly obvious that my quest for salvation was swiftly swept under the carpet, never to see the light of day. There was no follow up from those who were employed to protect me. The outcome of my situation, was as unknown as their ability to understand how to help me.

I realized that the issues I was facing as an adolescent were never going to be dealt with, let alone cared about. I was made to feel as though I was the headache of the school by people who allegedly had the students' best interests at heart. Due to the complete lack of clemency and understanding which I received from the staff at that school, it was clear they would never offer me the fortification or support that I so desperately needed. I continued to be treated as though I was the burden that no one wanted to waste their time with. It was as though the school deemed what had happened to me as acceptable behavior. I hadn't been validated at all. I only continued to be further victimized by the other students and staff alike.

It wasn't long after that realization that I felt as though I needed a dramatic change to my life and my present circum-stances. I also wanted to attain a greater focus on my own independence, which would hopefully lead me to that elusive place of peace that I was yearning for. I certainly hadn't been content with the answers that I received thus far. I thought my only redemption would be to seek a new beginning and make changes that would allow me to alter the course from that current pathway.

That change had to be a brand new beginning which didn't involve those hurtful memories of the past. I needed to break free and become my own person, who could live a life without the constant reminder of pain and humiliation. I knew there had to be a better way of life, away from those kids at school. I needed to make a move which could bring me closer to finding a connection between me and that supposed obscure lifestyle I wanted to plunge myself in to.

After a number of feisty discussions with my parents about me leaving school at the age of fifteen, they were determined that I wasn't going to leave school at such a young age. However, I continued to fight every single day until they finally gave in and allowed me to leave. Although, my parents made very clear from the start, once leaving school I would need to get a job straight away to contribute to the household.

I believed anything had to be better than going to a place every single day, not knowing if I would leave the school grounds to live another day. So naturally I agreed to their conditions. Even throughout the discussions and the arguments, I never told my parents the real reason why I wanted to leave school. Whilst my grades weren't great, I think they thought that I just hadn't applied myself to my studies, perhaps out of laziness.

Due to the bitter circumstances which surrounded my school years, to this day I never had the bravery to confide in them and express what my life was really like back then. I continued to find the power of shame much easier to deal with, as opposed to the power of truth which had the potential to set me free.

Once the decision was finalized for me to leave school, my departure from that high school was immediate. I couldn't see any reason for prolonging the inevitable. I was ready to move forward and take on any new challenges that may come along. I was excited by the opportunity of finding new prospects. Leaving school was like the opening of a door, which had the potential to lead me to places that I had only dreamed about. I then had the freedom to become who I wanted to be and leave that unrelenting misery behind me.

Although, I was saddened by leaving my two best friends behind. Nevertheless, they understood why I needed to make that dramatic and quick change to my circumstances. They still never really knew the whole truth about what had happened to me that day I was severely beaten, but they understood why I needed to leave school. They were very supportive and encouraging. Whilst it was also difficult for them to remain at that school also, I believe they had a greater determination to succeed in that environment, more than what I ever did or could have had.

My departure from school also meant that would also be the very last time I would ever see the ringleader. Whilst I was somewhat saddened by that, more so because I wasn't ready to say goodbye to those lustful encounters we shared, I knew he was no reason to stay imprisoned at that school. To this day, I have never seen him again, nor do I know which path his life has taken him on over the years.

As for my two friends, unfortunately once I left school, our friendship drifted apart. For a brief period after leaving, there was the occasional telephone call or catch up, but our lives continuously moved in different circles. Sadly, it would only be within a matter of months before we too, had no further contact with each other.

The Magic of Illusion & Discovery

Throughout the two years after leaving school, I worked at a variety of different places. All of the jobs that I had, and there were many, didn't seem as though they would lead me to any long term career prospects. Perhaps I was disillusioned by the prospects of finding a new life. Or maybe I had just expected too much. One thing I did notice though, it didn't matter where I went or what I did, the reminders of the past would continue to taunt me.

I thought by leaving school, I would be exposed to people with open minds. That wasn't always the case. Whilst most people overlooked the fact that I was gay, there were others who completely overlooked me. I think in their eyes, it was just easier for them to ignore me and pretend I didn't exist. To be honest though, I much preferred that. Whilst they still made sneering comments about my sexuality, at least I wasn't on the receiving end of more physical violence.

As one job succeeded the next, I found that I wasn't getting what I needed from life. Yet, I still wasn't entirely sure what I was actually seeking either. I just didn't feel satisfied. I would continue making excuses, just as I did in high school, to not have to go to work. That was probably more out of laziness, rather than the mundane jobs I was working at. To tell the truth, perhaps both aspects were contributing factors. At that point, it all seemed too difficult for me to commit to making the changes that I needed, in order to find a better life.

Through my extreme lack of enthusiasm, I started to think just how much damage was actually done to me over the years. No matter how much I tried, I just couldn't move forward and forget about the past. I realized I was lacking direction in every facet of my life. I guess like other people who leave school before graduation, set to embark on a new direction, I found myself asking the same questions over and over. *Where was my life heading? How can I change my destiny?*

I knew I needed to offload the resentment which I'd allowed to manifest inside me over the years, before I could truly set *myself* free. I thought leaving school would be a miracle cure to end the confusion. In fact, all I seemed to be left with was more unanswered questions and more agonizing uncertainty. I continued to question my inner most feelings which I had about my sexuality. Questions such as, *'Did I really need to change my sexual orientation in order to be accepted by society?'*

Maybe I genuinely did need to speak to someone about removing those 'perverted' thoughts from my mind, just as the high school Chaplain suggested. If he was so sure that could be done, I started to think that maybe I could do it myself. With those dangerous thoughts rattling around my head, I decided to become a person who I wasn't.

One afternoon on my lunch break, I was reading the local paper which had just been delivered. I noticed there was an advertisement for a new drama class which had recently opened in the area where I lived. At that time I wasn't really sure if I was ready to take on something new, especially a hobby that could have been so time consuming. However I soon realized that learning how to act, could be the perfect opportunity to learn how to take on another identity and become another person. It seemed to be the ideal solution to creating a 'straight' version of myself. In my mind, that was what I needed to do in order to be accepted by the world.

More to the point, I had always thought the entertainment

industry seemed so glamorous and had always wanted to be a part of it. I hounded my parents to let me take that drama class until they reluctantly gave in to my demands. As I was a little reclusive at that time, I told my parents that I thought it would be a good social connection. What I didn't tell them, was I saw that as a chance to meet other people who may have been in the same predicament as myself. More importantly, I secretly thought that may have been my opportunity to become the next 'big thing' on Australian television.

A few months before I started drama class, I vividly recall watching the movie, 'Cabaret', which starred Liza Minnelli. This movie centers around the character of 'Sally Bowles'. She was an American singer and dancer who lived in Germany throughout the early 1930's. She dreamed of becoming rich and famous as she worked at a club called the Kit-Kat Cabaret, a seedy clandestine establishment where she'd perform provocative musical numbers for a somewhat 'underground' clientele.

After watching that magnificent movie, I vividly recall hanging up bed sheets as makeshift stage curtains in our back room at home. I would then perform scenes from that movie for my family, miming along to all of the songs. To be honest, I became so engrossed with her character, I actually believed I was 'Sally Bowles'. I was so inspired and captivated by every aspect of that movie I just knew I had to take the chance with drama class. Even in that moment, I dreamed about leaving my makeshift 'back room theater' behind me and making my dream of acting on a real stage become a future reality.

During my first drama class, I remember thinking that I'd found something new to enjoy. It wasn't long before I realized, that class was indeed going to be the vehicle which I needed to assist me with taking on a new personality and pretending to be someone else. I continued to think that if I could act like a 'straight' man, I would finally be able to forget about the woes which held me back. All I needed, was to be shown how to be more masculine. I genuinely believed that's all it was going to take before I would be accepted by society. I hoped that would lead to a victory with a happy ending, which I had been searching for. Once I could master that illusion, I knew it was going be the start of a different road ahead, or so I thought.

Several months passed by and I was still enjoying the new adventures of drama class. I really wasn't sure if I was becoming more masculine though, or even if I started to think that way, but I hadn't given up hope. I always knew that I would be gay deep down inside, which I didn't have any issues with, but I knew I would continue to be ostracized because of it, if I didn't change myself in some way. I just needed to conceal my feminine characteristics a little more. I needed to at least pretend that I was more like the other boys who I went to high school with.

It wasn't long after I started that group, I became so heavily invested with drama class. There were even many times I would get dressed in my best suit and ask my mom to take portfolio pictures of me in the living room of our family home. Needless to say, after seeing how dreadful those pictures were once we got the film developed, they never saw the light of day again. Although, having those pictures taken gave me a sense of importance. Even to the point that I could feel an inkling of my lost self-worth returning. Life appeared to be slowly getting better than it had been for many years prior.

About a month prior to performing our end of year show, which was our rendition of The Wizard Of Oz, a new girl joined our class. She was an attractive girl with a big, bright smile and long straight blond hair. She had recently moved in to the area and wanted to continue studying amateur drama. She had a lot of experience with other drama groups, including performing several main parts in big budget productions. Without doubt, she was an asset to our class. Because of her incredible talent, she was immediately cast for the role of 'Dorothy Gale'. As for me, I played the part of the Scarecrow.

Within a month after she started, to my surprise, she and I very quickly become the best of friends. I enjoyed spending time with her and learning all about the productions she had previously worked on. I was also excited to be working alongside her, as she taught me many new acting techniques. I soon realized she could take on the world stage and maybe one day be seen on television, starring in her own hit television program if she desired. She was extremely talented, dedicated and passionate about the arts. She was simply divine.

One day after drama class she asked if I would like to go and see a movie that afternoon. I didn't think too much of it as we used to catch up after rehearsal sometimes anyway, so I agreed. As it turned out, we got to the cinema and the movie we planned to see had been canceled. So instead, we spent that afternoon talking and joking around, like we had done many times before. She had an outrageous sense of humor and made me laugh more than I ever had before.

That afternoon, we found ourselves sitting amongst the green, grassy knoll of the nearby local recreational oval. It was then I noticed she was acting a little different to her usual self. She was being rather suggestive with her mannerisms and a little too forthcoming with her sensual advances, which made me feel slightly uncomfortable. She continued to became quite expressive, even blowing me kisses and touching my inner thigh. I just thought she was joking around, however I soon realized there was no humor behind her intent. Her message was loud and clear.

It was obvious she wanted more of a physical connection than I was prepared to give. I had never been confronted by that type of bold affection before. I quickly wondered if I had given her the wrong idea of my intentions. Yet, I don't believe I did though. The more she continued with her overwhelmingly forward sentiments, the more I was retreating. I was unsure how to react to that unfamiliar situation.

She was unaware of the torment that I went through at school. She was also completely oblivious to the feelings I had for other boys. There were times I thought she knew, but just didn't mention it. I certainly never mentioned it to her either, in fear of losing our friendship. The one thing she did know though, was that I had no experience with girls. After I mentioned that to her, she was very upfront and said she could change all of that if I wanted her to. Whilst the forwardness of that comment shocked me, I made a conscious decision not to reply, instead, I bashfully laughed off her direct remark.

It was directly after her audacious verbal advances, when she slowly leaned over and placed her lips on mine. I wasn't sure of what was happening, as it all happened so fast. Confused, I didn't know if I was more stunned by her brazenness, or by the fact I was actually kissing a girl. Although, I will never forget the softness of her lips and the smooth skin on her face, which was unlike anything I had ever felt before.

The taste of her pineapple flavored lip balm enticed me to want to taste more. It was delicious. As for the kiss, I remember it felt somewhat contrived. I instantly knew that I had no burning desire to take that relationship any further though. In the heat of that moment, I should have been upfront and honest with her about my feelings. I should have told her about my feelings for other boys and the battle that I was fighting for my own self-acceptance. Instead, I said nothing. I chose to keep quiet and go along with the socially accepted way of life.

Perhaps I saw that as an opportunity to finally rid myself of the demons which I thought were holding me back. Perhaps I thought my earlier idea of living the life of a 'straight' man could have become a reality. Perhaps I just didn't say anything in order to gain a fictional sense of acceptance and equality. Whatever the reasoning was, I couldn't find the right words to let her down gently. By keeping silent, I knowingly entered in to a partnership with her, which I wasn't completely sure I wanted to be in.

Without thinking too much about the situation, we quickly became boyfriend and girlfriend. However, that was a concept which wasn't as foreign as I imagined it would be.

Surprisingly, I found myself in an emotionally comfortable place. But even throughout those very early stages of our relationship, I always knew something was missing, apart from the obvious physical differences between a man and a woman. I felt there was a limited spiritual connection between us. I soon realized, probably not unlike other people in a similar situation, being intimate with a person that you have no sexual attraction to is one of the most difficult emotions to deal with.

It was an extremely daunting feeling when we got to the love making stage of our relationship. I just knew that I had to do whatever it took to fulfill her desires. I didn't necessarily care if I was the best that she'd ever had. I just had to go through the motions and hope for the best. I look back now and I can see how totally hit and miss the sex was. From my perspective, there was definitely more miss, than hit!

Having said that, I legitimately enjoyed the intimacy and closeness that we shared. I just wasn't overly comfortable with performing those sexual acts. There was a definite sense of automation which accompanied the motions of what I was doing and indeed the feelings I experienced. As much as I told myself that was what society expected of me as a man, I could never bring myself to commit one hundred percent of my soul to her. I struggled with that on many different levels, because I did love her in many ways. However, I always knew that I wasn't *in love* with her.

She ultimately became my best friend over the two years we were together. Although, I knew deep inside that I had let our friendship down, due to me not being completely honest with her. However, there were so many similar aspects that we had in our relationship which compared to any other heterosexual relationship. We laughed together, we cried together and we shared so many intimate details of ourselves. With each shared moment, there came a different level of love and understanding. I wanted so much to break the bubble I was living in and whole-heartedly share my soul and innermost deep secrets with her, but I was too frightened.

For the duration of our relationship, there was only ever one aspect of my true self that I never shared with her. However, that caused me to hide the very core of who I really was. In turn, I surrendered the very thing I had always wanted, the freedom to truly live my life. I could never find 'that' appropriate moment to tell my girlfriend that I was same sex attracted. That only made it harder to break away from my relationship, however as time went by, I knew the charade I was living had to come to an end. I just couldn't continue living that double-edged, self-destructive lie any longer.

Living amongst that dishonest situation, which I created, wasn't fair to her, nor was it fair to me. I knew there was no other choice to make. At that time, as complicated as I knew it was going to be, I made the decision to end our relationship. Besides, there was nothing more complicated than the web of lies I was already living. Although the break-up was going to be difficult for both of us, in different ways, I couldn't continue holding her back from a life that she truly deserved to be living. I had to set her free so she could be honored in ways that I was unable to provide.

A couple of days later when we met for lunch, as we did every Thursday, I knew that was going to be the very day which I would deliver the devastating news. I also knew that once my words were spoken, I could never take them back. I could still see no other option but to finally be honest with her about my feelings. Although, back in that happy escape from reality, that conversation was something I should have had two years earlier. I acknowledged with the deepest of regret that it was I who was to blame for her wasting two years of her life, denying her from potentially meeting the real boy of her dreams.

That Thursday afternoon was a cold, rainy Melbourne winters day. I remember sitting alone, pensively staring out the window, watching each individual rain drop fall heavily onto the window sill. Each of those rain drops sounded like a fierce explosion going off in my mind. In turn, those explosions created an internal battleground whereby the war was against my heart and my conscience. I knew those very explosions may seem insignificant compared to the actual reaction I could receive after breaking the news to my soon ex-girlfriend that I was actually gay.

I waited, nervous and anxious. The beads of sweat were teaming from my forehead in a continuous motion down my face and beyond. I had no idea what I was going to say, let alone how I was going to approach the subject. Once she arrived, we sat quietly at the table for a few minutes. She could sense something was on my mind, but couldn't understand what could be so bad that I couldn't simply come out and say it.

As I sat silently looking in to her bright eyes, I knew what I had to do. I just didn't want to hurt her any more than I already was. I was about to inflict the pain and suffering that only a broken heart can bring, on a person who never asked for it or deserved it. I took a long deep breath in and opened my mouth to speak. Suddenly, the speech I was about to give seemed so inadequate. Just then, from the corner of my eye a single tear rolled down my cheek in amongst the sweat beads. She gazed into my eyes and gently squeezed my quivering hand. She sweetly encouraged me to tell her what was on my mind.

First and foremost, I told her that I loved her deeply. Then, without even thinking about what I was going to say next, the words, *'I'm extremely sorry to say this, but our relationship had to end, because I'm gay'* just blurted out of my mouth. It was almost as though I had no control over what I was saying. It was then the floodgates of my eyes opened and I began sobbing. Although in that brief moment, I was also relieved to have finally said those words. At the same time, my psyche was desolated. I knew I would never have the opportunity to take back those hurtful words, or the pain they caused her.

I couldn't believe I had just told another person, especially one who I cared so much about, that I was gay. It was almost like a massive weight had been lifted off my shoulders. However, that moment wasn't only about me. Feeling disgusted with myself, I had just abandoned that innocent girl of her hopes and dreams.

Just as quickly as she had reached out and taken my hand in hers moments earlier, she instantly pulled her hand away. She looked at me in amazement and disbelief due to the statement I had just made. My words were clearly still ringing in her ears. There was a distinct look of sadness and empathy in her eyes. With my tears still streaming down my face, I waited for her to speak or show any emotion. There was only an uncomfortable silence which continued to linger for a few seconds. She was obviously shell shocked and urgently trying to digest the destructive news I had just delivered.

I asked her to say something, anything. She couldn't open her mouth without choking on the words she so desperately needed to get out. Every time she wanted to speak, her words would come to a grinding halt. No matter how much she tried, she simply couldn't articulate how she was feeling. It was clear that there were no words that could describe the pain and humiliation she felt right at that moment. Those were emotions which I had thoughtlessly made her feel.

Her eyes then welled up with tears, just as quickly as the blood drained from her face. She was still speechless. I made her feel just as I had been made to feel by those bullies during my school years, inadequate and redundant. I never wanted to cause her the deep pain that I did right at that very moment.

My actions throughout our relationship were egotistical and

inconsiderate, but for the sake of us both, my words finally needed to be heard. It was never my intention to destroy the beautiful soul who was opposite me. Sitting at that table with my now ex-girlfriend, I saw beyond the look of tremendous sadness which had completely taken over her. Through her anguish, I could sense that her mind was abuzz. There seemed to be many questions that she wanted to ask, but couldn't bring herself to hear the answers which may have emotionally destroyed her.

In some ways, it would have been easier for us both had she not wanted to ask questions. However, that was only my selfishness for not wanting to explain anything to her. More importantly, I didn't want to risk further hurting her with more of the truth. I realized that the truth is a very powerful expression to share. In my experience, it can only be properly digested when those wanting to hear it have an open state of mind, whereby they can truly accept any words that are spoken in complete honesty.

Following further moments of inept silence, in a softly spoken and overwhelmed manner, the first and only words she was able to speak through her tears was a solemn, *'thank you.'* After a few short, shallows breaths she then continued to say, *'I'm grateful that you had the courage to tell me the truth, no matter how painful it was to process, for both of us.'*

I sat quietly, feeling numb and dumbfounded. Her gracious and reassuring words were not at all what I had anticipated to hear. I would have expected her to yell and scream at the top of her lungs or at the very least, slap me across the face and walk out on me. Perhaps that's what I had deserved anyway. Instead she seemed more at peace with the truth, which had essentially set us both free from a future life of unhappiness. Her unselfish philosophy was one of understanding, harmony and compassion. As she appeared to be coming to terms with my unwarranted disclosure, she went on to express that above all she wanted nothing more than for both of us to continue living the lives we were meant to be living, without anything holding either of us back.

I was incredibly relieved by that outcome, for both of us. I never intentionally wanted to hurt her. If the truth be known, I was probably just as perplexed as much as she was about that entire situation and indeed the circumstances which led us to where we were on that day. We both took that moment to sit and think of the time we shared together. We did have many good times, which paid a beautiful tribute to the love we shared for one another.

She once again reached out and took my hand in hers. We managed to find common ground in the hours which followed. Both she and I were aware that love simply doesn't instantly stop, no matter how much we wish it could. We both also knew that our lives would never be the same again. I had not only managed to break her trust for the future, but I had also temporarily taken away her zest for living a life that she loved.

With the most profound sadness and regret, I never saw or heard from her again after that day. She would also never return to our drama class either, nor offer any explanation as to why. Although, I knew that I was solely responsible for that happening. I had been the cause of her not continuing with all that she had been so passionate about previously. With every beat of my heart, I wish I could have been the man that she wanted and needed me to be. I have no doubt in my mind, or my heart, that she went on to find a man who would treat her like the Princess she was. She deserves to be showered with as much love as one man can possibly give.

After the abrupt ending of that relationship, there was a constant void in my life. However, I continued drama class until the end of that following year. For me, drama class was about having that escape to live a life through another person's beliefs. That was, until I met my ex-girlfriend, what I thought I'd wanted all of my life. The harsh reality of that situation showed me that

I needed to find my own life. I needed to live a life that was truthful to how I was feeling, without hurting anyone else in the process.

Right from the beginning, I knew that I should have never have become involved with a person that I couldn't offer my entire being too. I did love my ex-girlfriend. Profoundly, I realized the reality of my illogical thoughts at certain periods throughout my life made me believe it was easier to justify doing what was seen as 'acceptable' by the inconsistent standards of society. I needed to determine whether I was going to conform to a society which seemed to control the thoughts of others, or if I was to break away from those expectations. Because of the bitter-sweet experience that I had with my ex-girlfriend, the choice was obvious.

I never considered myself to be overtly masculine, certainly not by the values of society anyway. In a reflective mood, I couldn't help but think that there must have been times when my ex-girlfriend realized that I wasn't her lifelong perfect match. I often asked myself if she ever noticed the discreet sideways glance I'd give to guys as they walked passed, or perhaps if she noticed a twinkle in my eye when another guy looked at me in a certain way. Given her initial reaction when I told her I was gay, it was evident that she had been oblivious to any such occurrences.

I believe that sometimes that tiny internal voice we hear in our head can make us believe that we are going to have to live up to the expectations of what other people desire, without consequence. Unfortunately, that is what I had done and to this day, I still consider myself one of the lucky ones. I met a person who ultimately, through the anguish and suffering which I had caused, still only wanted me to live the life that I was born to live. Through her courage, I felt a brief moment of contentment.

Shortly after that period, the most crucial question which keep continuing to replay in my mind was, *'Why did I want to ever subject myself to living a life that is true to other people's expectations, whilst denying myself the right to live a life that makes me truly happy?'* As I searched for the answer, the only conclusion I could reach was the one from earlier, which reiterated that society, or our environment, should not and cannot determine who we are, or who we must become.

In the months that followed the break up with my ex-girlfriend, I found myself starting another new job. My track record with longevity in any workplace wasn't great. However, that didn't stop me from continuing to work in places which brought me no satisfaction or true purpose to my life. I continued waiting for the perfect opportunity to be handed to me on a silver platter. That was an opportunity which I wasn't actually convinced really existed in the first place.

In my mind though, even working at those monotonous retail and customer service jobs which had no future career prospects, I thought was still better than being at school dealing with the hatred of others, who would have been happy to see me dead. Yet, with every job I had since leaving school, the common denominator was that I couldn't hide from the enigmatic past. I was still subjected to bullying and being made to feel as though I was a second class citizen.

Specifically, in every job I had, there were always small groups of people who made uncomplimentary remarks about me being a 'sissy' or a 'queer'. Those perpetrators would also prey on others who were in the minority, such as people with different ethnicity or those who didn't conform to a certain dress code. Even so, in some ways, I felt more protected being in a work environment as there were managers who were trained and equipped to deal with these select groups of people, or so I wanted to believe.

One night when I arrived home from work, my dad asked to talk about an idea he had. Many years earlier, before becoming the high profile person he was, he used to perform his own magic and illusion stage productions. He went on to express his desire to go back onto the stage and as he knew of my exposure working in the theater already, he asked if I would be interested in becoming his assistant.

I thought that was the golden opportunity which I had been looking for. I didn't need to think twice about it and immediately replied 'yes.' Of course, I still had to work full time at whatever mundane job I may have had at that time, but I was so excited at the thought of going back on the stage again. I missed the adrenaline rush from performing, along with the admiration from the audience. It seemed as though a spark had been reignited from deep within my darkened soul. I was more than ready for that opportunity, even more so than any other opportunity at that time.

With no hesitation, it was decided, we would work together and come up with a brand new show. My dad and I rehearsed our show at every chance we got. There was so much to learn and so many tricks which needed to have perfect timing. I knew I was ready for that challenge. We incorporated an array of different magic tricks and impressive illusions. We performed everything from basic card tricks, turning water into wine, making rabbits and doves disappear and of course my most favorite illusion of all time, being cut in half with a chainsaw.

For a solid six months, we practiced our routine over and over until we finally perfected our act. I wanted that show to be the most grandiose illusion show that anyone had ever seen. There was nothing else in life which seemed to matter as much as that show. Once we believed we were ready to showcase our act to an audience, it was time to take that wondrous production on the road.

As we were preparing to start the publicity, I remember thinking how surprised I was to learn how many contacts my dad had within the entertainment industry. That was yet another aspect of his earlier life that I didn't know existed. Due to those vast contacts he had throughout Australia, we were booked solidly for two years, performing various shows all over Melbourne and country Victoria. It was because of that wonderful opportunity, I was once again slowly beginning to feel that same freedom as I had felt throughout the youngest years of my life. I was becoming more in touch with my feelings again. It was nice to mentally return to a place which ignited a long lost passion.

As much as I loved being on the road, I cherished being on stage more than anything. I felt an extreme sense of satisfaction from performing those magical shows with my father. There was nothing else on earth which could beat that tremendous feeling I gained from performing for an audience that truly appreciated our talent. I genuinely enjoyed being recognized for the hard work that my dad and I had put in to make our show one of the most spectacular of its time.

There was one show we performed which will always remain firmly embedded in my mind. That show was by far my most memorable to date. We had been booked to perform at an event for the Victorian RAAF (Royal Australian Air Force) base in Point Cook, Victoria. We planned to make that show our biggest yet. We even had new costumes made, which looked magnificent. My dad and I wore matching silver sequined suit jackets, which also matched with our bow-ties and cummerbunds. We both looked as though we were ready to perform an opening night musical on Broadway.

After weeks of waiting, finally, the night I had been looking forward to had arrived. We were only hours away from starting that performance at the RAAF base. I was unbelievably excited about performing what I believed was going to be the greatest show on earth. That night before the show, while we were setting up the magic tricks and illusions, I noticed a boy who was around my age, inquisitively looking around. He was tall, slim with dark curly ringlet hair and dark eyes that could pierce your soul when he looked at you. He seemed very intrigued about what we were doing, as he intently watched my every move.

As it turned out, he was the son of a visiting RAAF pilot. I didn't really take much more notice of him to begin with, as I just assumed he was curious about the show and what type of magic tricks we would be performing that night. As we continued setting up, he and I exchanged a quick glance, but before I could speak to him, he did a disappearing act of his own, which was quicker than any magic trick that I could perform. Once he'd gone, I didn't really give him another thought.

However, when my dad returned to the car to get our costumes, that boy magically reappeared. He slowly walked over towards me. After a somewhat menial introduction and a couple of forced words, he forwardly told me to meet him after the show, behind the auditorium where we were performing that night. Not really knowing or asking why he wanted to meet, I agreed anyway. I just assumed he wanted to ask me how the magic tricks were done, just like most other kids did too. He didn't wait around once I agreed to meet him. Again, he was gone. He seemed so very mysterious. That was a quality I found attractive.

Later that night, we performed our act. Just as my father and I suspected it would be, the show was a grand success. We even received a standing ovation from the crowd. That alone made me feel more exhilarated than I had ever felt while being on stage before. Until that moment, I'd never had a feeling that I could conquer the world if I wanted to. That show had sparked a fire in my belly that I not only enjoyed, but needed more of. Although, it never occurred to me at that moment, my night was going to get even better than I had ever expected.

A little while after our show had finished, like on other occasions, we would often mingle with the audience. That was our opportunity to personally thank the audience and ensure they liked the show. Rather, on that occasion, I saw that as my perfect opportunity to sneak away and meet that secretive boy.

Riding high from the rush of our performance, with excitement, I ventured outside to look for that boy who captivated me earlier. There he was, standing against the outer wall of the shed, staring directly at me. His intense glare penetrated deep in to my soul. I was in awe of his seductive and alluring presence. I gradually walked up to him, although still not completely sure of his intentions. I took my last step until I was standing directly in front of him. Before I could speak, all of a sudden, with a salacious look in his beautiful dark eyes, he reached over and passionately kissed me on the lips.

I was trembling with anticipation. Although, I never once fought him off. I gave in to what he wanted. That forceful kiss we shared was intense. It was fueled by our inexplicable desire to explore one another further. He then took my trembling hand in his. Walking at a slow pace with the muddy ground under our feet, he led me to a dark and secluded area, away from the auditorium.

I was again feeling how I did when I was back in high school. I had the same lustful emotion as I did when I was wrapped in the curtains with the ringleader, but without the trepidation. I wanted that boy more than I had ever wanted anything else in my entire life, which included the ringleader. I wanted him to take me to the utmost physical and spiritual heights, right then and there. I had never before experienced such emotional intensity and such demonic desire to be with one person, as I did right at that moment.

There was absolutely no doubt in my mind that he was more experienced with boys than what I was. With every move of his taut body against mine, I surrendered every fiber of my existence to him. Our bodies were tense as the adrenaline pulsated through our veins. Our breathing became sporadic as we softly and intimately touched one another all over. There was an electric feeling between us which I had only ever dreamed of experiencing. That moment was more magical than the magic I had been performing on stage. However, that was no illusion. That was extremely real.

I continued to experience explosive feelings from within. My mind was filled with thoughts of ecstasy as my heart was beating faster, with an intensity which paralleled to nothing else on earth. That boy and I had become one. I was stunned by his sensual moves which flared an eruption of unadulterated desire from deep within. Lying together in a secluded field of long grass, he not only took my virginity, he took me to a new dimension of life which I needed to explore further.

After what can only be described as a pure rush of excitement and satisfaction, our sweat covered bodies finally collapsed to the ground as we both struggled to catch our breath. I wanted nothing more than to stay in that close embrace we found ourselves in, but time wasn't on my side. My emotions were conflicted between desire and responsibility. I knew I couldn't be away from my dad for too much longer, but I never wanted to leave that precious moment either. I wanted to stay with him until I had again fulfilled his every desire, more than I just had. I never thought that surrendering to a person could feel so phenomenal. I was basking in a euphoric afterglow, which was second to none.

Unfortunately though, there wasn't time for an encore. After composing ourselves, we only enough energy left for one last passionate kiss. I struggled with the thought of leaving him, but it was time for me to miserably scurry back in to the auditorium where my dad was probably wondering where I was. As it turned out, I could have stayed away longer. My dad was too caught up with other people to even realize I wasn't even there with him. Although, I was still very happy with the short amount of time that I'd shared with that boy, because it became a spectacular memory which has lasted a lifetime.

After that encounter, I promptly realized whatever doubts I may have had about my sexual identity, those fears or concerns were finally put to rest, once and for all, never to rear their head again. I had finally taken a positive step towards my own self-confirmation as a gay man. Contrary to what I had been led to believe by my peers and my parents, there was nothing perverted or disgusting about what I had experienced with that boy. In fact, my soul felt more alive than I had ever known it to be ever before.

There was such a vast contrast between that boy and the ringleader. The ringleader used vile threats and degradation after I served my purpose and gave in to him. Whilst that other boy also got what he wanted, he and I knew we could only fill the need for the 'here and now'. We both enjoyed it for what it was, a fleeting moment of unrestrained passion. It was a one night adventure which we would both hopefully look back on and treasure for the rest of our lives. At least, I know I have!

For as far back as I can remember, I always wanted to live without the ongoing judgment from other people. What I was feeling after that night was as close as I had ever come to living that very life. I had a new found hope to know that at some time throughout my journey, I could rid myself of the shackles of guilt and worthlessness which I thought continued holding me back. At last, I felt as though I was growing in to my own identity. My thought process was changing. I was discovering that it was possible to live a life without lies or double standards.

During that phase of my life, I spent many sleepless nights thinking about events which had previously taken place in my life so far. That led me to thinking of my ex-girlfriend. As it turned out, there were many symmetries between what I did on stage with my dad and the illusion which I portrayed with her. Both required great skill and an enormous amount of energy. Both also involved only showing what I wanted to have seen. I soon realized that I invested too much time in to hiding who I was. I wasn't living a life of reality, merely an elaborate fantasy.

I also concluded that I had become a chameleon. I could

knowingly take on, or change my persona to anything or anyone I desired. I thought that I could be all things, to all people. Yet, it wasn't long before I saw the error of my ways. I learned that the notion of being true to myself took the most power and courage of all. I had mastered the illusion of allowing people to see what I wanted them to see. I realized there was no real magic in pretending.

Unfortunately, due to my father's decline in health we only had the opportunity to perform a few more shows. The traveling and hectic work schedule had taken its toll on him. Regrettably, it was time to retire our top hat and tails. I'll always be grateful that I had the chance of making those memories. I'm also thankful for the experiences I gained, at a time in my life which transformed me in many different ways. One of my major discoveries was that all it takes to change one's outlook, is being offered that one opportunity. My advice to anyone, is to never give up looking for that *one* lucky break, because if you do, it will never know where to find you.

I felt fortunate that my dad offered me that bright light of opportunity to join him on stage. It allowed me to slowly regain and rebuild my self-esteem. It also gave me a little more clarity and hope for the future. I felt as though certain aspects of my life were being put in to a rational perspective. For the meantime though, it was back to the everyday humdrum of working in a retail job at a bakery, which I was beginning to loathe. I so desperately needed to change my tactics. I also needed to believe in my own ability to make new opportunities work in my favor.

Once my dad and I finally stopped performing, I began to miss the life that we shared on the road together. There was no other comparison to the excitement I felt when we arrived at the destination of where we were going to perform. I enjoyed the continuous change of environment by traveling to unknown places, which brought with it the chance to meet many different people, from many different backgrounds to that of my own.

With a burning desire for new experiences smoldering inside me, I couldn't easily let go of the taste for change, nor did I want to. I gave enormous consideration to what I could do with myself to achieve a greater level of satisfaction, both personally and professionally.

Even though I didn't have too many decent prospects available, there only seemed to be one solution which I kept coming back to. I knew it was time to 'bite the bullet' and go back to the very place which I can only describe as my own private nightmare. I decided to return to high school and complete my graduation.

Everything New Becomes Old

In the summer of that following year, I enrolled to attend a different high school to where I had been previously. I was more determined than ever to graduate and obtain my High School Certificate. I was ready to seize every future opportunity which presented itself. I didn't deserve to be working in a dead end job that wasn't providing me with what I needed. I realized that I was destined for a better way of life. I wanted to be a person who would someday, in the not too distant future, make a memorable name for himself.

Before I knew it, the long awaited first day of school had arrived. There was only one question that consumed my mind that morning, which was, *'Was I actually ready to go back in to an environment that had taken every part of my dignity and myself self-respect?'* The only answer, was a surprising, *'Yes.'*

I was more than ready to embrace a new challenge and take on whatever was to happen. I was feeling more empowered than I had been in a long while. I wasn't going to waste away and let my previous high school experience tarnish an opportunity which could ultimately be, a positive and rewarding experience.

I believed my saving grace at that new high school was the fact I was slightly older than the other kids in my year. I had just turned seventeen years old. I had also been working for two years prior to returning to school, so I felt as though I had an edge of maturity over the other kids. There was no way I was going to allow myself to succumb to any ridicule or become the victim of any brazen bullying attacks once again.

I believe the first day at a brand new school for *any* child is particularly disconcerting. Even more so for a child who doesn't know anyone at all. For me though, I used that unsettled feeling to my advantage. Those new kids didn't know about my history, nor were they ever going to find out about what happened in that former life I once lived. I adopted a positive fresh new outlook, which didn't include any of the negativity from the past.

Although, all the self-motivational speeches I gave myself beforehand didn't amount to much. I was still a little nervous as I walked through the school gates, on my way to the first day orientation class. I noticed some of the other kids were looking at me with a curious look on their faces. Some others were whispering and some were laughing and discreetly pointing at me. For a fleeting moment I wondered if that school experience was in fact, going to be like my last. Unsure of what they found amusing, I persevered and brushed it off without becoming disheartened or showing too much concern. In the back of my mind though, I couldn't help but secretly think that a dreadful experience could have been waiting ahead.

To my surprise, my first impression was that most of the kids at that school were welcoming and seemed friendly enough. As well as being a little older, I also thought that being a little taller might have just given me the edge I needed to be left unchallenged. I had also lost weight over the years, which meant I wasn't 'that fat kid' any longer. Nevertheless, I wasn't taking anything for granted or leaving anything to chance. I was extremely cautious about how I spoke and who I spoke with, but more importantly, how I behaved. I was rather mindful of my mannerisms and realized I had to tone down my 'feminine' characteristics in order to find the uncompromising acceptance I secretly desired.

In some respects, I think going back to school was the best decision I could have made. That was not only because of the value it brought to further my education. I also needed to prove to myself that although I had a difference to most kids, I wasn't going to let them stop me from achieving what I wanted to do and indeed, becoming who I wanted to be. I believed that was going to be the stellar chance I'd been searching for to do just that. I only hoped that opportunity would allow me to achieve the greatness I felt as though I missed out on. I had a new found sense of liberation, which I was proud to wear.

It was almost one month after I started that new school that I felt as though I was settling in and adapting to my new surrounds. To be honest, I did find the first couple of weeks to be the hardest and the loneliest though. But as I was used to not having any friends from my last school experience, I wasn't overly bothered by that. What did bother me the most though, was not having anyone to share special moments with, or to laugh with. I had again become a loner. I was disheartened that not *one* person would extend their hand of friendship to a lonely boy who simply wanted a companion.

The reality of my loneliness was twofold. Although I had no one to call my friend, I wasn't being bullied or beaten either. As much as I wanted to put my previous school experience behind me, those memories continued to stay with me. Albeit they were in the back of my mind, but no matter how much I tried to let them go, they were obstinate. My only choice was to genuinely accept what had happened and try to move forward the best I could. Besides, when I was really lonely, I could still rely on those wonderful memories from those magic shows to invigorate me. However, I was beginning to sense that my good fortune was coming to an end. I soon discovered I needed more than those magic memories to stop my past defining my future. In fact, I needed real magic to stop what was about to happen.

A more few weeks passed and I had completely settled in to my new school. Although on one particular day, as I wandered around aimlessly, alone on my lunch break, I could see some of the other kids in the distance making fun of me. They were staring and blatantly giggling amongst themselves at my expense. I knew I just had to turn away and ignore them. I thought if a little teasing was going to be the worst that could happen, then I could deal with that. I accepted that I was probably going to be ridiculed by a few of the other kids anyway. Let's be honest, I would have only been fooling myself if I had thought differently.

It wasn't long after that episode, those same troublesome kids were becoming much more confident with their words than they had previously. They continued to snicker and make snide comments about me being gay. They took every possible opportunity to mimic my mannerisms with the hope of destroying my spirit. As difficult as it was, I knew it was best to continue ignoring them. I had to bide my time to see how far those bullies were actually prepared to push me to my limits.

Unfortunately, it was only a matter of time before their brazen teasing became more prevalent and virtually impossible to deal with. I again found myself hearing those same degrading words such as 'faggot', 'homo' and 'sissy' which had previously taken away my dignity and self-worth. From that point, I knew the barrage of hateful name calling was only going to continue to become more spiteful. I realized I needed to act in haste. If I couldn't find a way to stop those verbal attacks, I was already able to predict the gruesome outcome. I now felt as though I had to prove to the entire school that I wasn't going to become a subservient victim to their ridicule. More importantly, I needed to prove to myself that the situation I again found myself in, wasn't going to become the inevitable.

There was no chance I was ever going back to becoming that boy who was damaged, emotionally and physically. That boy who was left alone, with no will to survive. I tried as hard as I could to not let it affect me. My brain systematically went in to overdrive as I thought, *'What could I do to stop that situation from ruining me?'* To be honest, I wasn't sure if I had the inner strength to stop that undeserved treatment before it became even more unbearable. I felt as though my mind was perusing an internal high speed chase, with an undetermined outcome. I didn't know if I was going to escape that pursuit safely, or crash and burn again.

I gave great consideration to what I needed to do in order to survive their criticism. I still knew I had to act quickly before that unpleasant situation became totally out of control. Unfortunately, I didn't have many resources at my disposal, but somehow I just knew I had to devise a plan of retaliation. That plan needed to be one which would have a major impact on all of the other kids at that school. I wasn't going to let them think it was acceptable to bully me, or others who may be different to them, regardless of what that alleged difference was.

My master plan had to let the other sufferers of bullying know they were not alone either. Together, *we* were not going to remain victims of whatever vile treatment *we* were being subjected to, by those who intended to make our lives miserable. I had to effectively portray a message to all and sundry that *we* would stand together and fight back, united and collectively. Although, it silently appeared as though I was the one who was 'chosen' by the other kids who were also tormented, to make that stand. I believe that was because the other kids didn't know how to put a stop to what was happening to them. They too were scared, afraid and alone.

Due to the promptness of the avenging behavior from those other kids, I made the decision early that it was in my best interests to take matters in to my own hands. I wasn't sure I could rely on the support of the school to end that derogatory behavior, which seemed to be getting worse by the second. I didn't want to encounter the same failings I had previously with the Chaplain and teachers from my previous school. I wasn't going to be known as the burden that I was once made to feel by those who *supposedly* had the power to make a positive difference to a child's life. So it was up to me to put a stop to those injustices which not only had I been exposed to, but many other kids also.

Before long, I realized that it may have been too late to think of a positive solution. Before I knew it, those despicable two dimensional words I tried to ignore, became a three dimensional reality. Later that week there was as occasion when I was forcefully approached by one of the senior kids in the locker room. Luckily for me, that incident didn't come to fruition. I was saved by a teacher who was passing by on her way to class. That in turn, gave me a quick escape from a potentially volatile situation. Still, that type of scenario in the locker room had become all too familiar. I had to quickly re-evaluate my plan before a similar kind of alarming situation escalated into something more sinister. I sensed it was only going to be a matter of time before the next assault occurred.

I was right. Later that same afternoon I was back in the locker room putting away my books after class. Out of nowhere, I saw that same senior student from earlier, walking towards me. I knew I was in his line of sight. He kept walking until he was invading my personal space. He then stopped and stood over me. His shadow covered every inch of my quivering body. For that split second, I regressed back to my old high school days. I was incapacitated. There was nowhere to run or hide. I felt that same helpless feeling as when I was bashed previously. I couldn't believe I was going to allow that to happen to me, yet again.

Anxiously, I looked up at him. As I looked into his eyes I could only see a look of disgust. Although he wasn't that much taller than me, he was certainly much stockier than I was. I could feel his heavy breath bellow from his mouth, which was only inches from my face. His breath smelled of the most repugnant stench of stale cigarette smoke. That initial look of disgust in his eyes soon filled with enraged fire. His torrid demeanor was one of hatred. The only thing standing between him and I was his sentiment of sheer contempt. I stood breathless as I tried to conquer my fears and stay strong. I could only wish that another teacher would walk by and rescue me again, but unluckily that was to no avail.

As he physically looked down upon me, I grappled to find firm ground to make my stand. My heart was beating ferociously. I was terrified. He took one step closer, before forcefully pushing me in to the locker which was behind me. Scared, I didn't know how to react. I just wondered what was coming next. Then, he just continued walking passed me, sadistically laughing. With a tremendous sigh, I fell to the floor, then scrambled out as quickly as I could. I had become panic stricken. I thought, without doubt, I was going to be brutally attacked right then and there. With an horrible realization, I knew that wasn't going to be the only encounter I would have with him, or with his friends for that matter.

I felt as though time was running out. I still hadn't devised my grand plan of how I was going to protect myself. I had no idea of what I was going to do when I was confronted again. And I *knew* that it *was* going to happen again. I had been lucky to escape his fury on two occasions previously, but my luck could have ran out at any time. His intimidation tactics on that day were duly noted, however, I knew the events which would take place in due course, could be much worse the next time I was in his sights.

Whilst trying to negotiate my next move, I wondered if anyone was going to protect me. I wanted to believe that I had a guardian angel looking over my shoulder, but I wasn't sure if that was to be. Perhaps that situation may have been easier if I just let him unleash his cruelty and allowed him to bash me, without resistance. If I'm honest for a moment, I doubted that anyone at that school would have even cared if I was hurt, or worse, bashed to death.

Instantly, my mind became flooded with the memories of what had taken place in my younger years. I immediately became emotionally disabled, void of any feeling. I started to feel as though my life was again beginning to completely spiral out of control, ferociously leading me back to that same rock bottom sensation of hopelessness. The best way I can describe that powerless and terrified feeling, is when you intuitively know something really bad is about to happen, but are unable to stop it because you're not exactly sure of what is going to happen. That was the feeling which consumed me. There I was, back in that black pit of nothingness, too scared and weak too defend myself.

There was no question, that older boy knew I was terrified of him. He was drawn to my extreme sense of panic, like a moth to a naked flame. He also knew I had expected the worst to happen in the locker room, on both of those previous occasions. From his first intimidating taunt, he understood that he had total control over me, in which all he needed to do was look in my direction for me to become crippled with unparalleled fear. He took great pleasure in teasing me with the unknown. That look of pure evil in his eyes became his signature trademark. I realized he was biding his time before he would finally make his move and destroy me. There was no uncertainty in my mind, he enjoyed having that overwhelming power over me. He used that to control my emotions. He was the puppeteer and I was nothing more than his lifeless puppet on a string.

His actions only made me regress further back into my life. No matter how much I tried, I still couldn't let go of those memories of the past. I spent countless hours trying to ratio-nalize my thoughts. Over and over in my mind, I wondered how I could let that vileness happen to me again. I never once asked for it. Those thoughts only led me to a further wrestle with my conscience about becoming true to myself and indeed, the thought of giving up on what I had gone back to school for. I really hoped that new school was going to be different. The reality was such, that whilst it was a completely different school, the attitude and behavior of the students remained the same as I had previously experienced.

A few more tiresome weeks passed by. I was still enduring those same unbearable circumstances as I had been dealing with earlier. Little did I know, there was one particular day that week which was potentially about to become my most terrifying yet.

On that day as walking to class, out of nowhere, I was forcefully pushed to the ground from behind. At that time, I was unaware of who was responsible. As I tried to fight back, I struggled to turn around to see who that cowardice person was. During the tussle for my life, I saw from the corner of my eye that same boy from the locker room. He was the spineless person who did that to me. There he was, towering over me whilst I lay pinned to the ground by his extreme force. He was too strong for me to overpower. By all accounts, he was ready to inflict a brutal and inhumane act of torture. He grabbed my hair with a violent force, then pulled my head back to the point I thought he was going to break my neck.

Shaking from pure terror, I was motionless to retaliate. He had me restrained so tightly that all I could do was beg for mercy through the flood of my own tears. Yet, not even my tearful pleas of him to show me kindness were enough to waiver his condemnation. He knelt down so his face was perfectly aligned with mine. I continued to beg him to spare me and please let me go.

There was nothing I could say or do. My words were futile. They only seemed empty and meaningless to him. He knew I was unable to fight back, which made me an easier target for him to play with my vulnerability. He simply smiled as he relished in the delight of seeing me quiver with fearful anticipation. Without even realizing it, due to his terrorization, I lost control of my bladder. As he profusely laughed about that, in what can only be described as volatile tone, he looked directly in to my eyes and at the top of his lungs screamed, *'You're a cock-sucker! All faggots must die.'* I lay convulsing on the floor, saturated from the waist down in my own urine-soaked pants, too afraid to move.

Even before he finished that despicable threat to my life, his posse of mates gathered around cheering, as though they were at a football game. That entire situation was all too reminiscent of the last beating I received from my previous school. I thought that was going to be the moment when he would unleash his anger and serve me the most savage bashing that I would have ever received. Although, almost as quickly as it begun, he let me go. I nervously waited for what was to come next. As I lay stunned, I thought perhaps he was actually going to show mercy on me. As it turned out, he was again biding his time. I had once again been spared, but I wondered for how long.

It was obvious he seemed to enjoy the mind games more than anything else. He simply took great pleasure in tormenting me to the very brink of my despair. I can still hear his mates laughing in the background as he stood over me. They too, were waiting for him to plot his next coldhearted move. His parting gift to me was spitting in my face, which led to his mates following suit. As they disbursed, they continued to tease *'the fag who wet himself'*, which was immediately followed by the united bellow of their merciless chant, *'kill the fag'*.

I lay silently shaking on the ground, too scared to move away, feeling dirty and so incredibly humiliated. I was overcome with an inconsolable sense of devastation. It became apparent that his mind games were only going to continue, until the time was more appropriate before he sought his vengeance. That exploit left me not only severely traumatized and destitute, but physically fearing for my life. Without any hesitation, I knew my only option was to escape the confines of the school grounds. Terrified and overcome with sadness and devastation I ran as fast as I could, crying and suffering all the way home.

I was so incredibly troubled and riddled with exorbitant fear that I was unable to speak at all. The mind control which that boy had over me was nothing, compared to what would be awaiting my return to school. Because of that, I replayed the same question over and over in my mind, *'Was he all talk, or was he really going to kill me?'*

Up until that point, I thought I worked extremely hard to put the demons of the past behind me. Sure enough, those very demons were again staring me in the face, more ferocious than ever. I continued to be taken back to that same emotional carousel which I had been on ever since I was a young boy. It seemed as though I was destined to continue to live a life that was filled with sorrow, humiliation and torment. I never *once* asked for that treatment. It was always brought on by other people who thought that's what I deserved. I just wanted to be left alone so I could be just be me. I simply wanted to be happy.

In my deepest, darkest moments at that time, I wondered if living this life was actually a life worth living at all. I entered that same world of darkness once before, but thought I managed to see light at the end of that tunnel. Perhaps I was wrong. Perhaps I was led to believe that I was a good person who deserved better, by those I was closest to. Although, my reality was telling me that they were very wrong.

I wondered if those people who saw the good in me would still think I was a decent person, if they knew the truth about who I was and what was happening to me. Nothing else seemed as bleak as where I was emotionally. I didn't believe I would ever see that light at the end of the tunnel, ever again. I was trapped, inadequate and helpless. I was lost in a bottomless pit of obscurity. As I could see no reconciliation in sight, I gave even greater consideration to how I could overcome those recent events, which would set me free from the enormous pain and depraved sense of guilt that was killing me. All avenues of hope seemed to lead to nowhere. There only seemed to be one reoccurring pathway, which was again, the calling for my death.

Whilst I continued to grapple with the those thoughts of death, no matter how much serious consideration I gave to ending my life, I couldn't seem to find my own conviction to go through with that final act. Besides, I knew I needed to somehow fight back. I didn't want to become a victim of circumstance. In my mind, my objectives were very clear. All I wanted to do was return to school and obtain my Higher School Certificate in order to build a better life for myself. By taking my own life, I would defeat my own goals, no matter how far out of reach they seemed to be at that time.

As sad as it was to admit, I began to think that people who were different from what society expected, such as gay people, weren't worthy of an education like the 'straight' kids were. It appeared that due to my sexual orientation, I was deemed to receive a substandard level of schooling. I knew I wasn't a second class citizen, therefore, I wanted to prove society wrong. I realized that I needed to live through that experience, just to be granted my own personal victory.

It was several days before I returned to school. I once again found solace in that secret park near my house. It was there I realized the confidence I once had when I first started that new school had now been torn away. Before making the decision to return to school to complete my studies, I truly thought I had worked hard to make changes in my life which I believed were necessary for me to become accepted by others. However, I was now left to find the answer to a question, which at that time, didn't seem to have a definitive answer. I thought, 'Was I able to rebuild any part of my life after so much had already been taken away?'

Due to that last fearsome bullying attack, I found myself looking over my shoulder every time I left my house. I allowed myself to be become paranoid to the extreme. The anxiety and dread that I felt had a tight strangulating grip around my entire existence. My personal safety had again been jeopardized. Not only had I become scared of the *unknown*, but also the *known* was just as terrifying. I thought that every person who looked at me wanted to inflict harm upon me. I even felt as though those who *didn't* look at me only took pity on me because they were disgusted that I was gay. Regardless, it felt as though every single person who looked in my direction thought I was suffering a dirty affliction which needed to be dealt with, one way or another.

I tried every possible angle to ensure my safety was paramount, both inside and outside of the school environment. I even reported that latest incident of bullying to the police. However I was told, in no uncertain terms, until such time that he physically injures me, their hands were tied. According to them, apart from that bully's intimidation tactics, there was no 'proof' that he was trying to endanger my life. There was nothing they could do. It became evident that even the police department thought the same way as my previous school. Their only difference, the police didn't suggest that I make an appointment with a psychiatrist.

There had to be a solution to what I was subjected to, but I was running out of options. I continued to exhaust every possibility to make sure I was safe. As I didn't feel as though I had any further alternative, I decided that was the time to speak with other teachers, career counselors and even the school principal. I thought it was now in my best interests to speak with anyone who I thought would listen and proactively assist me with what I needed, but unfortunately, they too, dismissed me, suggesting that my situation wasn't as bad as I was making it out to be. My desperate cries for help only continued to fall on deaf ears.

By all accounts, the information I received from those people who were supposed to help, all had one common denominator. I had to wait until I was hurt or in the worst case, dead, before anyone was able to help me. Nevertheless, at that time, I still excluded telling my parents about my volatile circumstances. I thought if the police and school facility couldn't or wouldn't help, then what could my parents do?

It didn't take long before I started to lose complete trust in a system which was allegedly designed to assist those in need. As far as I could see, they didn't seem to be serving any greater purpose to anyone. My sufferings continued to be swept under an invisible carpet, deemed too difficult to deal with. The belief that I once had about my voice being heard, was rapidly starting to disintegrate. I started to wonder, *if I wasn't gay, would people care more about me or at least be more willing to offer an abundance of help to make sure I felt safe and secure?*

It wasn't long before I became that timid, withdrawn little boy again. My faith in humanity had slipped away. I appeared to have fallen through the cracks of society, without even being recognized. I was again that same little boy who was too afraid to try new things or explore new adventures, due to feeling nothing but extreme fear. I was made to feel tarnished, almost somewhat repellent. It was as though I wasn't entitled to a fulfilling life like the other kids. I had to miss out on the joys of growing up because people couldn't see beyond their own bias or hatred. I strongly believed that my only legacy to this world would be a damaged spirit which no one would ever be able to love.

As that exhausting school year continued, I dodged and weaved my away around the school grounds to make sure that I didn't come across those senior boys. To be honest, I had actually taken extreme measures to ensure that I wasn't making contact with anyone at that school, for any reason. If it meant that I had to walk down to the back of the school oval and around the long way to get from one class to another, that's what I did. I left nothing to chance. I couldn't face another degrading attack from those bullies. Their actions had taken its toll on everything that I once lived for. More importantly, my sense of freedom had now been taken from me also.

Whilst my avoidance of any other human being at school seemed to work for a short time, I always suspected my luck would run out. Unfortunately, it wasn't long before my luck did come to an end.

It was on an unusually hot Melbourne day, when I was again confronted by that senior boy who silently promised to take his revenge on me. Also, once again, I was in the locker room. As I turned to leave to go to my next class, there he was, with that same despising look he had toward me. His chest was inflated and the muscles in his arms were flexed. It was clear from his uncompromising look that he was ready to do more than intimidate me. He was about to demolish me. I froze in the anticipation of that moment. Stunned, I literally was not able to move at all. I believed that day was going to be my time to inadvertently say goodbye to life as I knew it.

In a panicked frenzy, I hastily looked for an escape. As I turned around, I noticed the swing-back doors to the locker room were suddenly locked by his mates from the outside. It was then, he slowly walked towards me with that same horrid look of disdain on his face. With every step he took closer, I could see the burning rage he had toward me smoldering in his eyes. He was that aggravated, I could almost feel the heat emanating from his eyes.

There was something which made that occasion feel different though. Something told me that his intentions were to do more than his usual campaign of intimidation. Perhaps it was his intense anger which made me realize it was a fight or flight moment. It became cemented in my mind that it wasn't just going to be another scare tactic moment. I had to either stand my ground the best I could, or be taken away from school in an ambulance, or worse, in a body bag.

To say that I was petrified was a gross understatement. I was trembling uncontrollably. The sheer anticipation of that moment had me unexpectedly blind sighted. That day had become the reality which I had been dreading for weeks prior. Petrified, I stood in awe of that beast-like boy who only wanted to break me in to a million pieces, for reasons that weren't justifiable to me at all. With quivering legs, I continued to try and stand tall the best I could, but I was sure my legs were going to give way at any second.

I felt as though my only redemption would be to surrender myself to him and let him pulverize me. In that moment, I became submissive to his command. I thought it best to allow him to do what I was too afraid to do for myself. At least he felt justified to take my life away from me. By having him destroy me, it took the onus off me having to make that decision myself. Besides, admitting defeat seemed like my only option, as I couldn't take any more of the distressing thoughts of horror which were furiously running through my mind.

With the last step he took before his imposing physique was standing directly in front of me, I felt an uncanny sense of calm and wellbeing. Perhaps I had come to the realization my life wasn't worth the air I was breathing. However, it was also within that split second, my mind set changed again. Perhaps that was because I didn't actually want to surrender to the peril of death after all. Maybe his direct threat to my life made me stop and think about what would be lost if I wasn't able to find my courage to fight back. Whatever the thought process was behind my motives, within those seconds I became so incredibly fueled by the pent-up hate and anger of my past. I then realized I didn't want my independence to be taken away from me, nor did I want my life to come to an end.

As he gradually brought his face down to mine, the more I felt my own unholy emotions taking over my entire body. Even so, I tried the best I could to remain poised and calm, but I was also conflicted with my own devious feelings from within. I was not only frightened by what was about to happen to me, but hideously enraged that I had knowingly allowed him to make me feel as though I was absolutely worthless.

As we stood in that moment, there was nothing but the sound of my heavy, pensive breathing between us. I braced myself as he opened his mouth to speak. Unsure of what he was going to say, he then asked, *'How's the filthy faggot today?'*

That was the moment I was waiting for. All of that capped emotion which I had inside me boiled over in to a display of rage that I couldn't hold onto any longer. Something inside me snapped and I lost all control. That feeling was similar to watching a volcano erupt with a severe and deadly force. I then raised my forearm to his neck, held him as tightly as I could, whilst pinning him against the lockers which were behind him. I felt nothing but resentment and hate towards him and indeed to those other boys from my past who made my life hell.

He was taken aback as he wasn't prepared for that unexpected onslaught. My forearm now had more of a powerful tight hold around his neck than it did before. If I'd pushed him any further back in to the lockers, I'm sure he would have stopped breathing. Although, I didn't care. I could already see there was no circulation to his neck, due to how white and colorless his skin had become. That only made me want to inflict more agony on him.

His once sturdy body became limp as he gasped for air. I saw that as my opportunity to take further control over him. I wanted to hurt him beyond repair. The more he struggled to overpower me, the more force I applied to his throat. As it was, the hold I had over him meant his feet were elevated several centimeters above the ground where we both stood moments earlier. His legs kicked through the air as though he was trying to tread water in the heart of a catastrophic tsunami. His calls for forgiveness meant nothing to me. His body becoming more lifeless as I clutched his throat with my other hand. With every move he made, my grip became more firm around his already restricted airway.

That strength I experienced was some kind of super human, animalistic strength which I had never experienced before. Incapacitated, he continued to squirm around, trying to maneuver himself in to a better position which would allow him to break free. He tried desperately to remove my trembling hand from around his inflamed throat.

Alas, there was to be no escape for that vile bully. I couldn't release him from my grip, no matter how much I may have wanted to. I needed him to experience that same type of pain and suffering which I had undeservedly endured from him throughout the year. I now had the power over him. I was in control. In that moment, I finally felt vindicated. It was as though my actions would have been justified had I wanted to snap his neck and kill him. My teeth clenched so tightly, I thought they were going to shatter. I looked directly in to his eyes as he continued to unsuccessfully struggle to break free. In that same foul tone of voice he used with me previously, I shouted through my clasped teeth as loudly as I could, for everyone to hear, *'The fag is fine, thanks for asking.'*

Once I let those words out, I released him from my grip, then forcefully pushed him down to the floor. I showed him the same mercy and the respect as what he had extended to me. He continued to hold his hands around his red-raw throat, gasping for whatever air he could get in to his lungs. Due to him being in an immense pain he couldn't say anything or even find the strength to retaliate. It was obvious that *he* was now scared of the unknown. He tried to scurry away, but it was evident that I had inflicted a vast amount of pain on him. He wasn't in any position to move.

I stood over him, but he was still powerless to defend himself. Whilst I felt empowered, I was also saddened by the sight of him helplessly lying on the floor. He was scared, frail and unable to come to terms with what had just taken place. In many respects, I knew that I was now no better than him. I had committed an act of violence toward another human being. That type of bullying was no different to what had been inflicted upon me all of those years prior. He remained lying on the floor, still unable to move. He was only an empty shell of a person, one he thought he would never be. He looked back up at me with fear and sadness in his eyes. All I could see staring back at me was a mirror image of myself. I knew all too well how it felt to be in that fragile position. Unfortunately, my vindication was short lived. I realized that I too, had become a violent predator.

Throughout those fiery minutes of battle, there was one other thing that surprised me the most. His mates, who were outside the locker room, didn't come to his aid at all. They merely stood outside, silently watching. To be honest, I would have expected them to intervene and try to stop me from hurting their friend. However on that occasion, there were no chants of victory, or no moments of glory from them. It appeared that there was no shared solidarity when push came to shove.

As I look back now, I certainly don't believe that violence was the only answer to solving my problems. However, due to extreme circumstances beyond my control, I unfortunately reached my breaking point. His deplorable actions sent me in to a rage unlike any other which I have ever experienced before. I never wanted to intentionally hurt that boy. In that split second though, my mind and body had been taken over by unadulterated fury. I thought the only way to get out of that situation was to fight back. The other alternative was to risk the possibility of having my own life taken away from me. It was certainly a fight or flight moment, which was twofold with a variety of different emotions.

It wasn't long before that incident that I had considered my options with regard to what course of action I would take to defend and protect myself. At no point were my actions, at that time, premeditated. Not in my wildest dreams would I have imagined that I could have been capable of taking the stand I did. I never thought I had the courage to confront, or attack a bully before. Although, whilst the act of what I did was somewhat courageous, I was left with a feeling of emptiness and empathy for that boy. My actions on that day will remain as a bittersweet feeling, that I will live with forever.

I have to admit though, I became concerned he might try to avenge me or seek his own retribution shortly after that attack. As scared as I was of that happening, it wasn't to be the case. He and his mates never crossed my path again. Perhaps they were more afraid of me, than I ever needed to be of them. I think I had proven my point to all the kids at that school, that if needed, I could fight back with anyone who had disrespected me. I also believe the rumors from that day would have spread like wildfire which assisted with me being left alone. That day brought back a sense of freedom, whereby I was able to roam around the school ground as I pleased, without hiding away. That achievement was more than I could have ever wished for.

It took a couple of weeks for me to come to terms with the feelings that attack left me with, they were both good and bad emotions. Just for a moment, I wondered how differently my previous high school experience would have been if I'd only found the energy, strength and determination to fight back with those bullies from years gone by. Once again, I found myself retreating to that happy escape from reality, but that time my visit to hindsight was only fleeting. I didn't want to dwell on the 'what if'. I only wanted to revel in my new found immunity.

That was the first time in my life I experienced an irresistible taste of rebellion. Although it certainly wasn't as glorious as I had dreamed it would be. I found it to be more of a humbling experience. I never wanted to hurt anyone in my life. All I needed was the validation and reassurance from those people around me. I wanted them to let me know that everything was going to be alright, regardless of whom I was or where I was headed in life.

With my own personal acknowledgment and acceptance for what I did to that bully now behind me, I was able to concentrate on what I had set out to do in the first place. Not only did I proudly finish the year at high school with a new lease of life, I accomplished what, at times, seemed to be an impossible achievement. I received my High School Certificate and graduated. That was an extremely difficult year, emotionally, mentally and physically, but one that was probably my most fulfilling, thus far on my journey.

One of the biggest lessons I learned throughout that year wasn't taught in the classroom. My school experience was much more than learning through the eyes of another person, about past events and how our forefathers shaped our current world. If I had taken away the text books, teachers and classrooms, I realized all I would have been left with was an education which taught me about people, society and the beginning of a journey to my own self-discovery. Whilst what I learned in the classroom was necessary, nothing seemed as important as the firsthand education I was taught by living the lessons of life.

I soon understood how important it was for me to take on and tackle every experience and every challenge that I had been confronted with, head on. Some of those experiences were good, some were not so good and some were even indifferent. Even those indifferent challenges had the ability to define who I would become. I realized that every experience I lived through had the potential to dramatically contribute to my own real life success story. I truly believe this opinion needs to be shared with everyone who is unable to yet see the reasons behind the experience they're currently living through.

Through the achievements I made and the lessons I learned throughout that year, from both real life and of course the classroom, I felt as though I could and would be able to positively contribute to society. I realized that I wasn't a burden.

Although, I still didn't know where my life was going to lead now that school had finished. I just knew that I was hopefully in a better position, both mentally and emotionally, whereby I could more easily assess and embrace the future challenges which would inevitably come my way.

At the Edge of the Rainbow

Shortly after leaving high school for the last time, I commenced working at another full time job. I was still unsure of what career path to take, so I decided that I would continue within the retail industry. I hoped that working back in a retail environment would provide the short to medium career prospects which I needed at that time.

I started working with an employer who was and still continues to be, one of Australia's largest retailers. That company would not only provide a stable platform where I gained valuable employment skills, but took me along the path that led me closer to my journey of self-discovery, which was unlike any other journey I had been on before.

I always appreciated working for that large national retailer. I was constantly surrounded by so many different and diverse people. It opened my eyes to a large cross section of the population whom I had never been exposed to before. Every day at work I would encounter more remarkable people from different cultures, different countries and people who basically just had different lifestyles to me.

Being employed in the menswear section, I discovered I had many hidden talents which I never knew existed. Apart from my wondrous abilities to superficially admire the male clientele, I realized I not only excelled at customer service, but also achieving daily sales targets through whatever I needed to do to ensure a sale was made. More importantly, I really enjoyed interacting with a vast array of people, both other staff and customers alike. I took pleasure from getting to know who they really were.

I was also excited by working with so many different people, as they all had very different personalities. It was there that I started to question who *I* really was. I noticed that my way of thinking was starting to change, for the better. My thought process was no longer a case of *who do I want to be?*, but more so, *who was I actually becoming?*

Although I was still quite young, I recognized I probably had some more emotional baggage weighing me down to that of other people who were my age. That made me reluctant to allow myself to personally get too close to anyone. I wanted to feel comfortable with their acceptance of me before I'd open myself up and share my experiences. However, I would randomly share excerpts of my humor and little snippets of who I was with my colleagues, but there was never any real depth or substance to my personality.

That time in my life was an enormous period of change. First and foremost, my main ambition was to try to exorcize the demons which had plagued me from a young age. I made the decision to let go of all of that the baggage which weighed me down. Although, I wasn't entirely sure how I was going to execute that. I even contemplated seeking advice from a professional counselor, however, I believed that I was able to rebuild my own life, in my own time. I wanted to try to heal myself first. I felt as though with every small step I took, there would be a bigger step just waiting to come to fruition, which would lead to my emancipation.

It was also no surprise that over a period of time my confidence had become impaired to a point that I found it extremely difficult to even look people in the eye what I spoke, or to even smile without covering my face. One thing was for sure though, I didn't want to fall back in to that trap as I had previously been, which was to continue living a life that was designed for other people's happiness. I wanted to create a life that was planned and intended for me to live. Without me having to undergo a complete overhaul of my existence, I knew that dramatic changes from within needed to be made first.

I believe the road to self-discovery can be a very personal and long route. Sometimes I was taken on a path with many turns and developments. To internalize my own being and dig deep to expose every element of who I was, after already having to deal with many different obstacles, was very confronting. That process was also one of the most painful, to say the least. That was the fork in the road where my life had led me at that exact point in time.

I felt blessed that my discovery wasn't so much about unveiling my sexual identity. Although, maybe I was a little slow on the uptake to know which team I was batting for, considering everyone else throughout my school years knew before I did. However, my discovery was more about uncovering and accepting myself, for who I was as a person. Then, I knew I had to somehow guide myself through the misconceptions and stereotypes of that life I wanted to be living, which were brought on by my peers, my parents and society. It seemed to be a big task. I understood that living true to myself would mean I may need to move mountains, but that was a challenge I was willing to accept.

I certainly never felt ashamed of the fact I was gay. To be honest, that's only a small percentage which makes up the huge picture of who I am. However, I carried the burden of shame for how society and my peers conveyed their messages of hate towards me, because I was gay. I was only a child. I never asked to be an outcast. That realization also greatly affected the outcome of what I had to endure every day, both in and out of school.

It was the belief of what other people thought constituted a 'normal' lifestyle which challenged my own views of what I wanted. Whether that belief came from the parents of those kids, the media or people in authority, my conviction was stronger. I knew I wasn't able to remove a part of myself which I had been born with. What I could remove however, were people in my life who wanted to have a negative and toxic impact.

Throughout my journey of discovery, I realized I had allowed people from my past to take advantage of my kind nature and abuse it for their own selfish gain. Those same people had conditioned me to believe that I was worthless and in effect, forced me to live in uncertainty and fear. Perhaps they too had been living with their own type of fear. Maybe they were scared of what they didn't understand, or possibly, they realized they were actually no different to me. Regardless of their reasoning, I found myself in a position where I needed to discover my own sense of belonging, without the preconceived notions from other people.

As time went on, I was settling in and enjoying my new job. I started to integrate with more people than I had previously. It seemed most people were more than happy to share an abundance of different stories and experiences. For the most part, I felt a true sense of belonging. That was a concept which was somewhat foreign to me as I had never really fit in before. I embraced their acceptance with open arms. I even found that I would share aspects of my life, with a little more depth than I had previously. I discovered that I was like a book, which was to be opened by the reader for the very first time.

One day as I was having lunch in the work cafeteria, another staff member from a different department asked if he could join me. I had seen him around the store and we would often just exchange a few polite words as our paths crossed. I thought it would be nice to have some company while I was eating lunch, so I agreed. We had never actually engaged in any meaningful conversation, until then. Little did I know, because of that lunch break we shared, my life was about to be changed forever.

During lunch, our conversation flowed particularly well. The more we spoke, the more we both found out that we had many similar interests. In fact, that lunch ended up becoming more like he and I were old friends having an overdue catch-up. The only thing missing though, was an endless bottle of wine. Nevertheless, over that lunch one topic led to the next. We then got on to the subject of nightclubs, when he asked if I wanted to go out to a club that following weekend. I was a little surprised by his invitation. I thought his advances toward me were a little forward. However, he went on to say that he socialized at a gay nightclub known as 'The Peel', in Melbourne's inner city suburb of Collingwood.

The Sir Robert Peel Hotel is one of Melbourne's longest serving gay bars. Over the years, that hotel has seen many interior transformations. However, it has always remained a dance bar which has kept up to date with the changing times over the years. 'The Peel' is a well-known institution amongst the gay community, featuring drag shows, a selection of the finest DJ's and an atmosphere that is second to none.

I probably seemed a little aloof when my colleague asked if I wanted to go out with him. More so, because I thought he was giving me some cheesy pick-up line at work. As it turned out, he was just being friendly. He wasn't trying to seduce me. He swiftly went on to say, that he and his boyfriend enjoy going to that club regularly. They could dance all night and meet all kinds of interesting people. Ultimately, they were free to be whoever they wanted to be.

There was never a question or doubt in my mind regarding his sexuality. He was slightly older than I was, but he was an openly gay and proud man. He spoke of his identity as if the entire world was gay. That was something which I certainly hadn't been exposed to before, but found refreshing, as I saw that there are actually people who have no fear of their individuality. Listening to him speak, I never wanted that lunch break to come to an end. I was fascinated by hearing his stories about life, love, along with some hilarious stories of his occasional misadventures.

The more he spoke of 'The Peel', the more intrigued I became. As he continued speaking, my mind began to wander with many thoughts of what that club could be like. His invitation seemed to be the perfect introduction to a life which I had been curious about for many years. It was also very timely. I relished in the opportunity to start exploring a lifestyle, which I was brainwashed in to thinking was filthy and taboo. The impression I was getting from him as he spoke, was that 'The Peel' and indeed his lifestyle was anything but that.

Without hesitation, I immediately accepted his opportune invite. I became extremely curious to not only venture out to my first gay nightclub, but to also step outside of my comfort zone. I was unbelievably excited and incredibly nervous, all at the same time. It was then arranged that we would go out that following Saturday night. Although, being as impatient as I am, it seemed as though that Saturday night couldn't come fast enough. I was so looking forward to being in an establishment where there were other likeminded people. The wonders of 'The Peel' seemed as though it could be a dream come true. I couldn't wait to enter that magical wonderland, which I hoped could become my new playground.

In the lead up to that night, I was more curious than ever to know what that club was going to be like. I imagined it to be a safe place, with a warm and welcoming vibe. I also believed it would be a haven where any person could be themselves without worry, negative opinion or fear. As appealing as that new endeavor was, in the back of my mind I was also a little scared of what the reality was actually going to be like. Thoughts such as, *'Could my parents be right about those places?'* and *'What was I to do if I arrived and I didn't like what I saw?'* rattled around my head. To be honest, I knew that if I didn't go, I would never have known what I could have been missing out on.

After a few short days, that Saturday night which could potentially change my life forever had arrived. I was ready to jump into the deep end and surround myself with whatever the night would offer. To protect myself from any lectures that my parents would have given about going to a gay bar, I lied to them about where I was going that night. As far as I was concerned, I had no alternative, but to lie. I wasn't actually sure if they quietly suspected that I might have been gay or not at that point. Although sadly, I wasn't able to be honest with them anyway, due to the fear of their judgment. Regardless if they were uncertain or not, I *knew* they wouldn't approve of me going to a gay bar.

For that entire Saturday afternoon, before I was about to embark on a new adventure that night, I couldn't think of anything else but 'The Peel'. I was so consumed with the idea of being free. I was beside myself with anticipation. I also have to admit though, as curious as I was about exploring that new way of life, my nerves had taken over my ability to think rationally. I became giddy by the thrill of the unknown.

At last, the time had arrived for me explore those very boundaries of that unknown. I was standing at the edge of the rainbow, still slightly unsure if I was actually ready to embrace the pot of gold, which awaited. I arrived in Collingwood shortly after 10:30pm. I wasn't sure what to expect if I went inside the club alone, so I thought it best not to tempt fate. I remained seated in a nearby park whilst I waited for my work colleague to arrive. Sitting in that park I could hear the music thumping loudly. By all accounts, from what I heard coming from the inside of the hotel, it sounded like any other nightclub which I'd heard about previously. Even from the outside, that hotel appeared to be like any other.

'The Peel' is an older style building, circa 1912. It looks like most of the other unassuming bars that are littered throughout Melbourne's inner city suburbs. Even back then, there wasn't anything to denote that it was a gay bar. Perhaps many who passed by were unaware of the type of clientele on the inside. Today, the world famous *'Peel'* hotel still continues to hold prime position on the corner of Peel and Wellington streets. With a bold bright rainbow flag flying proudly from the roof, the exterior facade still looks as majestic as it did back then.

The longer I waited for my colleague to arrive, the more curious I became about exploring the mysterious possibilities of that night. It was those possibilities which also had me trembling with an energetic restlessness. I was savoring the feeling of intense jubilation. I'd never felt those two very strong emotions before. Those combined feelings gave me a wonderful sensation of being intoxicated with excitement.

With every slow passing second that I continued to wait, I found that my anticipation was taking on more of a fear-like state. The world around me seemed to have gone silent, as I could no longer hear the music. All I could hear was the second hand on my watch ticking in time with my heart beat, which seemed to get faster. I felt as though I was about to lose my nerve. I thought if I had to wait much longer, my feelings of fear and anticipation would turn in to bitter disappointment. Before I could give any more thought to the situation, my work colleague finally arrived. Although still a little hesitant, I knew it was time to take that leap of faith which was long overdue.

That leap of faith had soon become an inevitable realization that it was time to confront my fears. I was now overcome with an anxiously eager desire unlike any other. The closer I was to entering, the more extreme my feelings became. My heart was racing like a sports car at the Grand Prix, which enticed me even more to want to walk in. As I stood at the front door, the beat of the music was pulsating through every fiber of my entire body. My apprehension wasn't so much about going to a nightclub. Those feelings were more about what I would find happening inside a *gay* nightclub. Was I about to enter a seedy, underground world of perversion? At least, that's what I had been led to believe it would be. I continued to become overwhelmed with excitement and curiosity. Once the hotel door opened, I knew there was no turning back.

That same fight or flight response I experienced back in high school, was again with me. Although, I felt as though I had already passed the point of no return. All that had been alluring previously, was now beckoning me to enter. My mind was still unsure, but my intuition overruled any rational decisions I should have made. My heart was now pounding like a drum in my throat. It knew it had to be now or never. With a quick gasp of air to fill my lungs, I proceeded to walk through the door. I then crossed the threshold into an establishment which seemed to be like walking into an abyss.

Even as I write, at this very moment in time, the ecstatic chills of that night consume my body again. The hair on my arm has literally risen, along with the appearance of tingling goose bumps as I recollect. I am immediately transported back, as those very clear memories are flooding into my mind as though that magical night only occurred yesterday.

I recall I was welcomed in to the club with the Fine Young Cannibals song, 'She drives me crazy', which was blasting throughout every corner of the hotel. The bright flashing colored lights and lasers were shooting around the room like a fireworks display at midnight on New Year's Eve. The dance floor was crowded with revelers gyrating to the intense beat of the music. There was a pulsating current, which was complimented with an electric atmosphere that further enticed me into that new uncharted world.

I remember I stood close to the front door, just in case that dream I was living quickly became my worst nightmare. Instead, I was unable to move due to being in awe of all that was happening around me. I stood silently overwhelmed, ensuring I observed every second so I didn't miss any aspect of that irresistible new discovery. I was looking at nothing less than what I can only describe as a sensory overload. My eyes darted all over the room, not to miss any of the visual feast which was on display. Although, those who were looking back at me must have thought that I was the one that wasn't accepting of their lifestyle. Little did they know, I was completely enthralled and couldn't get enough of what I was seeing.

With every inquisitive turn of my head, I couldn't help but stare at the myriad of different people. They all seemed so diverse, well, to me they did anyway. I had never been exposed to such a glorious sight before. Everyone in the club had their own individual look, which made them stand out in their very own unique way. There was a respective vibrancy like no other, which was connected to each and every person. It was obvious those people were living the life that they wanted to live, without any inhibition.

It wasn't long after we arrived that we were approached by friends of my colleague. As we pushed our way through what seemed like thousands of semi-naked people, we were ushered to a table in the back bar. That's where we sat with my colleague's boyfriend, along with an eclectic group of their friends for the entire night. I was introduced to everyone at the table, however at that time, I was so completely absorbed by my surrounds, I only pretended to be listening whilst the introductions took place. The one thing that did stand out though, everyone who was at that table was incredibly accepting and extremely friendly.

I remained sitting at the table, astounded, whilst listening to the witty banter which was flying back and forth. I could barely keep up with what they were talking about. Although, I soon learned that they would use the word 'she' when they were actually talking about a 'he'. Phrases such as, 'Get her! She's been entered more times than the lottery' and 'Check out the package on that one. There's more meat inside her pants than there is in a butcher shop' were being thrown around with gay abandon, pardon the pun. It was almost as though I was listening to a newly created language, one which I didn't fully comprehend. Nevertheless, I found it very amusing and enormously insightful.

In between those random outbursts of banter, I remember wondering how must those people live their daily lives? Did they work? Were they just as confident with whom they were outside of our current environment? Surely those weren't the type of people that would cower away from others in society and live a life of disgrace. I had so many questions that I needed answers for. Clearly though, that wasn't the time to analyze situations or compare differences. That was a night of letting go of any emotional turmoil from the past and celebrating a new lease on life. I knew that night would only be the beginning of a life which I couldn't or wouldn't let go of. I remained enthralled by every second of what was going on.

As the late night turned in to the early hours of the next morning, I vividly recall not being able to escape the feeling of just how surreal that entire night was. For as far back as I could remember I was the outcast. I was the person who others didn't or wouldn't relate to. All of a sudden, I found myself in an environment whereby people wanted to know the story of who I was. There was a genuine feeling of acceptance. That feeling was like coming home after a long period away. It was comfortable, familiar and welcoming.

That night was filled with laughter and the celebration of simply being. We danced to all different types of songs and talked all night until the sun had come up the next day. I learned many things about myself that night, including the value of genuinely being true to myself, whilst not giving up on creating the life I wanted to live. I also realized that I still had a long way to go to deal with my own self-acceptance.

However, that night was the glimmer of hope I needed. It was the absolution I was looking for, which would hopefully lead me to take the right path in life. I wanted to be living that life, which

I was watching others so passionately enjoying.

I had finally been exposed to a lifestyle which had been deemed wrong by most of the people in my life, including by those I was closest to. Whilst I only had limited exposure to the gay community, it was hard to believe that other people with the same sexual identity as myself could be so well adjusted. Yet, those were people who must have been so determined to take charge of their lives and celebrate their own individuality. I admired how those people did that without allowing the fear and hatred of others to have a negative affect on them. They didn't seem to waste time with people who would only degrade or disrespect them. That was something I had only ever dreamed of. I was inspired by their generosity and candor. That only affirmed I had been accepted in to a community, which I had wanted to be a part of.

That following Monday, I returned to work a new person. I was a little more confident and assertive with my composure. I believe that night changed me in a positive way. Later that afternoon, I saw my colleague and I couldn't thank him enough for showing me a side of life that, if it wasn't for him, I may not have discovered until many years later, if at all. I felt as though I quickly bonded with him, as we did share similar traits. I saw him as a person who I aspired to be like. He was funny, charming and knew how to live his life. He had very quickly become my new found big 'sister'.

As I spoke with him, I couldn't do anything else but continue to rave and relive that entire night's events. He was happy to know that I had a good time and again extended the offer to go out again in the future. Although he and his friends went out regularly, it certainly wasn't every weekend. He reiterated that the invitation was a standing offer which was available for me to accept at any time. Of course, that was an offer which I jumped at. I was very thankful to him and his friends for allowing me to share their night with them. It was and always will be a night that

I hold very close to my heart which I'll never forget. I always refer to, and consider that supernatural night to be my 'coming out' party.

Over the days which followed, I couldn't stop thinking about that night at 'The Peel' and indeed the questions I needed to find answers to. I really needed to know how it appeared easier for some people to survive the turmoil without having scars from the past, whilst being able to find acceptance in the world. On the other side of that question, I also needed to understand why some would let their unspeakable experiences secretly consume their lives, which may eventually destroy them. I realize firsthand how damaging it can be to deal with a difference, but surely there's strength in unity. I believe we'd all benefit if we could find the courage to share our stories, to not only help ourselves, but to learn from one another.

There seemed to be such a dramatic contrast with how people dealt with their sexual identity. Although, I knew there were many contributing factors to that also. I assumed that I would find the answers which would help me understand why the journey is different for everybody, in due course. Until I did though, I knew I wanted to go back to 'The Peel' by myself. I needed to start my own true journey of discovery. Perhaps then I would find the answers I was longing for, sooner than I expected. At the very least, I might have the opportunity to meet someone in a similar situation to myself, who might also be looking for an answer to their own question.

I didn't wait too long before I went back though. That very weekend I returned to 'The Peel'. Although I again found myself lying to my parents about where I was going. I felt terrible about having to deceive them. Yet, I thought it was better for me to lie to them and continue leading my double life. Unfortunately, that's what I had become accustomed to for many years during the entire time I was bullied at school, so I allowed it to continue. Deception had become an easier way for me to avoid dealing with the truth of my problems head on. Besides, I couldn't see the point in disclosing any information about my private life, which my parents could have potentially used against me.

I have to admit that I was a little nervous about going back to 'The Peel' alone, as I didn't know anyone. At least last time I was with other people who could have helped me if I found myself in trouble, or if I just needed to talk about the feelings of what I was going through. Nevertheless, I ventured back into that exciting world.

That time, I noticed there was a different vibe from when I was there last. Although the club was just as amazing as I remembered it, I was more vulnerable and on guard than I had been previously. I felt somewhat exposed. As I sat at the bar, alone, I noticed there were many more guys staring at me. I sensed they wanted a little more physical action than what I was prepared to give. Don't get me wrong, I never considered their attention a bad thing. In fact, I quite liked my new found fame. Being in those unfamiliar situations was all just a brand new experience for me, which I was more than happy to enjoy.

To be honest though, I wasn't entirely sure of what I was looking for that night. I had no expectations for anything to happen. I wasn't very wise or worldly when it came to understanding gay life, so I remained reserved. I sat quietly at the bar watching as some people found new 'mates' for the night, whilst others were happy to dance the night away. Also, like myself, there were those who were happy to just sit in a nonjudgmental environment and watch the events of the night unfold.

A few hours passed and I was still sitting at the bar, drinking a bottomless glass of Southern Comfort and Coke. Just as I was thinking about going home, I was approached by a handsome man in his early thirties. He was about six feet tall, muscular build, with sandy blonde hair. His face was perfectly framed by a soft three day growth, which complimented his boyish look and naughty smile. With a pronounced Irish accent, he asked if he could join me at the bar for a drink. As there was no reason for him not to, I agreed.

For the most part, he was happy to sit and talk about all kinds of meaningless topics, such as Melbourne's well known cafe culture, along with and other local tourist attractions. As it turns out he was only visiting Melbourne, from Ireland, for business. Although it wasn't his first time in Australia, it was his first time visiting that club.

I have to admit, as much as I love an Irish accent, he was at times, difficult to understand over the loud music. Because of that, I wasn't always sure what I was agreeing to throughout many of our conversations. Although, I was happy to go with the flow of whatever happened. When our conversation did became stagnant, we danced to a few of my favorite songs. Let me tell you, apart from his very sexy accent, he had some pretty sexy dance moves too. He brought with him a new dimension of 'Dirty Dancing!'

Ultimately though, that night we drank and talked ourselves in to the next day. As the night progressed however, one thing did lead to another. It wasn't long after that we ended up back at his hotel room. In a state of drunken passion, we intimately explored one another until we both collapsed on the bed, feeling satisfied. Although the sex wasn't the greatest, which was a shame considering the moves he was pulling on the dance floor. Nevertheless, the sex served a purpose which fulfilled a desire that I needed to have met right at that time.

Once our intimate act had finished, I quickly dressed, said goodbye and left straight away. Yet, I remember thinking just how easy it was to actually meet random men at a club and should I choose to, have sex with them and disregard them hours later. I quickly realized there was something not only very erotic about the concept of meaningless one night stands, but also just how empowered I felt by doing so. The fact that I could make a man please me and not give much consideration to his needs or feelings, seemed to be a secret delight.

Unbeknownst to me at that time, I was about to embark on my very own sexual revolution. One that was about to become a sexual independence which would bring with it a major change within my life. That change would ultimately alienate me from the people who I loved, trusted and needed the most.

An Age of Liberation and Defiance

I soon discovered there were many other gay nightclubs in Melbourne also. Most of those clubs were regular bars with music playing, alcohol flowing and dancing arenas. However, it wasn't long before I was also exposed to 'other' types of gay clubs. Those clubs didn't offer a wild dance floor, with pumping music and a fully stocked bar. Instead, those clubs provided infinite dark corridors, with even darker rooms surrounding them. Some of those dark rooms even had a waist high hole in the wall which allowed the opportunity to receive anonymous pleasure from whoever was on the other side of the wall.

During that sordid time of my life, I had consciously entered an unknown world of gay sex clubs and bath houses. I became excited by exploring those alternative clubs. That type of environment provided the perfect setting whereby I could meet similar likeminded men. I only frequented those establishments for the sole purpose of engaging in gratuitous, no strings attached and relatively carefree sex. I was able to seduce men without having to make inane conversation, or ever see them again once I'd used them and quickly discarded them.

Whichever type of gay club I decided to go into, I soon discovered just how sexually gratifying it was to be a fresh faced, eighteen year old boy on Melbourne's gay scene. It wasn't long before my innocent quest for friendship and acceptance was quickly overshadowed, by what can only be described as a lustful and devious age of sexual liberation and defiance, which was against all that was pure.

That new discovery brought on many new opportunities to express a new found freedom. I no longer wanted to gain acceptance from the masses, I wanted to be desired in a way which made me feel respected. There were many popular, good looking men at the gay bars who I wanted to know. I knew by befriending those men, it would only bring me closer to exploring that different way of gay life. Most of all, there was a plethora of other men who I wanted to have anonymous sexual encounters with. They too, would seek the same gratification from me, especially as I was young and naive. Back then, I was considered a delicacy of 'fresh meat' on the gay circuit.

Excluding the sexual aspects, I valued the experiences which were associated with a new lifestyle within a community of my own. That community was then and still is now, so incredibly welcoming and accepting to those who need to take refuge in a world away from hatred. The people I met at nightclubs would often extend their hand of friendship, without question. That gave me greater hope and inspiration to excel with any endeavor I wanted to take on in the future. However, along with that, I soon learned just how consuming that new lifestyle and community could be. I allowed that new found hunger of my sexual appetite to destroy the genuine offerings which were available through that community. Instead, I turned my back on that goodness. I had welcomed debauchery in to my life, which before long, I permitted to take over and control me.

At that point, I believe I had lost touch with the realities of the outside world, even more than I had before. It was one thing to live a life which I was born to live and another to live a life which I had chosen to live. As far as I was concerned, I decided that my new life would only revolve around partying the nights away in gay clubs, with gay people. That also meant that I chose to continuously use men as my own personal sex toys, before shortly tossing them aside once they served their purpose. Then, it was straight back onto the playing field, where I continued searching for a new buffet of playmates to devour.

That desperate cycle was both repetitive and dangerous. Yet, that had become my life. There was no room for realism to interrupt and give me the reality check which I so urgently needed. I became addicted to the very lifestyle which seemed to offer the freedom and release that I had craved so many years earlier. I couldn't, or wouldn't see how self-destructive I was becoming. In my mind, it wasn't long before I believed that I was the center of the universe. I believed the gay community revolved around me and my needs. Sadly, with that tainted accomplishment, I became a product of my own immortality. There was nothing or no one who could hold me back from what I needed to do, in order to fulfill my selfish sexual desires.

Also during that time in my life, I was still managing to somehow hold down a full time job. I was working all day, then going to gay clubs until very late at night. Not being satisfied with going to the club once or twice a week, I almost made a career out of nightclubbing. I ventured out to a different gay bar every night of the week. Many a night, I wouldn't return home until the very early hours of the following morning. I also found myself lying by omission when my parents made inquiries about my movements. I would tell them that I was out with 'work friends', or out at well known 'straight' clubs. I said anything to throw them off the scent of my deception.

As far as I was concerned, my family home which I once held so dear to my heart, had now become nothing more than a disregarded motel. To add to that, I quickly realized that if one gay bar in Melbourne was closed or unable to satisfy my needs, I could find another, which *was* able to satisfy my desires. On the occasions there were no bars open, I often found myself meeting random men in local parks around Melbourne and the inner city suburbs. Without knowing it then, I was living up to the distasteful expectations of how gay men lived, according to my parents. That craving for acceptance which I once wanted, had now completely disappeared. It had now been taken over by a craving for endless sexual satisfaction, which would continue to feed my demand for rampant pleasure.

Night after night I continued to leave my family home, whilst deceiving my parents as to where I was going and who I was going out with. I became possessed by my own egotistical inclinations. I would have done anything to ensure I got what I wanted, without regard for anyone or anything. It was no longer about the gay community revolving around me, it was now about the entire *world* revolving around me. I had an unquenchable thirst to be serviced by other people. I expected that same subservient courtesy to be offered by my parents too. I had reached a point with them whereby instead of not feeling *comfortable* enough to explain where I was going, it fast became a case of not *wanting* to explain where I was going. After all, I wanted to know who *they* thought *they* were to be questioning *me*?

All that seemed important, was going out and meeting a new man for the night. In some cases it wasn't even for a night, rather just a few hours, nor was it usually only one man. I found myself in a situation whereby I learned how to manipulate men. I used my youth and inexperience to take full advantage of them. I believed I had a power which was greater than anything in this life, which I used to make those unsuspecting men obey me.

Depending on what I wanted on any given night, I would lure men into a false sense of reality until they gave in and provided all that I needed. I would tell them how attractive they were, or how I was looking for something more than a 'one off' experience. Once I obtained that false sense of trust and they believed that my intentions were in fact, pure, I continued to take advantage of them. It was generally on those occasions I exchanged sex, for cash. If they refused to pay, I would lie to those men by shocking them with the news that I was actually under the age of consent. I continued to play on their morality until they unwillingly parted with their money, then, I would immediately discard them.

At the bars, the scenario was slightly different. I would *tell* them to buy me drinks with the promise of doing whatever they wanted. The more intoxicated I became, the less inclined I was to care about who they were, or what they looked like. All that was important was my belief that I was respected because they were paying cash to spend time with me. Once they paid for my services, I felt as though I had the power over them. I was then accepted for the person I finally wanted to be, or at least, the person I thought I was at that time.

Meeting men in bars, sex clubs or parks for random sex became more than an addiction, it had become a way of life. I loved the 'thrill of the chase' because of the instant pleasure it provided me at that very moment. My actions continued to be fueled by my growing need for anonymous arousal, along with an almighty need for that ambiguous feeling of respect. Those power games continued to provide a sense of exhilaration, which only allowed me to be satisfied by a variety of different men, at any given time.

Savoring the delights of one man after the next permitted me to be in complete control of them, or so I thought. It was rare I would even ask their names, nor would I engage in any kind of pleasant conversation before, during or after sex. It was simply easier to just thank them after I got what I wanted, before walking away and never seeing them again. I became a person who continued to use men as though they were nothing but lifeless dolls, without the involvement of any emotion. My appetite for all things sexual had only further increased, until I reached the point of being completely out of control.

As far as my family life was concerned, I continued living that double life. I had become very comfortable in my self-created world of deceit and deception, even more so, when it involved anything associated with my parents. I wasn't going to let them dictate their rules to me. I had become defiant in every essence of the word. I believed I was finally living up to the standards which I had set for my life. I made my own rules, which brought along with it the freedom I wanted. I finally thought I was making my own individual mark on this world. I considered myself the type of person who others only aspired to be like.

During that period, it was obvious that my parents were becoming even more visibly concerned for my welfare. They continued demanding to know where I was going and who was I going out with. I always refused to divulge any information, mainly due to the repercussions which the reality of truth would bring. Because of that, I was reluctant to share any part of my life with them. Besides, I simply didn't believe they were worthy of my answers. After all, it was my parents who considered that being gay wasn't an acceptable way of life. To me though, there was nothing else that mattered in this world. As long as I was happy with my secret life *and* my secret sexual identity.

Coincidentally, it was also during that phase of my life where I began to experiment with drugs. Whilst at school, I never had to be concerned with peer pressure, as I was never a part of any group. However, that rebellious period in my life was a time in which I could try new experiences. The drug scene was becoming somewhat rife, throughout the gay club scene in those years, which made it easily accessible.

There was a cocktail of drugs at my disposal, such as speed, MDMA and cocaine. For a brief time, it became second nature to 'indulge' before hitting the gay bars. There were often a small group of us who would meet at one of their houses and get 'high'. My very first introduction to drugs was being handed a rolled up five dollar bill and snorting two lines of finely crushed white powder. I almost choked as it went deep into my nose. I couldn't swallow quick enough to remove the repulsive chemical taste, as that grainy powder slid down the back of my throat. It was as unpleasant, as it was exciting.

I, like other people I knew within the gay community at that time, had experimented with several different recreational drugs. On those occasions that I was 'high', I felt as though I had no fear of anyone or anything. I had a feeling of complete inner strength. That can only be described as 'a power trip of invincibility'. However, that was also a feeling which made me frightened, even more so than actually taking the drugs.

That powerful illusion, strangely enough, made me stop taking hard drugs *almost* as quickly as I started. I had always liked to be in control of my actions, even when I was in my most self-destructive phase. After all, I still knew what I was doing. However, those drugs relinquished my feeling of total control. Besides that, I didn't *want* to succumb to peer pressure. I believed I had always been level headed enough to understand that if I continued using hard drugs, my life may have turned out very differently, or worse, it may have even ended.

Funnily enough, I realized that I didn't need drugs anyway. I had already sought contentment with the 'high' I received from being so heavily engrained in the gay scene. I was living and breathing everything that involved the gay lifestyle. As far as I was concerned, the world outside the gay community was still nonexistent. I continued to have no need for anyone who was outside the boundaries of the life which I had manifested. I also had no time for anything which was only going to hinder my sexual exploits. In many ways, hardcore anonymous sex was not only my best friend, but it was also my drug of choice.

Within a matter of months, my rebellious behavior had completed a volatile 360 degree turn. I had always wanted to rebel against the other kids and teachers whilst I was at school. Apart from the one occasion where I attacked that bully in my latter high school years, I never did have the courage or mental ability to stand up for myself before that day. Throughout my entire school years, I was conditioned to believe that it was best to dismiss my own feelings. Although, due to suppressing those emotions then, maybe the seed of rebellion was planted from all those years ago.

Perhaps that's why my resistance to anything other than what was 'gay' had come to fruition. It seemed as though that period in my life became my time to make a stand and rebel against anyone who would keep me away from my new self-obsessed 'gay' world. Maybe I had subliminally conceived those current events from back in my early childhood. Whatever the reason, there was no sign in sight that I was ready to stop my continuous destructive tirade. Night after night, I still continued to live out that same repetitious scenario. The concept of sleep had very quickly become a notion of the past, as I believed it only impeded my ability to seek the rush of excitement which I had still been yearning for.

Of course, by that time, my parents were beside themselves with extreme worry. The more they tried to reach out to me and offer a lifeline of salvation, the more I closed myself off from their plights. I had only become even more secretive, aloof and extremely disrespectful towards them. I continued to believe that under no circumstances did I have to provide any explanations to them. I had completely shunned them, both emotionally and physically. My attitude towards my mom and dad had become one of ambivalence. Every time I looked at my mother and father, I couldn't let go of the feeling of bitter contempt which I had allowed to take over my mind. I wanted to indirectly punish them for holding me back from living a life that I was worthy of. I thought my abrupt rudeness was all that they deserved.

Although I wanted my parents to know that I was gay, I didn't want to tell them directly in fear of being disowned or unloved. To ease the onus of being direct about it, I would however, make flippant comments and remarks such as, 'Some parents are so naive about their children', as I walked through the house flapping my hands around like a seal out of water. I wanted to overtly show off my 'gayness', along with my obvious disrespect towards them. Back then, I just didn't have the courage to face the issue head on, like a man. I still continued to see my parents as the people who wanted to suppress my personal identity.

I believed I was entitled to live my life, my own way. I longed for them to accept that. I wanted my parents to accept me for who I thought I was and let me live whatever life I wanted to. I didn't believe that was going to happen though, so for my part, I formed a life which would shut them out. I didn't want any hindrance or interference from them. If they wouldn't accept me on my terms, then I wasn't going to give in to their demands. I thought that I was old enough to know what was best for me. Yet, the fantasy of that idyllic life which I thought I was living, was a far stretch from the reality which I had actually created for myself.

My promiscuous and recalcitrant behavior continued for weeks on end. If anything, my attitude only got worse than it had been. I became a destructive, arrogant and very selfish person. My parents became so concerned for me, they were now on the brink of their own despair. They were troubled by what was happening to their young boy. Their demeanor was now similar to that of mine whilst I was at high school. They seemed helpless and unable to reach out to me. I never knew that emotional pain transference was something real, however, it wouldn't be long before I realized just how real it was. I recall one particular day, the events which will stay with me and haunt me for the rest of my life.

I was feeling particularly exhausted on that day. The long nights of endless partying and lack of sleep were beginning to catch up with me. I was mentally drained and devoid of any kind of physical energy. All I wanted to do was sleep. I had just arrived home from work, when I was greeted by a very somber, 'hello', from my mother. She was leaning over the kitchen sink, wiping tears from her eyes and clutching at her chest as if someone close had just passed away.

As I walked in to the kitchen, the air instantly became cold and sparse. There was a distinct feeling of unspoken separation, which resonated throughout our entire home. It was obvious there was something very wrong. Of course, I didn't believe it had anything to do with me. I was too blind and closed off to think that I could have caused that immeasurable kind of pain. I took a step closer to my mom, but was immediately stopped in my tracks by a single question. Whilst trying to hold back her sadness, she tearfully asked, *'How would you react if your son was gay?'*

In a heartbeat, my blood ran cold and my body became numb all over. I was speechless. With her sorrowful words ringing in my ears, my mind was racing at a billion miles an hour. I quickly searched through my scattered thoughts for an answer to her awaiting question. However, that only stirred more questions in my mind, such as, *'Did she actually know that I was gay?'* If so, *'How was that possible?'* I continued to pause in silence. I didn't know where to look, or what to say.

Whilst standing there, shaking, I still tried to hastily figure out the answer I should give. Due to the extreme terror I felt, I could feel my core body temperature drop to an almost dangerous and freezing level by the second. However, the sweat dripping from my palms was the warmest part of my body. In a shocked and frenzied state, I gasped for air. I realized at that precise moment I had two options. I could either confirm, or deny her, the answer to a question which had clearly caused her an inconceivable amount of pain.

In the unbearable silence that followed, she turned and looked at me with profound sadness, which was emanating from deep within her soul. That was a look which I had never seen from my mom before. She had a vacant, despairing disposition. It was evident that her entire world had just crumbled down around her. As I looked back into her eyes, through my own dismay, I could see she was unable to take on any more of the pain which I had so heartlessly caused. There was my mother, a broken lady, who was still eagerly awaiting any kind of response to her unfavorable question.

I continued to scramble through my own thoughts to provide the right answer, whatever that may have been. I wondered if I had I gone too far with searching for my own identity. Due to my extremely vile and hurtful actions, I managed to crush the spirit of a lady who I loved more than life itself. Regrettably, I showed the same lack of regard for her feelings, in the same way those school bullies had repeatedly done to me. I knew I could never take away her grief. It all seemed too late to make those despicable wrongs, right again.

In a cloud of my own confusion, I managed to remorsefully blurt out the words, *'If my son was gay I'd accept him and love him unconditionally.'* As soon as I finished that sentence, my mom turned her back on me, then walked out of the kitchen. She left, with no other words spoken. I could only hear the sound of her crying as she walked down the hallway in to her bedroom, before gently closing the door behind her.

I called out to her, but there was no reply, only more of that sullen silence. There I was, alone, standing in that moment. All that surrounded me was the trail of devastation which my words and actions had caused. I didn't know what else to do or say which could rectify a situation, which had evidently become one of the most painful memories in my family's history. I again called out to my mom. Alas, there was no reply. Her grief was now consuming her in silence. She was locked away in her bedroom, secretly mourning the loss of her once precious little boy.

That situation caused me to become overwhelmed with those same feelings of pain and loss which I had endured back in school. All that hurt, anger and frustration which I felt back then, I had just inadvertently channeled onto my mom. Those feelings of extreme shame and guilt from all of those years ago had again taken over. However, those feelings were nothing compared to what my mother was now facing. She also had to deal with having a son, who had callously manipulated her love and trust, for his own selfish gain.

In that very second, I realized that I hadn't made any positive changes to myself since leaving school. My life appeared to be nothing more than a vicious circle of pain, which I was now inflicting onto those who didn't deserve it or never asked for it. My selfishness had reached a new depraved level. I imposed in tolerable grief onto the very person who I was closest to. The word sorry, had become redundant and empty.

From that moment on, my relationship with my mom had changed dramatically forever. I never felt as though I was her precious little boy after that. I had become a monster, who ripped her heart out and cut it into a million pieces. I had not only disrespected her, I was responsible for solely destroying all that was good in her life. I knew I would never be able to rebuild that same level trust with her again. I wasn't even sure if the love she once had for me was still there. To be honest, I didn't feel worthy of her love anyway.

Of course, I knew it would only be a matter of time before my father would also find out about the conversation which took place. Sure enough, that very night I was sat down by my dad to discuss how I could become a decent heterosexual boy and leave that *disgusting* gay lifestyle behind me. During that emotionally disconnected conversation, he spoke with a distasteful tone which inferred that I was no longer his son. As far as my father was concerned, I *was* disgusting. As he continued to berate me, I knew more than ever, that I had thoughtlessly torn our family apart.

That was something which I had accepted full responsibility for. I knew I couldn't turn back the clock and erase the sorrow. Those fearful thoughts that I once had about 'coming out' to my parents were now put to rest. I no longer needed to find the bravery to 'come out', but rather, I needed to find the courage to repair a broken relationship. I caused more suffering with my despicable actions, more so, than if I had only spoken the words of truth from a time gone by.

I do believe my dad was disturbed by my sexual identity. He never actually understood how I could be intimate with another man. However in a fleeting moment, I couldn't help but wonder if my father was more disappointed that I was gay, or if he was more ashamed of having a gay son which might discredit his work within our community. As I listened closely to him expressing his unfounded opinions of my lifestyle, his sentiments quickly turned in to a speech about damage control. That conversation was no longer about helping me. He wanted to know what would become of him if that secret was made public. It became cemented in my mind that he *was* more concerned about his own reputation.

I understood that my actions were unwarranted and deplorable. I didn't dispute that at all. However, at no point had I ever set out to intentionally hurt my parents. I don't think that any same sex attracted child actually does. Yet, I believe that sometimes the reality of a finding the inner strength to 'come out' to a parent or loved one can at times, become too much to bear. Back in my happy escape from reality, I thought that perhaps if I had confided in them about what was happening during my school years, then that situation may have never occurred. Maybe we would still be perceived as the picture perfect 'Brady Bunch' family.

Still, the actual reality of that situation had caused my home life to deteriorate to nothing more than an emotionless shell of what it had once been. My parents often made snide comments about how distasteful the gay lifestyle was when they saw an article in the newspaper or a segment on television which involved anything associated with the gay community.

Although, I believe it was only through their emotional pain and upheaval that they continued to convey those words. Yet, their remarks were not as hurtful as what I received during school, but their ongoing messages were clear. It was obvious that their preconceived judgment was towards a lifestyle which they believed I had *chosen* for myself.

Many nights I thought about the ways in which I could change the unhappy dynamics of my family life. It was evident that the more I tried, the less inclined my parents were to accept or even want to know their gay son. I had been slapped across the face with a harsh dose of reality. It didn't take long before I realized that I wasn't as powerful and courageous as I once thought I was. I was still nothing more than an insecure little boy. The life which I had created, was not the life I was born to live. It was nothing more than a fantasy to make other people, including myself, believe that I was someone who was able to command respect.

It was with that thought I again remembered back to my school days. I was no closer to being respected then, to what I was at that moment. If I thought it was only going to be as easy as giving away my toys to gain respect, I would never have caused the tragic circumstances which had unfolded. I would have said and done nothing, but simply given in to the mind control of others. However, that wasn't the case. I had given away my dignity and self-respect by becoming corrupted, through an abstract sense of morality with the hope that I would be honored. I realized that I had merely been used again, by those who actually had the power over me. It was *them,* who had allowed me to believe that *I* was in control.

I began to wonder just how that current situation with my family would impact on the rest of my life. What type of existence would I live now that I'd lost all that was good in my life? Without a family, I believed that my life was going to be cold and cruel. I thought by living out that type of existence, my life would be much worse than I had ever experienced before. I somehow desperately needed to find someone who could answer my questions and explain what I was to do next. I found myself clamoring through that eternal battlefield of erratic confusion once again.

As much as I wanted to seek the answers from other people, those were recurrent questions which could never be answered by anyone else. As I shuffled though my thoughts, I concluded that I had gone through those experiences because I needed to. If there was no catalyst to my self-centered behavior, I may have continued a life towards my premature death. Perhaps it was also necessary for me to also understand that everybody's journey really is different. It became apparent that it was what those brutal lessons taught me about myself, which mattered the most.

Nevertheless, at that time, those experiences never made the journey any easier for me. Especially not really knowing or understanding why I had to go through them in the first place. The one thing that was clear though, for some people, their lives and support networks are vastly different to others. There are people who are shown unconditional love by those who surround them, which assists with their survival through even the toughest heartbreak. As I no longer had that reinforcement, due to my own doing, I needed to find a way to first rescue myself, then salvage my family life.

Although, I seriously doubted that I would ever completely re-establish the same type of relationship which I once shared with my parents. I singlehandedly destroyed that. Even though, I never stopped trying to please them, in many different ways. With my plights of forgiveness, I seemed to be only giving up more of my own individuality. I found myself losing my own personality, just to prove how sorry I was. I was unable to convey that for me, being gay was not a 'choice', but rather, that 'choice' had been made by a higher power in the universe, possibly even before I was born. Sadly as much I tried to affirm that, there was no alternative or resolution in sight, I had to simply agree to disagree with my parents. That still didn't make the painful situation of my home life any easier to deal with, for anyone concerned.

In life, the reality is, there's always going to be people who are accepting of certain things and others who are not. I realized that it was the poor choices that I made which inevitably determined my own future happiness, or as it was at that time, my own misery. That outcome was supported by my ignorant and egotistical decisions, which for the most part, selfishly stemmed from my need to openly exploit not only my independence, but also my sexuality. Regrettably, that caused my actions to speak louder than my words. However, that's what I believed was necessary, in order to survive a subjective society which seemed to prejudge and critique my every move.

One of the few regrets which I continue to live with to this day, was that period of my life. I became nothing more than a shallow, self-absorbed person. I took every opportunity to deceivingly prove to the world that I was an independent, mature and wise person. By doing so, I caused irreparable damage to the people who I loved more than anything else. They never deserved that treatment. I had inexcusably alienated the very people who I needed the most, to help me survive.

That alarming turn of events taught me that I had the morality to make decisions which affected my day to day living. I realized that other people can only guide us through life, based on their own experiences.

Then, hopefully their stories would help shape who we could become. Still, I believe life is something we all need to experience through our own eyes, good and bad. It's only when we can honestly accept our past failures, we can then genuinely celebrate our present and future success.

As much as I wished I didn't have to experience some of those difficulties back then, I believe I needed to draw strength from those events, which would hopefully make my future more positive. Sometimes life can be an experiment, which we hope will eventually lead us to the right path and ultimately provide an encouraging enrichment to our lives.

During that time however, the road behind me was littered with harsh lessons. I quickly learned that independence wasn't about walking through life alone. For me, it is about demonstrating that I am able to stand true to my own beliefs and my own principles. It's also about sharing and understanding myself, without malice, to gain acceptance.

I realized that I didn't need to project my own prejudice or superficial belief that I was greater than anyone else who walks the same earth as I do. I only hoped the road ahead was going to show mercy for my past indiscretions.

Moving Out, to Move Forward

As the weeks went on, the more apparent it became that my family life was never going to be the same as it had been. Those 'not so discreet' comments about the gay lifestyle continued to run rife throughout my parents' house. The words 'immoral' and 'unnatural' became second nature during most conversations. No matter how much I tried to move forward and capture the happiness we once shared, it wasn't meant to be. Due to my unjustifiable behavior I'd crossed many boundaries, which I thought I would never cross.

Because of my inability to reconcile with my family, more than ever, I needed to think about what the road ahead was going to hold for me. Through gut wrenching sadness and intense remorse, I thought it would be best for all concerned if I made the decision to move out of the house which I once cherished as my home. Sadly, my forever home was now just a house. I felt as though my unforgivable actions had tarnished every single memory which was ever made there. In the hope I may be able to recover any kind of relationship with my parents, plus find my own path, that period became the time to embark on a discovery of my true independence.

When I finally made the decision to leave home, I realized that becoming a truly independent person was a frightening feeling. With the dread of the unknown, I began to doubt my judgment. Before long, the 'what if's' had crept in to my mind, destroying the only shred of confidence I had left. Although, I still believed moving out was my only redemption to a state of affairs which otherwise may have seemed impossible to overcome. Removing myself from that challenging situation and becoming self-reliant, may have been the difference between mending a shattered relationship, or letting it drift into no man's land.

With the events that unfolded during that period, I often thought about that day when my mom asked me how I would react if my son was gay. I found myself questioning her motives. That led me to internally ask myself if I had in fact, been so overt with my mannerisms that all of a sudden it became clear that I was gay. Whilst I couldn't answer that question, one thought led to another. Maybe something more sinister had taken place, but what could have happened? With my mind again racing to keep up with my thoughts, I wondered if it was possible that someone had told her what I'd been doing and where I was going on those nights. But I wasn't able to fathom the notion that my own parents may have had me followed. That idea was absurd, or was it?

A few days prior to the day I was questioned by my mom, I remembered overhearing a telephone conversation one evening. At the time, I didn't think there was anything unusual about it. However, the memory and outcome of that telephone call hit me like a bullet to my brain, which devastated my world even more. The conversation which took place was between an unknown person and my mom. Whilst she was on the telephone, I only overheard snippets of the conversation, but my mom used phrases such as, *'And then what did he do?'* followed by *'Were you able to get close enough to see what he did?'* Suddenly, like a ferocious tidal wave of severe emotions hitting me when I least expected it, everything had suddenly fallen in to place. I realized that I *had* been followed by a person I was unaware of.

To this very day, I still don't know who that person was. However, I could take an educated guess of who was scrutinizing my every move then reporting back to my parents.

Regardless of whom that person was, with the detailed description of what my parents had received from that informant, my secret life had been uncovered. The information my mom received, was clearly what prompted her to ask that question several days later. I never challenged my mom with my awareness to that telephone call. As far as I was concerned, it was too late, the damage had already been done. The information that was shared became the catalyst which caused the path of devastation, that ended up demolishing the very core foundations of my family life.

Angry by the betrayal of trust from my parents, I wanted to know how they could do that to me. How dare they instruct a person to follow me and then provide a detailed report, as though I was a mastermind criminal at large. I understood that I gave them every reason to doubt my credibility by behaving in a manner that was, to say the least, malicious and disrespectful, but I didn't believe that gave them the right to invade my privacy in a forum that was unscrupulous. To say that I was livid, was an understatement. I continued to feel a building level of resentment towards my parents because of *their* actions. Although, I couldn't help but think, *'Was my reaction one of a double standard?'* I already knew the answer to that question before I'd finished asking it. Of course it was. Whilst I was seething over what had taken place, it didn't take long before I realized that I was powerless to react.

What was done, was done. I just had to deal with the fact that my privacy had been open for discussion and judgment. Having to come to terms with their act of dishonesty, which I now believe to be similar to that of mine during that period, was another life defining moment. All I knew, was that I needed to act quickly and make some life changing decisions to rectify my horrendous living and family situation. My decision to move out became imminent. I had to make it happen sooner, rather than later.

That following day, I spoke with my friend at work about the events which had taken place. I broke down and unashamedly divulged every disgusting detail of the life I had been secretly living. I knew if anyone might be able to understand what I caused, I thought he would be that person. Not so surprisingly, he was understanding and sympathetic, whilst reaching out with a genuine sense of compassion. He could see how dire my situation had become. He racked his brain to offer a solution which could be my lifeline. Out of the blue, within minutes, he had a promising solution. He suggested I think about moving in with two of his friends. As it turned out, their housemate had just moved out to live with his lover, so there was a room available at their apartment, in the beautiful bay side suburb of St Kilda.

I always loved St Kilda, which is only six kilometers south east of Melbourne's CBD. It's situated on one of the most picturesque points of the Port Phillip Bay. St Kilda is a trendy suburb which is filled with an eclectic array of people. Once known for its underground night life, it's now best known for its music venues, restaurants and beach. Not to forget the world famous tourist attractions of Luna Park and the vibrant cafe strip that is Acland Street.

I was thankful to my friend and excited with the prospect of possibly having a place to move to. However, it never occurred to me that I would be moving out of my home under such a dark cloud of emotion. I guess I always wanted to believe that the situation at home would work out for the best. I wanted to reclaim that happiness from days gone by. Although, it seemed as though that wasn't going to happen any time soon. So, I decided there was no harm in looking through their apartment. The next day after work I went to inspect his friends' house.

Located on a beautifully tree-lined street, I instantly knew that apartment was going to be my new home. That had been confirmed once I walked through the ornate stained glass front door. That wonderful apartment was a 1960's art deco ground floor unit, in the heart of St Kilda. One of the apartment's main attraction was the large bay windows, which allowed the sun to drench the entire living room. Those beautiful windows led out to a leafy, paved courtyard. Their apartment was furnished by a mismatch of relics from a different era. There was everything from 1950's wall art, through to modern neon lighting. The alluring sweet smell of vanilla candles filled every room. That was an apartment of not only style, but one that had a warm and nurturing appeal also.

Within fifteen minutes after the inspection started, my two new housemates and I agreed the room was mine to rent. Any thoughts I once had about *not* moving out of my parents' home, became a distant memory. That home was a sanctuary, where I was welcomed to move in with open arms. Being in the surrounds of that homely apartment, I knew was going to be the positive change I needed to get my life in order. Whilst I was elated to have found a new home, that feeling was slightly overshadowed by the thoughts of informing my parents I was moving out. I wasn't sure of what their response would be once I broke that news. However, I could now put an end to the strained living arrangements, which I believe we had all become accustomed to.

It was later that night, I returned home and I told them I'd be moving out. Their reaction surprised me a little. The news that I was actually leaving home didn't come as any great shock. That saddened me. Don't get me wrong, I wasn't expecting them to beg me to stay, but I didn't think they would be so blasé about it either. Maybe they knew the time was coming. Throughout that entire conversation, it was suggested that perhaps moving away was the best approach to sorting my life out, then I would be free to begin a new life. They further suggested that it was alright with them if I wanted to move out the very next day, which I did.

By that stage, it became obvious that it was the time to leave my family home and move forward with my life. Having said that, my parents also supported my move. Perhaps that was more so for their own benefit though. To be honest, when I told them I was leaving, I could see a vague look of relief on their faces. That's what saddened me more than anything else. However, they also knew that our current living arrangement wasn't working for any of us.

The following day as I packed my belongings into the car, my parents approached me on the street and wished me luck for the future. Our conversation was almost mechanical. There was a distinct feeling of finalization attached to saying goodbye. There were no emotional hugs or kisses. I felt somewhat displaced. I only hoped that moving out wouldn't completely sever my family ties.

My dad looked staunch and sullen. My mom had a vacant look of sadness on her face. I believe that wasn't how either of them envisaged me leaving home either. Although sadly, it was through torrid circumstances which I had created that led to that unfortunate reality. I understood that there had been words exchanged and feelings raised which couldn't be forgotten as quickly as they occurred. Still, it didn't make that less than perfect situation any easier to deal with though.

Whilst that was a major moment of emotional upheaval in my life, I have always considered myself fortunate that my parents never asked, or forced me to leave their house. Although, during our final goodbye there was a coldness to their tone of voice which implied that once the door was opened for me to leave, that door would never be re-opened for me to move back in. That only confirmed what I had already suspected. From that moment on, I knew the magnitude of damage which I caused, meant I was unable to turn back time, no matter how much I desperately wanted to.

I was heartbroken to be leaving home, especially as it seemed so quick. If only there was a way that I could go back in time to relive those months again. Alas, that wasn't possible. I had to deal with the circumstances that I had been dealt. Whilst there were no words or gestures of reluctance from my parents to leave, I had to believe there would be a way to overcome that tragedy. I knew it wasn't going to happen overnight, but I hoped it would happen. Although, even after the pain I caused, I was fortunate that my mom assisted me financially, if and when I needed it. To me, that was an indication that not all had been lost. In a strange way, I saw her offer of assistance as a chance that we may one day be able to mend our broken down relationship.

I also never realized the powerful feeling of freedom could also be one of tremendous loss and sorrow. I always imagined the day I left home would be a day of celebration, a coming of age. Whilst I never thought my departure was a celebration for my parents either, maybe that's how they perceived my move. To be honest, I don't think I properly thought through the idea of leaving, especially as quickly as I did. Generally speaking though, that's how I had been living my life, act first and think later. That was habit which I knew I needed to break, without delay.

Unfortunately with the rapid departure from my family home, that would also be the last time I would see or speak with my siblings for many years to come. My once close family bond had been obliterated. My relationship with my brother and sister had now become disconnected. It was almost as though we instantly became strangers. Sadly, that also meant there were no Christmas invitations or special celebration invitations forthcoming either. From my perspective, I never felt as though I was welcome to return to my once beloved home, not even to celebrate a special occasion.

That night, after moving into my new home, I was in a pensive and reflective mood. I wasn't overly talkative and just wanted to retreat to the solitude of my new bedroom. I was lucky that there was a comfortable queen size bed provided by my new house-mates, as I wasn't allowed to take my bed from home. As I lay staring at the plain white ceiling above, I was contemplating endless ways in which I could make amends. I continued to quiz myself about those recent events, but there was no result. I felt emotionally void. With all of the mindless thoughts whirling around my head, not one of them would lead me to the answer of how I could make things right again.

I reflected on how my life seemed to slip away so quickly, without me even knowing about it. That led me to think of my parents. I wondered if they too, were thinking about me. I wondered if they had even considered accepting my apology. I genuinely understood that I created that situation, but I simply couldn't believe, or accept that I had become an enemy to those who I once held so close to me. At that point, it was like I was watching a B grade movie in my mind. A sad pathetic movie, where I was the star attraction.

In the flashbacks which continued to run through my mind later that night, I relived my early school days. I wanted to pinpoint a definitive moment where I had allowed my life to be stolen. The more I recalled every single minute of those years, the more I still came up with nothing. To be honest, I don't believe there was *one* defining moment whereby my life changed. It seemed to be a progression of events which made my life slowly diminish.

Due to a myriad of untoward circumstances, I realized I had lost control of myself. Perhaps that was due to a collective of different occurrences which involved both my sexual identity and my weight issues. Although *I* wasn't concerned by either issue, those two factors seemed to shade me with pain and humiliation, which had been brought on from other people. Maybe I was too blind to notice what was happening in my early years. Perhaps I was just too naive to understand how to regain the control that I so urgently needed, in order to take charge of my life.

Either way, whatever the reasons were behind my circumstances, my life had changed so dramatically. I felt as though I needed to physically go as far back as I could to regain the harmonious balance that once existed, many years earlier. Sadly, that wasn't even an available option. I had become a person who was only trapped in the present, reliving the story of a prisoner from the past, with no foreseeable future ahead.

I tried as hard as I could to not take on the responsibility for how others had once treated me. I knew I had to redefine who I was before I could take a stand and accept that my past cannot be changed. I could only change whatever possible future that putrid past experience would leave me with. However even then, I wasn't sure if those changes would want to be witnessed by the people who I once shared my entire life with. At that moment, I made a solemn promise to myself, to never give up on making my parents proud. I wanted more than anything to become their precious little boy again.

Even from within the first week of me leaving home, there were countless occasions that I called to speak with my parents. I especially wanted to talk to my mom, because I was missing her terribly. However, it was painfully evident by the tone of her voice that she was still obviously very hurt by my actions. Our telephone calls were often cold, distant and hurried. All I wanted to do was tell my parents how very sorry I was and tell them how much I loved them both. Unfortunately, those calls were always cut short and finished before I got the chance to express my love. On many occasions, after I'd hang up the phone, my heart would literally ache due to the enormous pain those futile calls inflicted upon me. I would sit quietly on the floor and grieve for hours after. There was nothing more I wanted to hear, than the words, 'We love you, son'.

Whilst I still didn't hear those words, my determination for restitution never wavered. After several more of those distant phone calls, I thought I had a breakthrough. Whilst on the telephone to my mom one afternoon, we were sharing the usual strained conversation, when I emotionally broke down. I began sobbing and heaving. The distance that was between my parents and I had evidently become too much to bear. Through a river of tears, I offered an apology which was sincere and heartfelt. I begged for their forgiveness, but my words didn't seem to penetrate.

Instead, my honest and loving dialogue was only accepted with a nonresponsive, 'Ah-ha.' I then received the same reaction when I told them that I loved them both dearly. Again, the standard reply I received was that same unresponsive mutter of, 'You too', before an abrupt end to our telephone call. Sadly, as much as I needed to hear their reassuring words of emotion, they never once told me they loved me after I left their house.

I didn't want to continually force my apologies over the phone. Although I had no other option as my parents were seldom available for me to visit their house and vice versa. I needed my parents to understand that although I treated them badly, I *was* sorry and that I *did* love them to infinity and beyond. I prayed that time *would* heal all wounds. I only hoped that they would one day accept me as their son again. My perseverance toward hearing my parents say they forgave me, or even loved me, was at that time, only a dream. I simply had to continue to wait and find refuge through the universe, until such time when they would hopefully tell me that they forgave me.

After several weeks of living in St Kilda, I settled into my new home and thought that my life was actually going relatively well. Although I was still devastated as I hadn't made any inroads with my parents. However, I continued to wait for that magic moment to hopefully come to fruition. As much as I wanted it to happen, I tried to believe that when they were ready to listen to what I had to say, the time would be right. Luckily, during those few weeks, my new housemates had become a slight diversion from the pain I was feeling over the situation with my parents.

It wasn't long before the three of us became very good friends. Those two men were different to many other people to who I had ever met before. I believed I could learn many things from them both, in many different ways. One of my housemates, a twenty-seven year old, worked as a male model. His stunning looks graced the pages of many contemporary magazines, along with holding his own on any catwalk he was paid to strut down. That wasn't his only job though. His second job had a very different side to his modeling career. He also worked as a gay sex worker.

My other housemate, a twenty-nine year old, worked in retail management for a large Australian menswear chain. Their lives were not only vastly different from each other's, but also quite different to mine. However, there were similarities which we all shared along our individual journeys. That made for an interesting dynamic, as we shared our stories and learned more of each other and our backgrounds.

It wasn't long after I moved in, that one of my housemates and I started chatting about a range of different things. Whilst one topic led to another, we got on to 'coming out' stories. I soon discovered that he and I shared a somewhat comparable story. We had both once come from a loving home environment until that one day when the life changing moment of 'coming out' had adversely affected our family lives. Although whilst devastated by my own circumstances, nothing compared to the horrific nature of his story. I recall listening to him relive the graphic tales of his home life when he came out, which made me feel sad and sick to the bottom of my stomach.

At the age of twenty years old, he became the victim of bullying behavior and verbal threats from his very own father. Not only had his dad degraded him, but he also brutally bashed him. To make matters worse, my housemate went on to say, he was then forcibly removed him from his parents' home, with nothing but the clothes on his back. He was exiled into a life of disgrace, for simply being honest with his family, about who he was. Fortunately, once he was discharged from the hospital, his salvation was having a good friend to take him in until he was able to rebuild his life, which luckily he did. Whilst I'd heard of similar stories, I knew I was more fortunate to not be exposed to that type of violent or aggressive mistreatment by my parents.

My heart sincerely went out to him, as I couldn't even imagine how I would feel or what I would do if I endured a similar situation. Back then and even now, I can't understand just how cruel some people could be to their own flesh and blood. Sadly though, I understand heinous events such as those, still continue to take place throughout the world, with many individuals not surviving to share their horrendous stories.

I felt blessed that my housemates and I were brought together. Our journey at that St Kilda apartment consisted of sharing many other different stories and various life experiences. Hearing their tales made me understand that I wasn't alone in this world. I also learned that my housemates had helped others who found themselves isolated by situations that were less than desirable, due to homophobia. Their home had been respectfully known as a safe haven, for residents, visitors and strangers alike.

During one of our nightly conversations, they both spoke of past loves, one night stands and crazy nights out at the gay bars. I was truly captivated, amazed and inspired by their stories. Although, they could see that I had something else on my mind. It was obvious that I was missing the connection with my family.

I sat silently, dazing in to space as I relived happier times with my family. It wasn't until later that night, during one of our many deep and meaningful conversations, my housemates reiterated that reliving my past, wasn't going to assist in any way for me to move forward with planning my future. Whilst I'd already told myself that previously, their words hit me hard. I was a little dismayed by the boldness of their sentiment, but I knew there was truth behind them. It all just seemed to be a case of, easier said than done though. I appreciated their guidance and I valued their honesty, even if their comments were sometimes delivered with an edge of bluntness.

One night while I was thinking about my life, I started to think about the comparisons between my own life and the life of one of my housemates. I realized I had my own preconceived ideas about what I thought the life of a gay sex worker was like, considering I had never really been exposed to that side of life before. Whilst there were numerous occasions where I had accepted money for sex previously, my motives were for control and respect, not so much for sex or cash. Back then, I very naively assumed that people who exchanged money for sex as a career, must have come from a broken home or an abusive environment. I soon realized, that misconception certainly wasn't his story either.

His upbringing was one of acceptance and love, even after he 'came out' to his parents. They continued to love him regardless of his sexual preference. He believed that his parents always knew of his attraction to boys. However it was never mentioned until he was ready to reveal his story, in his own way, in his own time. Once he did tell them, at age seventeen, he regaled us with the story of how they sat around the dining table while his parents opened a bottle of champagne to celebrate their son's milestone. He was one of the fortunate ones. Many other people, including myself, only dream of that outcome. It was obvious he was extremely comfortable with his identity, both sexual and personal. He was a confident, educated and articulate man who had been fortunate to tour the world and meet many interesting people along his travels.

He was also a gentle, genuine soul who could relate to anyone who crossed his path. He was wise in a way that surprised me. Although, whilst he was a little rough around the edges by having 'street smarts', he also understood the value of life and the best way to live it. I admired him. His explanation for the other work he did, was simple. Whilst modeling paid well, he also enjoyed the money which he received from performing sexual acts, which in turn, greatly contributed to allowing him to have the lifestyle that he wanted. There was nothing sinister, or untoward about his motives. He was simply a humble person, who would provide a service in exchange for money, for a better lifestyle.

Listening to him speak, I learned something about my own character at that time. Although I had tried to gain acceptance from those in society for who I was, I realized that I inadvertently judged him for being a person who he was actually so far removed from being. I felt ashamed of myself because I misjudged him.

However, actually knowing him and understanding him, made my bond with him much stronger than I had ever expected. I also quickly learned the extremely valuable lesson of not judging a book by its cover, along with not judging a person by their profession.

Yet, there was also another dimension to him which I hadn't known of until many weeks after I moved in. I soon discovered that he had an alter ego who could rival even the fiercest competition. *She* was known as 'The Lady Of The House'. Whilst I wasn't overly surprised to learn that, I found the entire concept of drag to be fascinating. I really didn't understand much about it though. However, I'd often seen several fabulous drag shows around the Melbourne gay scene, such as, *'The Lipstix'* with renowned drag artists, 'Kerrie Le Gore', 'Miss Candee' and 'Doreen Manganini' at the 3 Faces Nightclub, as well as, *'Le Gore's Backyard'* at the X-Change Hotel.

At that time, whilst the drag shows I saw were amazing, I'd never really contemplated why a man would want to get dressed up as a woman and parade around in front of random strangers, lip syncing to other people's songs. I guess that was just another aspect of me which needed to have an education. I did however, find myself more than a little curious to know about that fascinating *other* side of gay life, which involved wigs, make-up, dresses and high heels.

It was during that conversation, my housemate instantly discovered there was about to be a change in me. A change that I didn't even know was going to occur, but because of a twinkle in my eye, he knew what was coming. It was also during that same conversation, it became clear there were so many other elements to the gay scene which I had never imagined. I realized that it wasn't, or didn't need to be all about drugs or finding a 'Mr. Right Now' for the sake of casual sex.

I have to admit though, I would have liked to have found a 'Mr. Right' during that period. Even so, I knew I had to sort myself out emotionally before I could start sharing my life with a potential long term partner. I didn't want to become involved with another relationship where I was going to cause pain to anyone else.

So for the time being, the idea of finding that long term partner was comfortably pushed to the back of my mind. Yet, I wanted to continue exploring that other dimension of gay life just a little more. I again asked my housemate to tell me more about the bewitching art of drag.

I couldn't help but become memorized by listening to him speak of the fun and freedom which drag provided him. There appeared to be many positives aspects regarding that unknown facet, especially the concept of being able to anonymously reinvent oneself. The more I heard, the more it secretly seemed as though all of my Christmas' had come at once.

With the new found knowledge of my housemates' alter ego, I wanted to, no actually, I needed to meet 'The Lady Of The House'. When I asked if I could meet *her*, he was more than obliging to accommodate my request. Without any hesitation, we planned to go to the *'The Peel'* hotel that coming weekend, where I would finally get to witness that miraculous person, behind those unbelievable stories. I have to admit, after hearing some of those outrageous stories of *her* persona, I really wasn't sure what I was getting myself in to. I thought if nothing else, it would be a well-deserved escape from all that had taken place from the previous weeks.

Even though I was fascinated by drag, one thing was certain, I knew I had no sexual attraction to the feminine side of drag. My sexual preference has always been for masculine men. Although, I still frantically needed to know more about the desire a man felt to get dressed up in ladies clothing. I wondered if it was the same craving for attention which I felt when I was on stage performing magic, or was it something more alluring?

Apart from those impromptu shows in the back room of my parents' house, where I portrayed 'Sally Bowles', I also vividly remember the day I was playing with the daughter of a family friend. I was about eight years old and she was about ten years old. She and I were playing a 'super hero' game in the backyard at my house. She had recently been to the Royal Melbourne Show and purchased the 'Wonder Woman' show-bag. It came complete with headband, wrist cuffs and of course, the lasso of truth.

Whilst we were playing that day, I told her that I wanted to be 'Wonder Woman'. She laughed at me and wouldn't let me wear the 'Wonder Woman' costume. After that, we exchanged a few childish words. Yet, those childish words soon turned in to me having a massive tantrum and throwing her out of my house. I was unbelievably upset that she wouldn't let me dress up as one of my childhood idols. Not surprisingly, because of that, we didn't speak for several months after. To be honest, I really hadn't thought about how much that day affected me, until writing about it now. Back in that bright world of hindsight, it's really not surprising that I'm gay, or even why I became so fascinated by the concept of drag.

Nevertheless, the weekend I was waiting for had arrived. It was the night 'The Lady Of The House' and I were heading off to 'The Peel'. About three hours before we were due to leave, the transformation of my housemate was about to begin. I was so excited. I never dreamed that the entire process of getting in to drag was such a meticulous and calculated activity. It seemed as though it was all about planning and designing with regard to the make-up, wigs, outfit and accessories. Back then, I never imagined that it could be so time consuming to look as fabulous as what all drag queens do.

After hours of being locked in his bedroom, which felt more like days, 'The Lady Of The House' was ready to make *her* grand entrance. Once the bedroom door opened, I choked. I remember looking in astonishment, with my mouth gaping. There *she* was, standing before me, a six foot something tall, statuesque figure with long flowing platinum blonde hair. *She* was wearing the shortest, tightest black cocktail dress, with what can only be described as the highest high heels known to man. They would have been at least seven inches high. I stood silent, in complete awe of that captivating beauty. I was floored. She was flawless.

Whilst I'd previously seen a couple of photographs of my housemate in drag, nothing compared to what I was witnessing in the flesh. Those pictures hadn't even slightly compared to the vision which was standing in front of me. I remained silent. There were no words I could muster. I just couldn't help but stare. The transformation which had just taken place was stunning. Meeting that new persona was almost like I had met an entirely different person. A person who already knew me intimately. It was hard for me to determine where he finished and where *she* had started.

Still trying to comprehend that miraculous change, I apologized for staring. *She* told me not to worry about that as *she* totally understood why I gave *her* that reaction. That was generally the same reaction as *she* received everywhere *she* went. Being over six foot six tall myself, I even felt slightly intimidated by that beautiful Amazon-like 'woman'. *Her* overwhelming presence implied there was nothing that could stop *her* from doing whatever *she* wanted. *She* appeared to be a dynamic diva, with nothing but an endless supply of money and an infinite amount of time on *her* hands. *She* could have easily been one of *'The Real Housewives Of..........St Kilda'*, if only there was such a television program made.

Her walk was powerful and *her* presence was beguiling. *Her* entire personality was vastly different to that of *her* male self. *She* was more forthright, with a poignant tone to the words *she* spoke. *She* was a force to be reckoned with. *She* exuded style and grace in every aspect of her character. To be honest, even I found that a little overwhelming to being with, as I didn't know what was to come out of *her* mouth next. *She* was particularly unpredictable. *She* had the charm of a Miss Universe, the wit of a standup comedian and the looks of a supermodel. *She* was glamour personified.

Once we arrived at *'The Peel'*, I wasn't sure of what the reaction was going to be when we entered. I knew that I was going to be safe, but I wondered how the other people who were at the club that night, were going perceive that overpowering beauty. More importantly, I asked myself, *'How was I going to react to the reactions of others?'* On the previous occasions I'd been to the gay clubs, I had only seen 'showgirls' engaging with the crowd once their shows had finished. Yet, 'The Lady Of The House' didn't perform in shows at all. She was simply all about being seen and heard, without having the stage presence. Because of that, I wondered if it was going to be difficult for her to 'wow' the unsuspecting crowd.

That was the moment of truth. The doors were opened for us by an overly familiar doorman. Without doubt, all eyes were instantly cast upon the stunning spectacular which was before them. There were gasps of amazement from the onlookers. Any concerns I had about the negative reaction of others, were quickly forgotten. We glided our way through the crowd in to the back bar. I was surprised just how popular *she* was. It appeared as though I was walking with a celebrity. Everyone who caught a glimpse of *her* wanted to say hello. They continued to touch that glamorous beauty which was holding onto my arm, almost as though they were touching royalty.

After a few minutes we arrived in the back bar. We were met by a slightly younger, overweight drag queen with the most bouffant hairstyle, longest false finger nails and extraordinary eyelashes to match. *She* was wearing transparent, glass-like high heels and a short silver sequined dress. *She* was sitting on a stool sipping beer through a straw from *her* schooner glass. *She* was also fabulous, loud and outrageous. With the way *she* commanded an audience around *her*, without question, it was obvious that *she* too had been to 'The Peel' many times before.

At that time, I had been somewhat naive to the drag community within the gay scene. However, I felt more at ease with it, the more I was introduced to other fabulous looking queens. Before long, 'The Lady Of The House' introduced me to that queen wearing the silver sequined dress. With raised eyebrows, *she* looked me up and down several times, turned me around, then lifted her schooner glass and said at the top of her lungs, *'Aren't you just heaven on a stick, darling? What a shame you're too tall to don a frock and high heels.'* I embarrassingly retreated from the conversation for a moment while I caught my breath.

All of the people that surrounded *her* laughed and agreed with *her* statement. I softly thanked her and laughed off her comment. Deep inside though, I was mortified to be the center of attention. If there was ever an occasion that I wanted the world to open up and swallow me, it was then. Although, apart from the extreme embarrassment *she* caused me, *she* seemed to be harmless enough. I didn't really care *that* much about the 'too tall' comment she made, as I didn't believe there was malice behind her words.

Besides, she thought that I was *'heaven on a stick'*. Which I later learned was a slang term for being extremely pleasing to the eye, so with a compliment like that, all was forgiven. I just had to quickly learn that some drag queens were very quick off the mark with making witty comments, regardless of what the intention behind them was. That was a learning curve that I took great delight in understanding more of.

For the most part of that night, I quietly sat back as an observer. I was enthralled by watching all the drag queens who were parading around, wearing next to nothing, showing off their bodies. They all looked so remarkably glamorous. I continued to watch as they talked to the other patrons of 'The Peel.' I was no longer awkwardly confronted by that unknown art form which was drag, but more so, I found myself bemused whilst laughing and openly interacting with 'The Lady Of The House' and *her* friends.

Whilst sitting around that table, I admired the presence which both of those queens had. Their ability to positively capture anyone who come in contact with them, was unlike anything I have ever seen before. Generally, all it took were statements like, *'Hey sexy, tell me you want me!',* before those curious men would come over to the table and sit down for a chat. Those two drag queens, along with almost every other drag at *'The Peel'* that night, used their attributes as a supernatural power, which captivated people. It was extraordinary. I continued to sit and watch, as I remained in awe of all that was happening around me.

It wasn't until a few hours later, I couldn't help but think about the comment that other drag queen made, about me being *too* tall for drag. However, at that moment, that particular thought was only fleeting. Although, that would be a statement which would later come back in to my mind and plague me for weeks after. I couldn't understand why I was deemed *too* tall to be a drag queen. Anyway, I didn't give it another thought, that night.

As for the rest of that night, we continued to laugh and dance well into the early hours of the following day. I also had the opportunity to meet some of the most incredible people, who were not all in drag either. Having seen that wonderful art form of drag in an up close and personal forum certainly opened my eyes to see inside a world, which was inside another world. I was again smitten by not only the gay scene, but all of the different elements which made up the colors of that beautiful rainbow, that formed a community.

In the weeks which followed, I remembered back to what that drag queens said about my height. I became mildly disturbed by her conclusion that my height would be a disadvantage for drag. I even asked *myself* the question, *'Do I honestly believe that I'm too tall for drag?'* and of course my answer was no. As far as I was concerned, there was no height restriction enforced for being a drag queen. After all, it's not like I wanted to play the role of an *'Oompa Loompa'* in the movie, 'Willy Wonka and the Chocolate Factory'. Don't get me wrong, that's not meant as an insult. Some of my best friends are actually *Oompa Loompa*'s!

It wasn't until about a month or so later that I spoke with my housemate about why I had been deemed *too* tall for drag. I needed an answer which would justify that other drag queen's perception. It seemed that throughout my life I was always being held back, or made to feel as though I couldn't achieve something, for one reason or another. Secretly, the idea of dressing in drag *was* appealing to me. It appeared to be the perfect opportunity for me to take on any personality that I desired, simply by putting a mask of make-up over my face.

For days after, I persisted with wanting to know why I couldn't dress in ladies clothes and take on another personality. All my housemate could offer me in the way of an affirmative answer, was the reassurance that I could be whomever or whatever I wanted to be. By the way, that was the first time he ever offered to assist me with the transformation, but I graciously declined.

As appealing as his offer was, I wasn't really sure I wanted to dress up as a 'lady' at that point. I just wanted to know why I couldn't do it, if I had wanted to do it. Apparently, with that same twinkle in my eye as earlier, my housemate dismissed my unwillingness to take him up on his proposal. Ultimately, he did know better though. Secretly, I did wonder if dressing in drag could be an opportunity which was too good to be true. Perhaps I could, yet again, reinvent myself and no one would know who I actually was. Whilst the whole idea of being in drag was appealing, at that time, I still wasn't convinced that it was for me.

I didn't believe I was ready to be the center of attention. My confidence was still very fragile from the events which had taken place with my parents. I didn't want to delude myself in to believing I was ready to take on something new, only to discover I would fail. Although, no matter how much I didn't want to think about drag, I couldn't think of anything else. I simply couldn't let go of the notion that dressing in drag may provide me with what I thought I needed. It was a thought that relentlessly continued to be at the forefront of my mind, every single day.

After more consideration, I realized that drag was in fact, an ideal way of disguising all the pain and resentment from the past. Not only from my younger years, but also from those events which had more recently taken place with my parents, which continued to still been at the front of my mind. I truly thought that drag could be one of the closest opportunities that I may ever get to be able to hide myself away for a few hours and be showered with attention, just as my housemate had been.

It was throughout the darkest periods of my youth, I'd secretly fantasize about becoming another person and seeking revenge on those, who at one point, made my life an unbearable existence. There were times that I used to sit alone in my bedroom and think of different scenarios that I could play out, if I was to ever see those other kids from my childhood again.

Whilst there were never thoughts of hurting or inflicting pain on them, for me, it was more about the feeling of superiority. At the very least, I often wondered how fantastic it would make me feel if I could degrade them in a way which made them question their worthiness to live. I wanted to take back the power which I had relinquished. Perhaps that notion of drag could allow me to do that, but on a different level. I saw dressing up as a possible way to reclaim my own sense of self-worth, with a blazing victory.

From Darkness, to Diva

On a beautiful, bright Saturday afternoon, I rushed home from work to speak with my housemate about his offer to transform me into the divine diva he knew I wanted to become. I'd thought of nothing else that day and indeed since we went out that Saturday night several weeks before. My thought process had been taken over by my desire to become someone else. I was excited and consumed by that notion. I had psyched myself up with anticipation, to the point I believed that I could have even been the next Prime Minister of Australia if I wanted to be. Although, first things first, I needed to explore that burning desire, which was to release my inner 'woman'.

At first, my housemate was a little bewildered by my change of heart, although he was very accommodating and very patient with me. He was excited that I finally decided to be honest with myself about doing drag. For the next few hours we looked through make-up palettes, wigs, shoes and dresses. I became even more excited about undergoing that transformation, so much more than I initially thought I would be. Amazingly, I could feel another part of my personality just waiting to emerge. I couldn't wait to see the final result.

Similarly to when my housemate was getting ready, there was so much that was involved in the drag process. There was foundation, mascara, false eyelashes, lip liner and an array of different face powders. Not to mention the abundance of accessories, which I also needed to perfectly match the couture once I was made over. That transformation was going to be a change of gigantic proportions. With every brush stroke of make-up which was applied, I could already feel an unbelievable metamorphosis taking place.

To say that I started feeling slightly overwhelmed, was an underestimation of how I actually felt. I became unexpectedly tense and nervous with all that was going on. I realized just how much I wanted that make-over to happen. I only hoped that I looked as amazing as my 'The Lady Of The House' did, once my housemate finished creating his masterpiece. Whilst he was busy shading, contouring and coloring my face, I remembered that there was an integral part of the drag process I'd forgotten about. That was, I needed a drag name. That name couldn't be just any name. It had to resemble and compliment the character that I was soon going to become.

There were many impressive drag names which I thought of using, such as 'Tess Tickle', 'Krystal DeCanter' and even one of my personal favorites, 'Taylah Made'. Nevertheless, those names were either already in use, or I didn't feel they matched the persona I wanted to represent. After a lot of deliberation, I decided my new alter ego name would be 'Angela'. I adopted that name in adoration for the infamous 'Angela Channing'. She was the steely, domineering owner of the Falcon Crest wineries, from the 1980's American television soap opera, Falcon Crest.

I needed my drag personality to be vastly different to that of my own. I decided on a character which could hold her own and fight back, if and when it became necessary, just as Ms Channing would have done. I wanted to be taken notice of, without exception. I secretly hoped that I could channel the character of 'Angela Channing' through my veins that night. I needed to embody her strength, power and wisdom.

As my housemate and I were discussing my new persona, several hours had already passed. He was now adding the final applications to my newly made up face. Once my make-up was completed, I then stepped into a long black sparkling evening gown, complete with a black faux fur wrap. I also had the most magnificent fire engine red false finger nails applied. As for the finishing touches of the outfit, I was draped in an abundance of glamorous sparkling diamante accessories. I couldn't contain my excitement any longer. It was almost time for the grand reveal.

Although I couldn't see the wig when it was placed on my head, I knew it was a golden brown color. That color actually complimented my natural hair color and skin tone. Apart from the excitement I felt, I was so incredibly nervous to see the final result. Even more so, I was desperate to see what dramatic changes had taken place. It was also a surreal feeling knowing that I was wearing ladies clothes. That alone, was a stark contrast to how I normally felt dressed in jeans and a t-shirt. Although at that moment, I didn't feel too different from being myself.

It wasn't long before the time had come to see the final result of how that overhaul turned out. The more my housemate prolonged the unveiling, the more anxious I became. He positioned the mirror in front of me, but covered it with a bed sheet. He gave me a countdown until it was time to unveil my new look. As he got to number one, he fiercely ripped the sheet away.

With a gasp of surprise and an instant tear dwelling in the corner of my eye, there I was, standing tall, with a new found glorious appearance. I couldn't believe how different I actually looked. I kept staring at myself, amazed. As I continued looking into the mirror, I didn't understand how a completely different person's image was reflecting back. Every single aspect of my face and body was transformed into an image which was immensely different to mine, under the make-up.

To be honest, I had the very same reaction I did when I first saw my housemate in drag for the first time. That was, it was hard to see where I finished and where 'Angela' began. Both *she* and I melded perfectly into that newly created form of what was about to become, my new liberation. I continued admiring myself. I wouldn't say I looked like a high fashion supermodel, but I certainly didn't look like 'Angela Channing' either, for which I was somewhat grateful. However, there was something alluring about my look, which was fascinating and moderately sexy.

It wasn't long before I felt my new persona taking over every inch of my entire body. By undergoing that process, I received the desired effect. I was ecstatic with the outcome. Finally, I was well on my way to becoming a brand new person, albeit, for one night only.

The best way I can possibly describe that new found personality, was like having an 'out of body' experience. It was almost as though my spirit left my body and in return, I inhabited another person's. Almost immediately, my entire outlook on life changed. Within seconds, I had forgotten about my woes. I had adopted a new level of self-determination, which, because of that, meant there was nothing that could hold that new persona back from doing whatever *she* wanted.

I not only had the height of an Amazon, but had the look of a supernatural being. Along with that, my new look brought out a fierce attitude, similar to that of Ms. Naomi Campbell. I felt unstoppable. I was primed to set Melbourne's gay scene on fire. I became excessively hungry for attention. I wanted to feel the same adoration which my housemate felt that night he was in drag. I too, wanted to be a celebrity. I continued to feel a building sensation of empowerment inside me, all because of my new look.

I felt ready to take charge of my life for a change. I became self-absorbed with my own reflection, as I couldn't stop looking at the powerful beauty who stood before me. All of a sudden, my housemate said it was a waste to be dressed for success, but not going out to show it off. He suggested we go out to 'The Peel'. As fantastic as I looked and as on top of the world I was feeling, after hearing his suggestion, I immediately started to contend with a moment of fear and weakness. The reality of leaving the house and being seen by other people, was slowly becoming too much for me to comprehend.

I wasn't sure whether I was actually ready for public exhibition, or as I thought in that moment of weakness, public execution. Even though those extreme feelings of empowerment and courage seemed easy enough for me to believe whilst I was at home, the reality behind that false sense of heroism was somewhat different. The idea of going out only brought me back to the harsh reality that I was still the same person under the make-up. That feeling of invincibility had quickly rushed from my body, to become a feeling of total terror. I truly didn't believe I had the nerve to be seen in public.

Strangely enough, in that same moment, that feeling of fright became a deep, lonely and overwhelming feeling of insecurity. It was then I remembered back to how the other kids at school would tease and torment me for being different. My stomach began churning as I recalled those hideous names the kids once called me. I thought I had already shed those evils of the past. Perhaps I hadn't. Maybe those kids still held an uncanny spell over me that was unbreakable. All I could do in the seconds that followed, was to find a myriad of excuses to not go out. My anxiety levels were going from moderate, to maximum.

For any person who's been at the hands of bullies, for whatever reason, I believe they may truly understand that irrational state of mind which can take over. It's almost as though I was having a passive aggressive struggle with myself. During that time, I was inclined to second guess myself. I believed that I would never live up to the expectations of other people, regardless of what their expectations were. I felt as though people would continue to make fun of me and belittle me. No matter how much I told myself I didn't need the approval of others, I was still unable to accept that I was worthy of having a decent life with high self-esteem.

Trying to find the will to overcome those negative thoughts, I was left dealing with an emotional struggle of acceptance, which was again, agitating around my mind. The feeling of dishonor which I had for my life seemed to be stronger than my desire to succeed. Irrespective of what I wanted from life, it appeared as though I had still been dictated to by those insidious voices of my past. I wondered, *'Is this how life was always going to be? Was I always going to think the worst and let the bullies from my past determine the course of my future?'* I so desperately wanted to answer no, but the internal conflict that was going through my mind wouldn't concede.

That entire situation became too much to accept. I asked my housemate to leave me alone. Once he left the bedroom, I sat quietly, disappointed and ashamed. Whilst I looked at myself in the mirror, I wondered how it was possible that one minute I could feel enough confidence to take charge of the world. Then, in a single heartbeat, how I could became so defeated. One voice in my head continued to take me back to an emotional place from my past where I didn't want to go. The second voice was encouraging me to break free from the past and start living life the way I was born to live it. That was a struggle which became too much to convey. Those inner voices continued to devour me. All I wanted to do was scream at the top of my lungs.

I became disheartened and confused. I knew I needed to break free from those painful memories of ridicule, but those were memories which seemed to be the hardest to forget. What made that situation even more difficult to accept, was I actually did think that I had already dealt with those issues previously. Obviously I hadn't, or else the doubt that was in my mind wouldn't be so strong. I seemed to have fooled myself with a false sense of determination. Denial had again, let me believe that I had moved forward. I wanted nothing more than to shut those voices out and enjoy the opportunity to try something new, without any reservations.

That aggressive power-play between my conscience and my hopes continued. I sat for a few minutes more and gave great consideration to whether I should actually take that leap of faith and go out. I took another look at myself in the mirror. The more I looked deep in to my eyes, the more I knew I somehow had to find the courage to genuinely move forward. I didn't want to feel sorry for myself any longer. I realized I had to reclaim ownership of my life. With that very thought, appeared a bright twinkle in my eye, which gave me the hope that I needed. That sparkle confirmed my spirit wasn't entirely destroyed, it was only slightly bent and a little bruised.

I also realized that finding the *real* me was going to be difficult, but not entirely hopeless. It was going to take an enormous amount of energy on my part to leave the past exactly where it belonged. I wasn't 100% sure of how I was going to do that, but I wanted to have the determination to at least try. Just before my housemate walked out of the bedroom earlier, I remembered what he told me. The wrath of his words came flooding back. He said it was all about taking one step at a time. If I could do that, I would once again find my confidence and my courage, but most of all, I would find the key to unlock my own self-acceptance.

Amongst other things, my housemate knew how to motivate me for my own good. He wanted me to be the person he knew I could be. He inspired me more than words can express. Reliving his wise words, I was more empowered than ever to make that dream of going out in drag become a reality. Although, I have to admit, the bottle of wine we consumed also assisted with giving me the strength to find my courage.

With one final look in the mirror, I decided I did in fact, want to take that leap of faith. I walked out of my bedroom and told my housemate to grab his coat. We were going out to party like it was 1999. Without any further procrastination, we found ourselves in a taxi cab heading to 'The Peel', to have the night of our lives.

As we got closer to the club, I could feel my heart beating like a drum. Out of nowhere, that crippling voice of doubt was back to haunt me. It had slowly crept back in to my mind. Those voices enjoyed toying with my emotions. I realized I could no longer allow them to have the credibility they craved. Somehow, I needed to find a way to stand proud of who I was and what I was doing. I only hoped that I hadn't set myself up to be ridiculed by those in my own community. I needed their support more than ever. Without proving to myself that I could do things, I was never going to unleash a positive new future. I had to remain focused and stay strong.

Once we arrived at 'The Peel' I knew it was too late to panic anyway. I simply had to prove to myself that was the first step to confronting both my fears and my doubts. I needed to resign myself to the fact that I was indeed, good enough to be accepted *and* genuinely respected. I had to do whatever it took to block those voices out, which were still trying to fill my head. There was no option, but to start genuinely believing that I was the megastar which I wanted to be that night. I continued thinking that night was going to provide me with my moment in the spotlight.

With those optimistic thoughts cemented in my mind, I took a deep breath and composed myself. In a random fleeting moment, I remembered back to my drama class days. In those classes we were brainwashed into believing that we must adopt the character that we were playing. To live and breathe the character wasn't enough to make it believable. We had to physically become the character in its entirety. That positive affirmation was all I needed. I truly believed that I was ready to portray the real 'Angela Channing'. Although, whilst I may have seemed composed from the outside, I was dying on the inside.

With one shaky foot in front of the other, which wasn't a

pretty sight wearing high heels, we slowly walked to the door. My head was held high. We were welcomed by the regular doorman, who didn't even recognize me. As he opened the door, I took my first step inside. Just as I walked through the doors, in that instant, I lost my nerve. I dropped my head and looked down to the floor. Once inside though, I managed to quickly regain my composure. As I slowly looked up, all I could see was the crowd which started to surround us.

They were gazing straight back at me, with a decisive sense of admiration. That was truly an amazing sensation, one that I had never experienced before. I received a multitude of compliments, as I was ushered to the bar. Those people who surrounded us actually wanted to know who I was, but more importantly, they wanted to know why they hadn't seen me out before. They continued to question why I wasn't one of Melbourne's elite drag performers.

That night *was* my time to experience the notion of being a celebrity. I felt as though I was walking the red carpet on an opening night. It wasn't long after we arrived, that my character had taken completely over. I then became the center of attention. 'Angela' was engagingly radiant as *she* charmed the crowd with *her* wit. I was not only accepted by my peers, but also felt an irresistible sense of love from all who continued to shower me with affection.

Standing as a two-hundred and twenty-six centimeter drag queen, I had no other option but to stand tall and not be missed by anyone. More to the point, I didn't want to be missed by anyone. It was also hard for me not to be the center of attention. Whilst I never enjoyed that kind of attention before, I certainly had no issue with accepting the praise of other people that night.

There I was, looking extraordinary. I was surrounded by almost everyone in the club. I wanted people to gravitate towards me, which is exactly what continued to happen. I knew I had to make the most of that positively intense experience, in all of its entirety. From the beginning to the end of that night, I had drink after drink bought for me and danced most of the night away. There were also many people who just wanted to stop and say hello to the towering beauty who stood before them.

Although, I have to admit, some people found it difficult to comprehend the vision that was 'Angela', due to *her* overpowering nature and statuesque appearance. Even though, once they realized I wasn't as intimidating as they first thought, they relaxed and became comfortable with engaging in conversation. With each and every person who wanted to say hello, my hand was immediately extended. Which was then quickly followed by the words, *'Kiss it'*, which they were more than obliging to do. That night, those words quickly became my signature trademark.

Throughout that entire night, I gained an absolute understanding of how it must have felt to be one of the popular kids at school. I finally found the vindication which I yearned for during my school years and beyond. At no point did I give any consideration to the person I was, under the make-up. As far as I was concerned, he didn't exist at all. All I wanted to do was remain in character and enjoy that night for the fantasy that it was.

That delicious admiration continued with every new face that appeared in front of me. I remember feeling renewed. Even under that tremendous amount of make-up, I had been reconnected with that little lost boy who was buried deep within, before he became emotionally damaged. Finally, I had become the person who I wanted to be. For the duration of that night my character didn't falter for one second. It was as though 'Angela Channing' really was living inside me. Due to the positive response from the other patrons who were at *'The Peel'* that night, it became apparent that I could do no wrong.

My housemate was so impressed with what he had created, if not a little jealous. Nevertheless, he supported me until the very end of that spectacular evening. He knew that feeling of emancipation would be just what I needed to kick-start and embrace a new positive way of life. In fact, I think he too, was secretly getting the same exhilaration as I. Although he wasn't in drag, I suspect he enjoyed watching the spectacle that was. Amongst other things, that night I learned what it meant to have the captivating power of a drag queen. By all accounts, drag queens are an illusion, who completely capture the attention, mind and senses of all those who look on.

It wasn't long before the night turned into the very early hours of the following morning. Sadly, it was time to leave. I was lucky that I wasn't Cinderella, who had to be home at the stroke of midnight. If that was the case, I would have missed out on what can only be described as the best experience of my life.

I slowly staggered out of the club, due to having sore feet from dancing rather than the amount of alcohol I'd consumed. With my head still held high and my sunglasses on, I didn't even care how awful I must have looked in the harsh sunlight of that day. I felt as though I was standing on top of the world. Nothing else could have compared to how I was feeling. Words seemed inadequate to describe my delightfully euphoric state.

One thing was for sure, I was sold on the concept of drag. It seemed as though I'd waited my entire life to feel that type of true freedom and acceptance. I was completely overcome by the response I received. I even had the pleasure of meeting some of the most gracious people, who assisted with further developing my drag persona. I felt as though I had been truly celebrated by my community. That night will remain as a golden memory, which I shall cherish for my entire life.

The Promise of a New Life

With a new lease of life starting to emerge due to me slowly overcoming my fear of rejection, I felt as though I was ready to embark on a new adventure. I didn't want to be a person who watched the world pass me by. That kind of existence was no longer sufficient for me. I wanted to participate in life.

You may recall earlier, I mentioned I had inherited a 'free spirited' gene from my mom. That time in my life was a rebirth. I began concentrating on what was coming next in my future, without anything or anyone holding me back. I had been through such a emotional transformation over those previous months that I knew if I continued with believing in myself, I could only achieve great things in life. I realized that those positive words that my housemate had spoken, had now been implanted in my mind forever. Change really did start with one step at a time. There was no reason to lose sight of what was becoming important to me. I was genuinely starting to enjoy my new and improved positive outlook on life.

At that stage, I was still working for the same large national retailer. However, my focus on career and change had now shifted to the forefront of my mind. I was content and happy enough with the progress that I had made within myself. But I knew I needed and wanted to change more aspects of my life. I knew that if I didn't make another change soon, I would have been stuck in the daily routine of life, not really living or achieving whatever it was that I wanted to achieve.

For the first time in a very long time, I was beginning to learn how to see my lifestyle from a different, more positive perspective. Of course, I still enjoyed nights out at clubs with friends, both in and out of drag. Because of that, I was exposed to a myriad of fantastic people and brand new experiences. I was fortunate that those I surrounded myself with gave me the opportunity to learn more about personal development.

Whilst they provided their words of encouragement, I still had to find the tools myself, which could implement the changes I needed. I knew other people couldn't make those alterations for me. However, that alone appeared to be a positive turning point which slowly began to outweigh the pain from my younger years. I reaffirmed to myself that I wasn't actually alone on my journey, contrary to the belief I once allowed to overwhelm me. Naturally, I was still guarded with my feelings and had not wanted to get too close to people. Although, I felt slightly more confident that I could overcome that with time. Again, I needed to move one step at a time and enjoy living in every single moment I had.

Above all, my priority was to heal myself from the impairments of the past and not just from the playground bullies who continued to leave me reeling on the inside. At that time, my relationship with my parents was still strained. I couldn't foresee that bond repairing itself to where it had been while I was growing up, certainly not anytime in the near future anyway. I could only presume that my parents still loved me, but perhaps it was now a different kind of love.

It seemed as though it was almost a conditional type of love. One that really didn't extend to having a gay son. Especially a gay son who caused them pain and who could have easily brought disgrace to his family.

As I step back into that happy escape from reality for just a second, I don't believe the only factor at play was my sexuality. I had also said and done some very despicable things that no matter how much I wished I could have taken back, it would never mend our broken relationship. I just knew that I had to work with what I had been offered by them at that time, as limited and as discouraging as that was.

That was probably the first time in my life I actually sat down and thought deeply about the direction my adult life had been taking. I wasn't thinking of reactive ways to fix a situation, but rather, thinking of ways to take a proactive approach to better myself, along with the quality of my life. It's almost as though I was troubled by that question we're asked when we're young, *'What do you want to be when you grow up?'*

Whilst I still had no definitive answer for *that* question, it seemed as though I had achieved a lot since leaving high school the second time around. There was still so much more of life to explore though. I hoped that I would continue to be offered new opportunities. Although, it was blatantly obvious that those opportunities wouldn't come knocking on my door. It was up to me to seek them out and make them work for me. Whatever those new opportunities may have been.

I even contemplated what type of impact a career change could have on my life. Although I really enjoyed working with the diversity of different people that I had been, it seemed pointless to think too much about making changes to that aspect of my life. I was only at a crossroads with everything else in my life.

There were still so many characteristics of myself that I wanted to retain, such as my new found liberation and value system which was more positive that I imagined. I also wanted to find love and build a life which I could share with another person. I assumed when the time was right, that's when that wonderful experience would happen. Until then, I just needed to remain grateful for the things that I did have. Although I didn't have much in the way of materialistic goods, I only hoped my principles would assist me with fulfilling my aspirations.

The one aspect of my life I still truly enjoyed the most was drag. Yet, I wasn't sure where a career as a drag queen would lead me. I knew that performing in drag shows wasn't for me. Although I have great admiration for those who do perform, I never saw myself on the full-time club circuit. Besides, I don't believe I had the bravery or quick witticism to perform in that arena. Being a performer in a drag show was something that absolutely terrified me. Those same feelings still scare me, even to this day.

However for the short term, I decided I was content enough to go out in drag and be seen as a social figure, without performing. Although, I sincerely knew that at one point in my future, my drag persona would take on a life of *her* own, in one form or another. I just wasn't sure what that form would be. So, I thought it was best to place that idea on the back burner.

It was shortly after, one of my housemates was talking about taking a lucrative employment opportunity in Sydney, which he had been offered. I had been to Sydney for holidays and always had a great time. Those holidays were usually with my family though, so, I wasn't old enough to appreciate my time there. One thing I did know, Sydney always seemed to have such a mystique about it. I knew there was a secret side to that city, which I needed to explore more of at some point throughout my life.

The job offer which was made to my housemate was far too good to pass up. Besides, I think he had already decided to say yes, even before he returned home that night. Without any hesitation, he decided to make the move. With the realization of him leaving, I became terribly sad. Naturally, I was happy for him, but I wasn't sure of what was going to become of me without his wisdom and guidance. Above all though, I simply didn't want my best friend to leave.

In the weeks that followed, he and I often joked about me moving to Sydney with him. The more we joked, the more serious our discussions became. The idea of living in a new city was appealing, although, I wasn't sure if it was the right move for me to make at that time. After a few more days, it became more than obvious that he was deadly serious about his extended invitation to move with him. The reality of our once meaningless banter, now meant it was time to make a serious decision to either stay in Melbourne, or move to Sydney. I had to think very carefully. That was an opportunity which could again, potentially change my life forever.

For days after, I remained so incredibly undecided about leaving my job in Melbourne and starting a brand new life in a new city. Once upon a time, I probably would have jumped at the opportunity to go, as I believed Sydney was the gay lifestyle city, of all cities. I knew there seemed to be more possibilities there, which could potentially compliment my new way of thinking and indeed, my new way of life. I became excited about the prospect of a new beginning, but there were also other considerations I needed to think about.

I wasn't sure if I wanted to leave our other housemate behind either. Although my bond with him wasn't as strong, he still provided me with many insights which assisted me with my reinvention. Whilst I had so much to thank him for, I wasn't sure if that was enough of a reason to stay. As it turned out, a friend of his was looking to move closer to the area which we were living in. Whatever my decision was to be, our other housemate had a backup plan for us leaving. He was happy for me to make the move if that's what I wanted. He even subtly encouraged me to go, as he knew it would be a positive move too. I invested a lot of time in to making that decision. There were still many other things to consider also, such as work and of course, my parents.

After a few more days of intense thinking, I woke up one morning and I knew I had to make that bold move. The pros outweighed the cons. It was confirmed. I agreed to move to Sydney with my housemate, where the promise of a new life awaited. That very morning, I went to work and resigned. I also remember the day I called my parents to let them know my plans of moving to Sydney. I think that came as a bit of a shock to them, especially my mom.

One of the first questions she asked was, *'Are you in trouble? Is someone making you move away?'* I found that to be a particularly bizarre question, as I wasn't sure what type of life my parents actually thought I was living. After all, I wasn't involved with a drug cartel or the underworld. I had many times previously, extended the offer for them to come and visit me, but time after time my offer was declined, without valid reason.

Whilst there appeared to be a moment of concern for my welfare, the duration of that telephone call was again, what I had become accustomed to, strained and distant. Although, I still sensed they were concerned about me moving interstate, which to me, implied they still loved me. Yet, I couldn't seem to convince them that the offer to move to Sydney was extended through positive circumstance. Not one that involved any force or coercion for me to leave the city in which I was raised.

I tried to make my parents understand that making that move was something which I needed to do for myself. I could find no other words to reaffirm to them the reason for me wanting to move. It was clear from the start they didn't approve, but I just knew that I had to make that move anyway. Besides, my relationship with them didn't seem to reconnect at all during that time, so there hadn't been much holding me back from leaving. If anything, I hoped by moving, that would only one day bring us closer together.

Within three weeks my housemate and I were primed to leave, but nervous about saying goodbye to our hometown of Melbourne. It all seemed to be happening so quickly. The weeks of anxious waiting were over. Our moving day had finally arrived. We were ready to embark on a new unknown adventure. Possibly the biggest that either of us had ever faced before. We hoped that moving to a new city was going to be full of new prospects and offer an optimistic direction for both of us. A complete lifestyle change seemed like a dream come true. We could at last free ourselves from whatever we once thought held us back in Melbourne.

Without question, I resigned myself to believe that it was the *right* move for me to make. Although, I couldn't help but think of some of those stories which I'd heard previously, about Sydney being one of the hardest cities to make a name for yourself. Hearing those rumors hadn't deterred me at all. I was more than ready for a change and in fact, to begin a new chapter in my life. Moving to Sydney could be exactly what I needed to entirely cut myself loose from my younger years. It seemed as though it was the perfect opportunity to allow me to blend into a city which was big enough for me to remain unknown, for as long as I desired. I anxiously awaited to embrace the new challenges ahead.

Due to my housemate needing his car, we decided to drive to Sydney. The road trip was entertaining, yet exhausting. Along the way we stopped at well-known Australian tourist attractions such as *'The dog on the tuckerbox'* in Gundagai and of course, Parliament House in Canberra. We took countless photographs, which served as a journal of our adventures. For the most part though, we drove nonstop. Finally after twelve hours on the road, we arrived in Sydney. The tiresome mood of my housemate and I suddenly became one of incredible excitement. We had entered a curious, but magical new world.

Once we arrived, I knew my first priority was to find work, quickly. Thankfully, our saving grace was that my housemate had already previously arranged a place where we could stay. Whilst that was only a short term arrangement with a friend of his, we still had to contribute financially. At least by having short term accommodation that provided us with enough time to get settled and find a new home of our own. There was no time to waste with sightseeing, at that moment anyway. It became all about finding an income.

Luckily, it was only a matter of days before I found work as a waiter at an American themed cafe called 'The California Cafe'. In its heyday, that cafe was one of the most vibrant, iconic diners situated at the top end of Oxford Street, away from the hustle and bustle of the city end of the street. Over the years, that cafe had undergone several transformations. Although predominately, the décor remained the same. It featured everything from pictures of Marilyn Munro and Elvis Presley, to Sunset Boulevard and Venice Beach. Along with an American themed menu and of course, personal 'in booth' jukeboxes on the walls.

Whilst that was not only a wonderful place to work, that job was exactly what I needed for the short to medium term. With my existing savings and a stable weekly income, that allowed us to move into our own home almost immediately. As great as it was having a friend's house to move into on arrival, it wasn't ideal living with two other people in a small two bedroom, older style, third floor unit.

Even back in the mid 1990's, rental prices in Sydney were expensive. My housemate and I didn't have much cash to spend on rent. However, we still managed to find a very small, two bedroom apartment. Fortunately, it was within walking distance to Oxford Street, in the inner city suburb of Darlinghurst. Whilst our new apartment was centrally located, the interior was very basic and a little dingy.

The apartment block was a 1940's style, dilapidated brown brick building, with narrow windows, which looked out into an even narrower back alley. Many nights we were woken by the sound of police sirens shrieking down the street, in pursuit of drug affected people or the occasional sex worker 'getting to know' his or her clients. Even so, for us, those experiences only added to the excitement of living in our beautiful new city.

Even though Darlinghurst did have some rather dubious

areas, it wasn't hard to submerse myself into the Sydney culture and gay lifestyle. There was so much more of an eclectic mix of people that I had been exposed to, more than what I'd ever seen in Melbourne. I was also fortunate enough to work directly on Oxford Street, which at one point, was one of the gayest and most exhilarating streets that you could ever find yourself on. Back then, Oxford Street was also affectionately referred to as, *'The Golden Mile'*. What a bright, sparkling mile it was too. It had a unique and dynamic flavor which was second to none. There was everything you could ever wish for in that area from bars and clubs, to restaurants and shopping.

The bright neon signs which flashed along the streets added an international feel to that cosmopolitan street. Every single night of the week there were people out and about having dinner and enjoying after work drinks, which would usually involve bar-hopping from one club to the next. No night out on Oxford Street was complete without ending up at the 'Albury Hotel', to watch their world famous drag shows.

Oxford Street knew how to turn on the charm and the excitement for both locals and tourist alike.

That street was an idealistic place where you could forget about any labels which people may try and pin on you. Everyone could truly enjoy who they were. The vast assortment of people who frequented Oxford Street, also made that street come alive. To be honest, the main reason I enjoyed working at that cafe, was because of the people. There was always someone willing to share a story about their life and where they'd come from. I have to admit though, it didn't take long before I became totally mesmerized by my new life. I quickly became a regular face along the *Golden Mile's* array of gay nightclubs. As I was working in an industry which never closed, bars such as, 'The Midnight Shift', 'The Albury' and 'The Stonewall Hotel', had all become my home away from home. Those familiar surrounds complimented the backdrop of my lifestyle. Back in those days, Oxford Street really was the epitome of the quintessential Australian gay lifestyle.

Apart from more expensive rent, it was also no secret that the cost of living in Sydney was much more expensive than Melbourne. Quite often, money was tight for my housemate and I. Although, we didn't really want for that much, nor did we ever go without. It was obvious to us both, that the quality of our lives was better in Sydney, rather than what it appeared to be back in Melbourne. We were living in a city which embraced us, just as much as we had embraced it. Neither of us had any regrets, whatsoever.

After about eight months of living in Sydney, my housemate and I decided it was time to unleash 'The Lady Of The House' and 'Angela' on a new found audience. I fondly recall spending many a night at the Grosvenor Club, or as it was lovingly known, 'The Taxi Club'.

'The Taxi Club' was a respected institution of Sydney since the late 1950's. Originally established as a social venue primarily for taxi cab drivers, which provided them a place to meet, socialize, or have a bite to eat during, or after their shift. In those early days, 'The Taxi Club' was also one of the only few 24 hour venues available, throughout Sydney.

In the later years, 'The Taxi Club' became a popular venue for various cabaret artists, including the magnificent showgirls of 'Les Girls'. That club became a haven for them to party after their performances around the vivacious inner city suburb of Kings Cross. It wasn't long before 'The Taxi Club' became one of Sydney's leading clubs, predominantly for the gay and lesbian community, the trans community, drag queens, cross dressers, as well as for the admirers of the aforementioned.

That was a venue which was literally a melting pot for all of society, in an embracing and accepting fashion. Without question, I always knew I would be guaranteed to have a good time there, regardless of whomever may have been there, on any given night. Every night of the week, they offered inexpensive alcoholic drinks, played all the latest music and offered a unique ambiance which compared to no other place at that time.

Unlike my first outing in drag, there were no feelings of trepidation when we arrived at *'The Taxi Club'*. It was a very different feeling to that of going to *'The Peel'*. That time around, I was more confident and aware of myself. I knew I had what it took to be the center of attention again. There was however, a brief underlying thought of how 'Angela' was going to be perceived by that new city. Although, that thought was still a far cry from the immense doubt that I had once struggled with. Even before the negative thoughts crept in, I managed to quickly banish those annoying voices in my head. I had started to truly believe in myself. Needless to say, as I suspected, there was nothing to fear or to be concerned about. I was welcomed into *'The Taxi Club'* in the same fashion as I had been in Melbourne. That night out was only the beginning or many more nights to come.

It was during that period, I came to the realization that hearing *those* voices in my head wasn't a negative cogitation. Those were only voices which kept me grounded in times of adversity. They gave me something to strive towards, which was my own acceptance and success. One of the most valuable lessons I've learned in life, is that there are always people who will put you down and make you feel as though you can't achieve what you really want. Sadly, those were the type of people who once wanted to take away my spirit and cast negativity toward me. Yet, I've now learned there was no valid reason for me to surrender my soul and allow those people to have the credibility which they crave. I also believe those people to be worse than any voice that I've ever heard in my head. It was apparent that it was them, who was missing something in their own lives.

Sometimes we encounter people who are too quick to use negative words, such as, *'you can't'*. Let me tell you, I am actually living proof that *you can* do what you want. Every time I hear those negative words now, either spoken by another person or even in your own mind, I make every effort to believe that I *can* and I *will* achieve whatever I want to do. Through my experience, there were and still are occasions, that without being challenged by negativity, I could never better myself or prove my own self-worth. I realized that it takes belief in myself, to make others believe in me too. It only takes one person who believes in you, to change the entire direction in which your life travels.

I also believe we are all responsible for making tremendous events happen. I think we need to believe more in our own ability to take charge of who we are and the success we want to achieve. Although, that isn't as easy as it sounds. Sometimes it does appear easier to believe the negatives of what people say or how they act towards us. Having said that, no one has ever traveled the road of success, without ever crossing the streets of failure. In times of uncertainty, I always remember, for every negative charge, there's always a positive spark.

That era became one of the most empowering and enlightening periods of my life. I managed to sincerely move forward and start making a decent life for myself. I wasn't being held back by people or memories that insisted I conform to a specific way of life. For me, that time was about exploring the joy and excitement of not only welcoming, but accepting new challenges in to my life.

Also during that part of my journey, I was fortunate to meet more of the most amazing people who helped heal my spirit, in ways they could never imagine possible. They offered me ongoing encouragement to continue to be the best person I could. Their unveiled inspiration was something which I needed to keep myself on track, not only for the immediate future, but for the longevity of my survival.

Questioning the Unanswerable

By that time in my life, which was about twelve months later, I'd completely settled into Sydney and considered that was now my home. My life had turned around considerably. I felt more complete than I had ever felt before. However, there seemed to be only one facet which was missing. Whilst I felt complete with the friends I had around me, I felt the time was right to start sharing my life with someone who was special to me.

Many times before, I'd heard from other people how difficult it was to find true love in a city which seemed to be all about 'Mr. Right Now'. It became evident, even as I walked along Oxford Street that Darlinghurst provided many accessible places to find that instant sexual release, if that's what you were looking for.

There was no doubt I was living in a city which could be wicked. However, I wanted to know how I could find something longer lasting and more meaningful than two minutes of *'oh baby, yes!'*, followed by ten minutes of *'wow, that was so awesome'*, whilst I got dressed, before leaving wherever I may have ended up. Don't get me wrong, I wasn't adverse to the occasional one night stand, but I certainly wasn't entertaining the idea of going back to a time where sex had ruled my life. I had greater expectations for myself and different motives, than I had back then.

I couldn't help but wonder, *'Was living the gay life in Sydney nothing more than one fuckfest after the other?'* Surely I wasn't the only person who was interested in companionship and romance. My quest to discover that answer, and so much more, had just begun.

I pretty much knew what I was looking for. I wanted to find a man who shared the same ideals as me. I strongly desired to settle down and live that infamous idealistic lifestyle that I had so often read about in stories or even seen on television programs such as 'Queer as Folk'.

From the outset of my mission, I thought that looking for a potential partner in a gay bar was probably going to be an unlikely option for me to actually find my soul mate. Although, I had heard stories of that happening before. I genuinely wanted to know if there *was* any truth behind those stories. Could single gay men actually find love in a nightclub? I believed that had to be more than an urban myth. With a curious mind, I embarked on an expedition to find my potential mate. I wanted to find that *one* person who was right for me. More importantly, I needed to make that one connection with a person who also wanted to build a life with a long term partner.

There was many a night that I sat at a bar, scouring the room for my ideal partner. I was hopeful I would find a like-minded man who would be more interested in getting to know a person, rather than engaging in quick meaningless sex. Disappointingly though, many of those nights I would either leave the bar alone, or have one beer too many, before I was back at their house for the one thing that I hadn't been looking for, sex. Generally once those encounters had served their purpose, I would inevitably hear the words so many of us have heard before, '*Thanks, you were great. Would you like a shower before you leave?*'

I became doubtful that I would actually find 'Mr. Right' anywhere. However, I wouldn't allow myself to believe that I was the only person living in the gay capital of Australia who was also looking for love. True to my style though, I continued looking for love in all the wrong places. I had more luck with finding all the 'Mr. Right Now' men of Sydney. It was because of that, I again teetered on the verge of promiscuity. However, I managed to stop myself from following that sordid road, on which I'd once traveled.

I merely wanted to find a man who would make my world shake with excitement when I saw him. I really didn't think that was too much to ask for. As weeks turned in to months, I was still no closer to finding the man of my dreams. Whilst I had encountered some very charming men along the way, our synergies weren't at the same place, at the same time. Their idea of a relationship was one drink, then off to bed, then out the door. If I was still at their house longer than an hour after sex, they assumed I was ready to move in. That was a concept which made those men very nervous, but it was fun to linger before leaving, just to 'take the piss' sometimes.

However, at that stage, the prospects of finding my soul mate still weren't looking incredibly good. I remembered a friend once saying that love finds you when you aren't looking for it, or at a time when you least expect it. Maybe that was true. Maybe I just needed to go about my daily life and wait for that magical moment that a handsome man would find me waiting for him. Whilst that idea seemed a little farfetched, I had nothing to lose, so I continued to enjoy each day as it came along.

Although, in theory it may have appeared that I sat back and waited, however, the reality was that I actually hadn't given up on finding my true love. I just didn't let the notion of finding love consume me quite as much as I had done previously. Deep down, I knew that when the time was right I'd meet that special man, fall in love and live happily ever after. At least that's what happens in fairy-tales. Yes, even in gay fairy-tales, it happens too.

Apart from lacking love, I realized my life was gradually becoming how I always dreamed it would be. Making the change to a new city gave me greater inspiration to follow my dreams. That was a time in my life when I hoped to finally, once and for all, be able to let go of my agonizing past. There was a new vision of polarity in sight which I wanted to see materialize. Little did I know, but that was to be a vision which would later in life become a reality and lead me to the very path that I remain on today. Yet, before I found that path, I needed to mend other parts of my life which were still in ruins.

I was desperately missing the lost love of my parents, which I so badly wanted to recapture. I just thought that it was going to take more time. However, I wasn't sure that amount of time was ever going to be on my side. I also wanted my parents to share in my excitements and triumphs, as I became a man they could be proud of. More importantly, their youngest son, which they could be proud of.

Whilst I still continued calling my mom often, that same detached situation never changed. The meaning of those calls still seemed pointless. Considering she thought I was living in a city that perhaps wasn't suitable, I stayed in contact to let her know that things were going well. I wanted to reassure her that I hadn't actually become a drug dependant person who was living on the street in a notorious underbelly world. Unfortunately, that seemed to be the perception from my parents for anyone who lived a 'chosen' lifestyle and moved to Sydney.

The one aspect I never became accustomed to whilst speaking on the telephone, was hearing the pain in my mom's voice. Although she never said much, it was the tone in which she used, that I found difficult to cope with. I was even able to accept that our conversations would remain somewhat unnatural and contrived, almost without purpose. However, I was beginning to lose hope that my parents actually cared about me at all. I never considered I would ever feel that type of resentment from a parent, as I did during those years. Because of that, I could never forget that I was the reason why they felt the way they did. That only made it harder for me to let go of the hatred and resentment I felt for myself.

All I wanted was for my parents to dig deep and tell me everything was going to be alright, and of course, tell me they loved me. Even if they didn't entirely believe it, I still needed to hear it. There was not one instance that I didn't tell my mom I loved her when we spoke on the telephone. Sadly I still only ever received that same dismissive reply of, 'Me too'. My reasons for wanting to hear they loved me, were just as selfish as my reasons for causing the damage I had. I needed their forgiveness, for me to be able to live wholeheartedly again. Hearing those words, 'Me too', only resulted in an awkward silence from my end of the telephone. I didn't know how to reply to that. Perhaps the fact I was living in another state from my parents was a case of out of sight, out of mind. I often wondered if the expectation I had of one day being a happy family again was just a pipe dream. I still couldn't find that answer, which I thought continued holding me back from emotionally moving forward.

I understand for some parents, it can be difficult to accept their child is same sex attracted. Although, I knew my story was a little different. I had not only been a disappointment to my parents because I was gay, I also behaved in a way that was callous. Yet the one aspect that I couldn't accept, was to live with the feeling of not knowing if I was ever going to be truly loved by my parents again. That had become a thought which was at times, too excruciating to live with.

Throughout my darkest periods, I questioned what my life would be like if my parents completely disowned me. Yes, it was no secret that I made poor choices, but I continued living with those consequences. However, the relationship with my parents was diminishing with every conversation we had. I felt as though we'd become nothing more than strangers, with nothing in common to discuss. That's not how I wanted my relationship with them to end.

I believe like most children, myself included, in times of adversity I needed to have the reassurance from my parents. I needed to hear that things would have an optimistic outcome. From an early age they always told me that regardless of what cards are dealt in the game of life, there is always a solution to every problem. Perhaps as far as my parents were concerned, I became the exception to that rule.

The older I became, the more I was able to understand that some questions simply have no answers. At least, not at the immediate time when I needed to find them anyway. In life, it's common knowledge that we don't always find what we may so desperately seek. Whilst that isn't fair, I continued to believe I needed to trust my instincts.

Two of favorite sayings which seemed to be the most applicable to many situations at that time, were, 'It is, what it is' and 'Que Sera, Sera, (whatever we be, will be)'. I strongly believe that people are who they are and that some events in life happen, simply because they do, without explanation. That was the state of mind which I allowed to take over. I believed when the time was right, I may perhaps find the answers I needed.

I also realized that many of the situations I found myself in, which seemed to be coincidences, were more like occurrences. I considered some of those to be validations, provided by the universe, acknowledging that the right path had been taken. Although, some were just abrupt reality checks which I needed at the time, because I thought I was greater than the universe. Unfortunately, I understand those analogies don't help those, who like myself, have an inquisitive mind.

That old saying about life being too short, it's more than a saying. I understand firsthand that it's a reality. There were occasions where I wasted too much time looking for something that may not have been there, right at that particular moment.

But again, by trusting my instincts, I believed that if I was meant to know the answer, it was going to find me and when it did, it would generally slap me across the face harder than I had ever expected. I only wish I could have found the answers, to what was about to happen next in my life.

An Unexpected Coming of Age

Whilst I impatiently waited to receive many answers from the universe, that hadn't been the only thought on my mind. My desire for a new change was again, begging me to look for my next challenge. As I still wasn't any closer to locating the man of my dreams, I questioned whether or not my job at the cafe was impeding my ability to meet that elusive man. Working at a cafe which was open twenty-four hours a day, seven days a week, it was difficult to work the extreme rotating hours that I had been, as well as maintain extracurricular interests.

I knew something had to change. There didn't seem as though there was enough time for me in my life any more. Besides, my lifestyle became a little too unhealthy. If I wasn't working or sleeping, I was still bar hoping night after night. Whilst I enjoyed the social aspect of work, I knew there were other work and life opportunities that I was missing.

It wasn't long after that realization, I resigned from that job. Once again, I found myself starting a new job, with a recycled career path. I decided to go back to my roots of retail. That change would also see me take a step back from living within the gay scene.

Starting a job that was outside the precincts of the gay scene, I didn't realize just how insular I had become from the rest of the world. I had been working, living and breathing everything associated with the gay lifestyle, to the point I was again living as a product of my own environment. Although at least that time around, my life was more affirmative. I wasn't causing destruction as I did with my previous escapades. For me, being gay didn't define who I was as a person. However, it was easy to let the gay scene define me, if I had wanted it to.

Once I started my new job, I enjoyed having regular retail hours again. Although, I found that having to start work early in the mornings was a difficult adjustment to make. I was no longer able to finish work at midnight, then go out and party all night at the bars. The reality of not having to get out of bed at an unscheduled time for work the following day was now history. My life became more regimented and controlled, which I liked.

There were many benefits to having a job with more organized hours. I believed that was a constructive change, as I knew I needed to find more stability and structure within my life. If I was going to live in the real world, with real responsibilities and away from Oxford Street, then other possibilities to further enrich my life may develop. I remained especially hopeful that the same could be said about my love life too.

At that point, I gave even greater consideration to seeking a partner. Although I became ambivalent, I hoped he was also still waiting to find me too. One thing was very sure, I certainly didn't want a life that revolved around bar hopping, one night stands or only catching up with friends at night in a club. I still fantasized about having dinner parties and lazy Sunday lunches at home with close friends. I wanted to create memories with a partner, not just relive old moments with friends.

I was then, and will always be a proud supporter and advocate of my own gay community. The gay scene provides a safe haven away from the sometimes, unpleasant realities of life. It's a place where you can truly be yourself and have no concern about how you'll be perceived. Although for me, it was, and still is important that I continue to associate with a variety of people, from all walks of life. If I'd only remained within the confines of Oxford Street and gay clubs, I knew I wouldn't be able to educate society that being gay was no different to that of living a 'straight' life, apart from the obvious differences, of course. I needed to show society that I didn't need to be constrained in one environment to make a difference in the world.

Whilst I certainly never ever felt lonely living within the gay scene, I needed to experience other ways of life and broaden my own horizons too. The idea of travel still fascinated me, more at that time than it did when I was back at school. I continued dreaming of places I wanted to visit, which I heard people talking about. I would daydream about how wonderful it would be to travel to countries such the United States of America and the United Kingdom, just to name a few. I had always been intrigued by those two countries, more so because whilst I was growing up, that's generally where my favorite television programs were made.

When I was younger and needed an escape from the reality that I once lived, I used to fantasize about what my ideal life would be like. Apart from one free of misery, those thoughts generally involved a partner and I traveling to see the wonders of the world. I hoped I would one day make that dream finally come true. Firstly though, I needed to find a partner. That notion seemed so much easier said, than done.

I'd never really had the companionship of an intimate lover before. At least not one where mutual desire could break all of the rules and have no boundaries. I desired the type of love that was an explosive emotion which could only be shared between two people who are completely united. I yearned to have that proper connection with a man who I could mentally, physically and emotionally surrender myself to and know that he too, would offer the same in return. I needed to find that unconditional love, without regard for what society had deemed acceptable. I wanted to be loved and adored in ways which broke all of those stereotypical rules. I hoped that sometime in the future I was going to find that very man. I knew I just needed to remain patient.

Before I knew it, a few years had quickly passed by. At that point, I was still no closer to having a partner to share life with. However, unbeknownst to me, the universe had something else planned for me at that time. The idea of finding love and pursuing that greater freedom which I was enjoying, seem to become much further away than I could have ever expected. I was about to undergo a dramatic turn of events which would drastically change me and the way I viewed life, forever. That phase in my life, which I was about to embark on, was going to become much more than a coming of age story.

It was no surprise that my life always had an unusual way of changing in a new and sometimes vastly different direction, without giving me any notice of its intentions. Sometimes those directions were caused by decisions I made, alas, others were caused by those occurrences I spoke of earlier, which I merely had no control over at all. Those were generally instances whereby I was completely powerless to react to events, no matter how much I wish I could have had control.

After a particularly long and exhausting day at work, I decided to have dinner at one of my local haunts, 'The Courthouse Hotel'. Over the years that hotel has become an icon on Oxford Street and is home to many of the locals and tourists alike. It offers a non-exclusive atmosphere which has an old style charm for patrons to enjoy a comfortable environment, without a pretentious crowd. Perhaps not so coincidentally, it's also across the road from the imposing sandstone building of the Darlinghurst Courthouse.

Immediately outside the hotel is the cosmopolitan 'Taylor Square', which is a forecourt area, often filled with *colorful* people from all different walks of life. There is a buzzing, electric ambiance which surrounds this area every night of the week. Both 'Taylor Square' and 'The Courthouse Hotel' are perfectly positioned next to a major road junction, where Oxford Street meets Flinders Street and Bourke Street. That location also serves as a convenient meeting place for friends to meet before a night out on 'The Golden Mile'.

That night, I sat and watched the endless congregation of people on the street, whilst I enjoyed my dinner. It was also that night, I vividly recall a feeling that literally crippled my body for a matter of seconds. I had never experienced that kind of pain before. Although the feeling was fleeting, the affect that it had over me was profound. It wasn't an ache or twinge. That sensation was deep and intense. It shot through my body like a bolt of lightning. I wasn't sure if I should be concerned enough to get medical treatment or let it pass.

I decided to let it pass and continued eating my dinner. Although, I remained cautious just in case I experienced the same symptoms again. Luckily, that feeling didn't return. Yet, I couldn't help but continue to wonder why I was stuck by that overpowering sensation. I was just thankful there was no encore. Once I finished dinner, it was still reasonably early, so I decided to take a walk down Oxford Street on my way home and get some much needed air back in to my lungs.

As I walked through the streets, I observed other people who were also enjoying time with their loved ones over dinner. That made me reflect on my own lack of love life. Although, I was grateful for learning the life lessons which I had, even if some were harder than others. Nevertheless, I was still craving to have an emotional connection with someone special. I felt as though my life partner was never going to materialize. I hoped I hadn't set myself up for more heartache, by having those dreams of a man who simply didn't exist.

As I walked, I continued to watch the array of people. Some were holding hands, others were laughing, but for the most part, they appeared to be fondly sharing their lives with one other. At that moment, my blissful reflective mood changed. I felt a heart-breaking pain from deep within my soul. That uncompromising notion of distress was almost as though I had been grieving for something. I found that impression unusual, because nothing in my life had changed. Surprisingly, that was twice in the same night that I experienced irrational feelings, which I couldn't explain. I became a little concerned and decided to walk straight home.

Once I arrived at my apartment, I sat restfully on the couch whilst I caught my breath. I was still somewhat shaken from the dramatic change of my emotions. I still could understand the heightened sensitivities which had taken over my body. I decided the best thing I could do was relax and clear my mind from the physically and emotionally draining events which had taken place throughout that day. I settled in for the night and began to look forward to watching my favorite television show at that time, 'Melrose Place'.

I would have normally enjoyed the company of my housemate and other friends for that typical viewing of Tuesday night trash television, and it certainly didn't get much trashier, or more fabulous, than 'Melrose Place'. Usually, we would gather around the television and watch in awe of what was going to happen next to that radical group of twenty something year old people who lived at an apartment complex in Los Angeles. That was a television show with the most extreme story lines, which had us believing what we were watching was actually happening in real life. Like most people at that time, we were always excited about our Tuesday nights, *being a bitch!*

However, on that particular night I found myself all alone, even my housemate was working out of town. It had been the first Tuesday night in a very long time that I was not spending it with other people around me. For an unexplained reason, I still felt surprisingly out of character and thought it best not to be around people anyway. Yet, I couldn't shake the undiagnosed feeling that there was something more ominous going on inside my body than what I had imagined.

I tried not to think too much about it though. Perhaps I was just feeling sorry for myself. Seeing those happy people from earlier, out for dinner, enjoying themselves made me realize just how much I wanted a lover. Although, I wasn't normally one to let other people's happiness affect me. If anything, I too would celebrate their happiness. I also tried not to over analyze my thoughts or feelings, but rather, simply made the excuse to myself that I must have been feeling tired and run down.

At 8:20pm that night, I had ten minutes to spare before viewing my night of wonderfully trashy television. Within those few minutes I decided to call my mom and say, hello. It then occurred to me that perhaps I was just missing my family and that's why I had been a little out of step with life that night. I thought hearing my mom's voice may at least ease the unparalleled sorrow I was feeling.

As I dialed the telephone number, I could feel my heart start to beat faster for no reason. I was hoping that call wouldn't be another cold conversation, because I already felt dreadful enough. After a few rings, my sister answered the phone. She and I went through the motions of the usual small talk that two people who don't have much in common usually do. I then asked to speak with our mom. There was a pause from the other end of the line, so I asked again, just in case she didn't hear me the first time.

A few more seconds of unexpected silence passed before my sister spoke again. There was an uncertain tone in her voice, one with hesitation. She proceeded to tell me that our mom was in hospital, followed by her hastily spoken words, *'There's nothing to worry about. She's only having a few routine checks as she was feeling tired due to her white blood cell count being low.'* I paused, in shock. I asked, *'Will she be alright?'* to which the reply back was, *'Yes, but she just needs to rest.'*

My parents had recently moved from our family home, into a new house. Although their move wasn't far from our old house to their new one, I appreciated that moving house could be tiring and stressful. I just assumed the relocation had taken its toll on my mom and she probably needed some time out to escape the woes of moving. It had also only been a few days earlier that I sent my mom a greeting card to let her know I was thinking of her and that I love her.

Whilst I was on the telephone that night, I asked my sister to ask mom if she received that card. My sister was unsure if it had been delivered, but said she'd ask for me. I then asked my sister to tell our mom that I love her and I would call her back in a few days to see if she was feeling better. After those words, there was nothing more to talk about, so our telephone call ended with the standard, 'See you later.'

Once the call finished, I was still in disbelief that our mom was in hospital. Although, as I was assured there was nothing to be concerned about, I apprehensively continued watching television. Although I didn't absorb much of what I watched because I was thinking about my mom, hoping she was in good spirits. Yet, there were several moments at that time which I wondered why I hadn't been told by my family what had happened earlier. Reluctantly, I had no other option but to take faith in what my sister said and believed that there was nothing to worry about.

That night, just as I was about to go to bed, at 10:30pm the phone rang. I didn't know who would be calling so late. When I answered, there was nothing but an eerie silence on the other end of the line. I could only hear excessive shallow breathing. I continued to say, 'Hello', but there were still no words spoken. I became a little concerned. Finally, in the distance, I heard a soft, fragile voice on the other end of the line. That voice was barely recognizable, to the point I had to ask whomever it was to speak louder, so I could distinguish who was calling. Again, the telephone line went silent. I could still hear that same cavernous, unnatural breathing in the distance. Just as I was about to hang up, all of a sudden, an inaudible, fragmented voice on the line said, *'I have something to tell you.'*

As I strained to hear those words, I realized it was my sister. I waited for the conversation to continue, however there was only more ghostly silence. My chest muscles were becoming tighter with every second that went by. I could now feel my own breathing become restricted. I wasn't sure why, but I knew something wasn't right. I waited in silence. I needed to hear whatever it was she was trying to say. With a superficial, breathless string of mumbled words, I could only hear a person who was trying to speak through extreme anguish. It was obvious my sister was feeling an inconsolable amount of pain. But why?

Every broken word she tried to speak sounded as though she was holding back a river of tears. The only jumbled words which formed any complete sentence were vigorously rushed. It was then, she proceeded to tell me something that no child ever wants to hear, *'Mom has passed away.'*

That news was delivered only two hours after our initial telephone call. I was so immensely confused. How could those events have gone from *'She just needs to rest'*, to her then passing away? I sat in aching silence. There were no words I could even find to speak. Without even saying goodbye, I scrambled to hang up the telephone. I then took it off the hook so no one else could call. That news left me distraught, troubled and consumed by a dangerously volatile string of heartfelt emotions. I was unable to digest a single word of what I had just heard.

I felt as though I had been dropped in to a bottomless pit of blistery burning hot fire. I was left with a million questions running through my mind. In reality, the only question which I actually needed the answer to was, *'Why was my mother dead?'*

I fell to the floor in arrant disbelief and confusion. My body, limp and motionless as I lay still, staring at the colorless ceiling above. My entire life flashed before my eyes. That situation seemed so very inconceivable. My mind took over and tried to block out those words, which continued to haunt me.

I continued to lay on the floor, unresponsive to everything. My entire body was numb, paralyzed from the enormous shock. There seemed as though there was nothing else in the room with me, only a gigantic weight pushing me further down in to the floor. That feeling was compounded by what I can only be described as a pillow, forcefully covering my mouth, not allowing me to inhale one solitary breath of air. I continued to be completely paralyzed. The extreme emotions which crippled me, were not only of grief. An intense state of dread, shame and guilt had also accompanied my heartache.

All of a sudden, the only sensation I felt was that excruciating pain, which I unexpectedly experienced earlier that night. That very pain hit back into my soul with a harsh aggressive force. The only difference was, that catastrophic sensation didn't last a few seconds. It continued to linger for many hours after. I begged for the agony to stop, but it only continued drastically tearing every single part of my fragile existence to shreds. That relentless torment was ravaging every fiber of my body. The world as I knew it had just imploded and impaired any sense of normality which I had, only a few hours earlier.

Those feelings were very different and more severe than anything else that I'd ever experienced in my life. I continued to be raped by profoundly chronic feelings of remorse, devastation and a complete state of gross powerlessness. There was no rationalization for the death of my mother. She was the lady who carried me in her body for nine months, then nurtured me after she gave birth. She raised me and looked after me through good times and bad. Regardless of how she felt towards me up until she passed away, I have to believe, even to this day, that she loves me. I am still her precious little boy, her son, her flesh and blood.

That acute pain was more than I was able to bear. I continued to lay on the floor in the fetal position. My stomach churning with every short, one dimensional breath I took. It was at that unforgiving moment when I came to an extremely abrupt realization. I knew I would never have another opportunity to rebuild the once loving relationship which I shared with my mom. There was no going back in time. I had to live with the fact that I selfishly obliterated our relationship, with no chance for redemption. It was too late. My mom will never know how truly and wholeheartedly sorry I was for the heartless pain I selfishly caused her.

I began sobbing uncontrollably. There was a deep heaving from within my broken soul. I felt an unconscionable feeling of supreme hate and resentment. Those emotions accompanied the fury I not only had for myself, but for that entire situation. I was unable to control what had happened. Every solitary tear that fell from my eyes, felt like the excruciating pain of a blunt knife severing its way to deep inside my heart.

There were so many words which I had left unsaid. More than anything else, there were so many mixed feelings which I wanted to resolve. Regrettably, the time for my sincere words and heartfelt actions were taken away. With the deepest regret, I realized that I would never again have that opportunity. The cold harsh reality of my mom's death was slowly starting to sink in. Apart from not be able to express my words to her, I also realized I would never be able to kiss her, hug her, touch her or hold her ever again. She was gone. Not even my memories could provide the solace I needed.

All that remained, was my mom's lifeless body, which used to house a beautiful lady who didn't deserve the agony I put her through. She had left this world and was ready to explore another. Hopefully she had been taken to a world without further pain and suffering.

My static body still lay wilted and doubled over on the floor. That night, for many hours after, I continued mourning for the loss of a lady who I had always relied on to be my guiding light throughout life. Even through the toughest, darkest hours of what I put her through, she was a beacon for all that was good in life. Even through our estranged years, she inadvertently gave me the inspiration to better myself.

Perhaps without her ever knowing it, she is still the one person who continues to inspire me to be the person I am today. Back then though, I so desperately wanted to tell her how sorry I was for being the son which I thought she never wanted throughout those early years. She never asked to have a self-centered son, nor did she ask for, or deserve, how badly I had treated her. I only wish that she was still in the realm of the living, to see the son I hoped she would be proud of.

I lay awake that night, feeling nothing but a tremendous amount of guilt and remorse for the emotional turmoil which I caused my loved ones. I often speculate, even as I type this, if my mother's passing was one of peace and sanctuary. Although I'll never know the truth of that, I can only hope and pray that my mother didn't pass with the negativity that I once cast upon her. I also sincerely hope with all of my heart, that her spirit is around me today, still shining her light on my road ahead. Yet, I truly believe that she is.

The memory of August 15th 1995 will remain deeply embedded in my heart and soul for the rest of my life.

For any person who's lost a loved one, they will truly understand the type of emotional abandonment that's associated with death. It's more than a private feeling of extreme weakness, anger, denial and in my case, disgrace and guilt. Death is final. One of the hardest lessons I had to learn throughout that period, was to accept what had happened and try to survive that experience the best way I could. As difficult as it was, I was determined that I would not allow that grotesque experience to survive me.

It was several days after receiving that intolerable news, I began thinking more about my mother's passing. I still wanted to know why no one in my family had told me that she was in hospital earlier. If I hadn't called to speak with her that night, I may never have known she was even in hospital. That alone, would have made that bitter experience a lot more unimaginable.

I also needed to know how long my family knew of her illness. I began to wonder if I was somehow being punished by my family for not being the person they wanted me to be. Although, I doubt they could have been so cruel to do that. Yet, I couldn't shake off that distrustful feeling that my family had in some way betrayed me by withholding that information. Because I was unaware of the circumstances regarding my mom, I was inadvertently made to feel redundant by those who I thought I could have trusted, especially in times of crisis.

Although the relationship I had with my mom wasn't entirely intact, she was the one common denominator which united us as a family. I assumed that with the devastation which had taken place, that would have been enough of a reason to once again reunite us as a family.

Sadly, with each grief stricken day that passed, the next seemed even more surreal than the last. I continued aimlessly wondering through an obscure cloud of despondency, unable to find any perspective. I was incapable of regaining control of my reality. I still felt motionless, as though I was trying to walk through deep water from a freezing Arctic pool. There appeared to be no way of coming to terms with what had happened. I became further consumed with sorrow and rage by the death of my mother. The distressing actuality that I was never going to have an opportunity to say my final face to face goodbye to her, was too much to grasp.

In the midst of everything which had taken place, I had also started that new job. As I wasn't as financial as I had been previously, I knew I had to start thinking about how I was going to return to Melbourne for my mom's funeral. That was something I felt as though I needed to do on my own, so borrowing money for an airline ticket wasn't going to be an option. After checking my bank balance, I only had enough money saved for a return bus fare, along with a few nights accommodation at a budget hotel. The following day I booked my bus ticket to make the pilgrimage back to Melbourne.

I continued living in a dazed state. I was still at a complete loss over what had happened. It was then, I realized I also had another puzzling circumstance to contend with. It occurred to me that it had been many years since I last saw my siblings. I wondered if the reality of receiving a warm reception, was going to be the reunion that was too good to be true. To be honest, I actually wasn't sure of what their reaction was going to be once I returned. There had been many different events that had taken place over the years. I was unable to determine the outcome. I wondered if we would actually be able to set our differences aside and simply celebrate the beautiful life that was. I hoped that we could. I couldn't help but ask myself, 'Was that going to be a reprieve I hoped for?' I was undecided about that too. I just had to wait until I was in that moment to see what really took place.

It was only a few short days after the death of my mom, I endured a sleepless and uncomfortable twelve hour bus journey from Sydney to Melbourne. I vowed that I would never do that again. It was only due to extreme circumstances that I had no other choice but to take the bus. Finally, I was back in my hometown of Melbourne. I returned to the city which stirred my emotions more than I had expected. I was happy to be back, but melancholy and anxious because of the somber reason I was there in the first place. I felt unbalanced and distracted by the memories of my past. My return was a bittersweet visit to a former life which I had once known.

Shortly after arriving, I checked myself in to the only accommodation I could afford. It was a small, run down hotel situated on Little Collins Street, in Melbourne's central business district. The rooms were clean enough, however the walls were paper thin. The pungent stench of musty wet laundry, like it had been left in the washing machine for days, filled every corner of that hotel. If I didn't know any better, I would have assumed they rented their rooms out by the hour at that establishment. Although, it served its purpose while I was there. Besides, I never received an invite to stay with my family, so I had to make the best of what was on offer.

Once I eventually settled into the hotel, which was on the Sunday of that same week, I called my sister to confirm that I had arrived. The telephone only rang out. As there was no answer, I decided I'd call back later. It was important that I spoke with her, as I also needed to find out the details regarding our mom's funeral service, which was due to take place that following day.

As I couldn't get the answers I needed at that time, I decided to leave the hotel and take a break from the 'not so picturesque' surrounds of my 'not so well appointed' hotel room. Moments later, just before I walked out the door, the telephone rang. It was my sister returning my call. After the usual strained pleasantries, she proceeded to tell me that she was with our father, who was also in hospital. I felt a sense of disturbance by hearing that. For many years, including the time we had to stop performing our magic shows, our dad suffered with a heart condition and deteriorating health, but with rest, he always recovered, fighting back to his usual self.

My sister went on to explain that his stint in hospital that time was different from previous occasions. Our dad had taken a turn for the worst, even more dramatically than ever before. In the seconds of confusion which followed, I realized that the loss of his wife, our mother, had not surprisingly taken its toll on him.

She then told me that dad requested to speak with me. As she handed the telephone over to him, I became a little nervous. Although he was very difficult to understand, due to his rapid decline in health, he seemed capable of making sparse conversation. I only had the opportunity to speak with him for a few minutes, however that was long enough for me to understand what he was trying to convey. In those brief minutes, we had one of the most compelling and deep conversations which we'd had for as far back as I could remember.

Whilst listening to my dad try to piece his words together, I could tell that he was only a fraction of the man he once was. His breathing was labored and his words were slurred. Although, he delivered a bona fide message, which was loud and clear. I can still hear his powerful words echo through my ears. He told me that I was to never give up on finding happiness and although I had 'chosen' a life that he disagreed with, I was still his son and that's all that mattered to him. His honest words struck me to my very core.

It became obvious by his tapered breathing and disorientation, that his life was slowly slipping away while I was speaking with him. Still, I wasn't ready to say goodbye to him. Whilst I felt exonerated by his words, I needed him to at least physically see the person I was becoming. It all seemed too late though. During our conversation, he also spoke of angels which came to visit him. He went on to say that those angels stood at the foot of his bed every night, inviting him to leave this world and take refuge in the afterlife.

As I was on the phone to him, through my tears, I found myself encouraging him not to give in to the temptation of death. I needed him to fight on. I told him that as a family we would unite and mourn the loss of our mother, together. The last sorrowful words I said to my dad before hanging up the telephone were, *'I'll see you tomorrow and then we'll be reunited as a family. Even if mom isn't there in body, she'll be there in spirit. I love you, dad.'* With those words, that call ended. I hoped that he could find whatever inner strength he needed to survive, even for just a little bit longer. Although, I couldn't help but sense that he would be unable to find that strength.

It was almost one hour later, my sister called to let me know that our father had let go of his life and was finally at peace. He suffered a severe heart attack and he too, had passed away. He was now on his way to be reunited with our mother, to bask in an afterlife of eternal prosperity. Once again, the world as I knew it had come to a grinding halt. The uncontrolled emotions which were already running high throughout my entire body, had now become too inhumane for me to even deal with.

On August 20th 1995, at the age of 24, I became an orphan. Both of my parents were now dead. I found myself not only grieving for the loss of one parent, but now, for both of my parents, in that same week.

Once again, throughout my darkest hours during that period, I found myself thinking that the death of my parents was karma giving me a good hard kick where I probably had needed it the most. I couldn't understand why life had dealt me a hand which seemed so impossible to take hold of. As much as I tried, I couldn't make any kind of sense out of the situation which had unexpectedly unfolded.

Besides my own anguish, my heart was also full of pain for my sister. It was she who was left to deliver the heartbreaking news to me, not only once, but twice. I couldn't even imagine how she found the strength to do that, whilst she was struggling with her own undeniable grief.

I became lost within the darkness of an unending depression. I never knew how I was going to find my own inner strength, which I drastically needed, in order for me to deal with my raw and unrestricted emotions. The events which had taken place left behind nothing more than a hideous path of destruction, which literally turned my life upside down and tore my spirit apart.

My soul was completely exposed to vulnerability. In an irrational psychological state of shock, I couldn't help but think that everyone in my life was going to abandon me, or even worse, die. One thing was certain, I needed to find a way to survive that horrendous loss, but I simply didn't know where to begin.

The Final Farewell

I remember as though it was yesterday, the unsettling day I called my employer to inform the store Manager that I needed to extend my bereavement leave. I was nervous about making that call, because it was still a relatively new job for me. However, given the circumstances, I was sure he'd be understanding of my situation and accommodate my request. Whilst on the phone to him that afternoon, I remorsefully explained what had happened. I then proceeded to let him know I couldn't return back to work until the following Monday.

There was a pause from the other end of the telephone. To my disbelief, I then heard an overt snicker, which was quickly followed by the words, *'Yeah right'*, in a doubting sarcastic tone. To add insult to injury, he then requested, in an offensive manner, that I fax both of my parents' death certificates to him as justification for my leave extension request. He went on to say, *'Without those certificates, my extension wouldn't be approved and my employment would come under review.'* Shocked, I sat silent for a few seconds. I became dismayed and angered by not only his words, but also his barbaric request.

I never had much to do with him since I'd started work there. However, it promptly became clear that he was a person with no compassion, or empathy for what I was going through. I couldn't understand why he needed me to prove that I actually wasn't 'living the high life', as he presumed, whilst I was in Melbourne.

Confused by that 'so called' Manager's request, it was blindingly obvious he was also a person who had no morality. Who was *he* to think it was acceptable to question my integrity and interrogate me as though that catastrophe was a way for me to get out of work? I couldn't believe his contempt. My parents weren't even buried yet. The more I thought about his attitude to my situation, the more disgusted and outraged I became.

By then, I was totally consumed by diabolical rage. I slammed the phone down in his ear with as much force as I could muster. I wasn't going to allow him, or his blatant insensitivity, add to the strain of what was already an extremely arduous and stressful week. Somehow, I knew I quickly needed to put his callousness out of my mind and remain focused on the actual reason I was in Melbourne. Fortunately, I had no further contact with him until I returned to Sydney. However, dealing with him was probably a better option, rather than concentrating on the harrowing days that were waiting ahead.

The events at that time seemed to be happening incredibly fast. Before I knew it, the first of two days that would further change my life forever had arrived. It was Monday, the day of my mother's funeral. On that morning, I received an early telephone call from my sister to see how I was feeling. I was touched by her concern for my wellbeing. I was still dazed and emotionally exhausted, just as she had been too. My body still felt as though it was dead on the inside. There was no feeling, only an abysmal emptiness, which was consuming every part of my very being.

My sister and I continued to exchange a few more minutes of vague conversation. She then expressed concern that our brother may seem distant toward me at the funeral. To be honest, I expected that to happen, after all, we were all in terrible shock. She proceeded to tell me that since the death of our mom, he was not only struggling to come to terms with her passing, but *may* direct his anger toward me because of her death. As he was the oldest child, I could understand that he would feel the most resentment and bitterness over our mom's death. I just had to remember not to take anything personally and let the grieving process take its course. However, that day was as much for me, as it was for him too.

I later discovered that my brother and sister were at the hospital on the evening that our mom passed away. They were both by her bedside, keeping vigil, until such time as they stepped out of the room for a few minutes to compose themselves. Sadly, it would be within those very short minutes after they returned to her bedside, to find our mother had let go of this world and was moving towards her final resting place. I believe she saw that as the perfect opportunity to bid her final farewell and graciously rise in to the mystical spirit world. Unfortunately, by that time, not even the machines which kept her alive could turn back the clock and revive her. She released herself from that current state of pain and suffering, which had ultimately taken over her life.

After learning that my siblings were at the hospital, I couldn't even begin to image how horrendous it must have been there, and indeed, in the hours which led up to the time our mom silently said goodbye. I knew my siblings would have done everything in their power to make her as comfortable as possible before her passing. My heart went out to them both. To sit and watch our mother, a lady who was dying from cancer, diminish hour by hour, minute by minute would be nothing less than emotionally annihilating.

As devastating as it would have been for me to see our mom suffering in hospital, I still only wished that I was informed about what was happening, before it was tragically too late. I only wanted to have one final opportunity to at least kiss her and say farewell in my own way. I believe that is the right of any child who has to say goodbye to their dying parent. I needed to have that closure. For me, I thought that could have been a vital part of my own grieving and subsequent healing process.

Whilst on the telephone to my sister earlier, I had taken heed of what she mentioned, about how my brother *may* react towards me. In some ways, I couldn't help but sense my sister was trying to tell me that our brother blamed me for our mom's death, because of the choices I made in life. Whilst that wasn't the case and there was no blame from him, I certainly didn't want to be held responsible, nor did I want our mother's funeral to be about which sibling was feeling the most pain or grieving the most. I wanted that day to be a special day for our beloved mom. That had to be a day for us all to pay our respect to the lady who had lived for her children. She was a lady, who was the only mother we'll ever have.

Later that day, after barely tolerating the forty minute train journey from my city, I arrived at the funeral home. Whilst on the train, my thoughts were undeniably fueled by sadness. That same irrational mindset from the previous days was again beginning to take over. I thought that perhaps I wasn't welcome to attend her funeral. As I made my way to the Chapel, I remember the extreme apprehension I felt as I walked down the long paved driveway. I could do nothing but stare vacantly in to the depths of the tall pine trees, which were perfectly aligned. In the distance, I could only see silhouettes of the mourners surrounding one other, offering their condolences. That surreal sight was something which I had only ever seen in movies.

I never thought I could feel such a tremendous wave of emotion, as the one which had taken over my entire body throughout that day. As I reached the end of the driveway, I tried walking into the Chapel, but had to stop as I'd became stricken by colossal heartache. Somehow, I knew I had to be brave and remain strong. With every step closer I took to those gigantic Chapel doors, my blood ran cold. I became impaired by the fear of the unknown. I was scared of what was waiting for me beyond those gigantic carved wooden doors. With one small step at a time, I finally found the strength to walk inside the Chapel. Nervously, I stood in the silence, as I looked around. I couldn't help but think the worst. I expected to be judged by people who I hadn't seen for a number of years.

I soon realized they were able to overlook whatever bias they may have had. The mourners embraced me at a time I needed to call on their strength. I believe most of the people who attended the funeral always suspected that I was gay anyway. It was also a blessing they seemed unaware that my relationship with my family had deteriorated, due to my past behavior. As I continued to walk further in to the Chapel, I knew that was going to be the moment of truth. I found myself standing face to face with my brother and sister. They were my siblings, who I hadn't seen for almost six years. I became dizzy and nauseous. I only hoped that our reunion was going to be one that was welcoming, as opposed to the treacherous thoughts which I had manifested in my own mind.

We stood in awkward silence for a few seconds. To be honest, I don't believe any of us actually knew what to say to one another. Whilst it was apparent there was a definite sense of separation between us, there was no anger or animosity. There was only a void feeling. Almost as though we were three strangers who happen to find themselves united by sadness and isolated by their own individual grief. Unfortunately, my siblings and I shared minimal words and contact throughout that day. However, our respective pain spoke volumes, where our words had failed.

It was evident that we were all dealing with heightened sensitivities and emotional distress. As much as I longed to know the answers to all of my previous questions, I knew that wasn't the right time, or the right place. Actually, I didn't even know if there would be a right time or place. That entire situation was again, one of those occasions I had to trust that the answers would find me in time.

Not unlike most funeral services, family members were seated in the front row of the Chapel. The casket, in which my mother laid, had been magnificently dressed with a stunning array of flowers, including one of her favorites, the Iris. The service which was conducted was as beautiful and as dignified as the lady that we were there to pay our respects to. Every aspect of our mother's life was covered in the eulogy, which was delivered by the priest. That service was a true celebration and reflection of the life, which had sadly been taken away from us. As far as funerals go, I believe that my mom's was delivered with perfection.

Once the service finished, there was to be a private burial at our mother's final resting place. The location for that was about thirty minutes from where the service was held. It was at that very moment, I felt a further detachment from my siblings. There was no offer extended for me to go with them. I was again excluded. In my mind, it was made clear that I wasn't welcome to attend. Feeling deeply saddened and unworthy of being my mom's son, I was left abandoned. Those feelings were not the emotions I wanted to contend with on her special day.

Once the mourners started to disperse, I stood staring at the coffin, which had already been loaded into the hearse. I remember wondering if it was at my mom's request that I didn't attend that private service, or if it was in fact, my siblings who wanted to exclude me from showing my respects and saying my own personal goodbye. It never occurred to me to confront my siblings in search of the truth. I just accepted that the pain I caused over those earlier years was the reason behind the decision. To be honest, I don't believe that either of my siblings would have been so hateful to purposely exclude me. Although, the truth behind that decision still remains an enigma.

I continued staring at the coffin, feeling totally lost and dejected. I didn't want to cause a scene in front the mourners, who were left paying their final respects. Rather, I turned and walked away from the congregation that was forming around us. If the truth be known, I was more embarrassed that I wasn't invited to go with my family. Needless to say, although that wish wasn't granted, several months after the funerals I made my return to Melbourne. I made it my ambition to visit my parents' resting place, pay my respects and finally say goodbye in my own way, at my own time.

Once the funeral service was over, feeling weary, I caught the train back to the city. For the duration of that journey, I sat and reflected on my mom's life. I cried as I recalled the memories of growing up. I remembered the look of pride on my mom's face when I first started primary school. The chicken and salad rolls she'd buy for my after school snack. The cuddles we shared whist watching television. The sweet sound of her singing that lullaby, 'Morningtown Ride', by Judith Durham and The Seekers, before I soundly drifted off to sleep.

During those reflections of a time gone by, I soon realized I had many loving memories, which will continue to last a lifetime and provide comfort when I need them most. Unfortunately though, I also realized that once I had become an adolescent, there were no more of those glorious memories ever made.

When I finally returned to my hotel room, I sat peacefully, for a few minutes anyway, on the corner of the bed. All of sudden, my oppressive emotions got the better of me. I was no longer enjoying the wonderful memories of my past. The only memories which came flooding back were from the not so distant past. They were now at the forefront of my mind, virtually eating me alive. I felt no relief from the torturous pain, which continued burrowing its way in to my soul. Like a scorching hot iron against pure silk, those hateful memories crumpled, then destroyed my delicate existence. I became so incredibly despondent. All I could do was lay on the bed in hope those detestable memories would vanish.

Later that night, I experienced an overwhelming sensation that I wasn't alone in my room. That experience was in complete contrast to those feelings of anger and bitterness I felt earlier.

Suddenly, I felt a sense of calmness and serene tranquility covering my body. I don't know what that entity was, but it seemed to be looking over me. The atmosphere in my hotel room became one of love and peace, which surrounded me. Whilst I still wanted to be angry about the passing of my mom, no matter how much I tried, I simply couldn't. That calm feeling of peace remained with me for the duration of that night. I couldn't explain what that entity was, although, I would like to have believed it was a supernatural energy from my mom, protecting me.

The following day was my reprieve between funerals. That was a day in which I needed to collect my thoughts and try to rationalize life. Whilst I felt more at peace than I did, my mind was still spinning like a carousel at full speed. My emotions continued to be like an out of control roller coaster, ready to derail at any second. It seemed as though I could do very little to take control of anything. I was alone, struggling my way through an unknown land of limbo. I was dealing with an infinite amount of emotions, not only towards my parents, but my siblings also. As much as I tried, I couldn't clear my mind to find the center of peace.

Then, before I knew it, Wednesday had arrived. That was the day of my father's funeral. It was surreal to return to the same Chapel where my mom's funeral was held, only two days earlier. I wondered if I was going to have to endure the same interactions with the same people who attended our mom's funeral. For the most part, the majority of those same people who I hadn't seen for many years, were still sympathetic towards our loss. There were only a rare few who wouldn't speak to me at all. I was a little upset by that, but I didn't push the issue with them.

My father, a proud man, was still involved within the community until he was admitted to hospital and subsequently up until his passing. I noticed that there seemed to be a different gathering of people to those at my mom's funeral. There were many more business associates and community leaders who attended my dad's service. Many of those people I'd never seen before. I never knew if those people were my dad's friends, or just people who wanted to viciously relish in my father's passing. Yet, it was still nice to see many of the same familiar friendly faces from the previous Monday, who had again come to pay their respects to my dad.

Our father's service, just as our mother's, was beautifully delivered. Once again, my siblings and I had taken the entire front row of the Chapel, along with a select few close family friends and other associates of my fathers. There were however, a few differences on that day. On that, the second most difficult day of my life, I found it hard to believe that one person could be so judgmental, vicious and vocally upfront with his point of view.

Before the service commenced, I walked through the Chapel to take my seat. From several rows back, I could hear snickering from someone who deemed me as a 'deviant'. That person obviously didn't believe that I should have attended my own father's funeral. I found his actions inappropriate, to say the least.

That day certainly wasn't the time or the place for closed minded people to air their opinions. It became apparent, by that person's standard, it was acceptable for him to criticize the boy whose father had just passed away, but it wasn't acceptable for that same boy to live true to his own life. I was stunned.

The memory of his hypocrisy and blatant disregard for respect, has sadly stayed with me until this very day. Back in that happy escape from reality, I should have requested him to leave the service. Unfortunately, sometimes it's only after the fact, when you're more affected by the disgusting actions of others.

During that day, I was also still a little upset that my siblings and I didn't reconnect as much as I hoped for. I didn't think that my sexual identity played *that* much of a part towards the distance that separated us. I just think that we had lost touch with each other as a family over the years. It was obvious that our lives had taken us all on a very different journey.

Once our father's funeral service finished, I was again on the train going back to my hotel room. I never asked if there was a private service being held for our dad, nor was I told of one. With all that had taken place, I felt as though the events of that entire week seemed to be moving as though they was being played on fast forward. Unfortunately, I also didn't feel I resolved as much as I wanted to in that week. I never had the opportunity to sit with my brother and sister to talk about our feelings, or indeed, the events which led us to where we were at that time.

I believed there was still so much left unsaid, to both my parents and my siblings. Even more so, there was much more I needed to explain to my brother and sister. I felt I needed to justify the actions of my youth in some way. I wanted them to know what my childhood was really like, but those words would stay unspoken forever. Coincidentally, that period would be the last time I would ever see both of my siblings together again. As usual, life would later unfold in its usual bizarre fashion. Alas, I never had the opportunity to truly make the peace I so desperately needed to, before time ran out.

After that very affective and emotional week, the time had come for me to return home to Sydney. I was still incredibly shell shocked from what had been a whirlwind of assorted emotions. I wasn't looking forward to going home, because more than anything, I wanted to remain close to my parents. Even in death, I hoped they continued to hear my pleas for forgiveness. I could only pray that they took clemency on me, before finding themselves in a beautiful, grand place of peace. It was unfortunate that it took the death of my parents to put my life in to perspective. For many months after the passing of my mother, I was still unable to come to terms with not being allowed the opportunity to say a simple goodbye to her.

I still understood that I wouldn't have been able to change the outcome, but at the very least, I wanted her to hear me say, *'I love you, mom'*, just one more time. I realized that it's the simple pleasures which mean the most. To have had that opportunity, I would have a final memory, which may have blocked out some of those more painful memories of the past.

It goes without saying, but there were many varied feelings connected with losing those people who I loved, respected and admired. Whilst I was searching for my own innermost strength, I realized there was one of two possible avenues I could have taken, in order to heal myself from the hurt I was so brutally exposed to.

The first alternative, was to allow myself to give in to the negative emotions I felt for the loss of the very people who gave me life. It could have been very easy to again self-destruct, just as I had done previously. Without battle, I could have easily given up. Then, before long, the time would have come where I would have just been another 'John Doe' lying on a cold hard slab in a mortuary, waiting to go in to a nameless grave. If that path was the one I'd taken, then my legacy to this world would amount to nothing.

However, the second alternative, was to reflect on and celebrate the lives that were. It was difficult to overcome those gross feelings associated with death. However, I couldn't allow myself to become isolated from all the wonderful things, which I sometimes overlooked in life. I wasn't prepared to negate the warm feeling of reaching out and touching another human being. Or even the simple things, such as walking through a park with my shoes off, feeling the lush green grass beneath my feet.

More importantly, I realized that no matter how big or how small the simple pleasures are in life, they are just that, simple and delightful things which bring pleasure. Without experiencing the simple joys, I would have lost my ability to connect with my soul again and in turn, I would have lost my ability to relate to other people. Those are people who continue to bring meaning to my life, just as I hope I do for them also.

Throughout those atrocious memories of the past, that was a time in my life where I began reflecting on how those experiences would further assist me with growing in to the person I am today. I knew I had to make bold choices, which I could take with me throughout my journey. I asked myself, *'Was I going to take a path that closed me off from everyone and everything, until I died?'* The answer was a definitive, *'No.'* If I did in fact, take that gloomy path, I would probably eventually do harm to myself, if not take my own life.

Through whatever determination I could muster, plus surviving to uphold the memory of my parents, I realized there was another way to live life. I decided to adopt the 'take every day as it comes' attitude. Of course it was going to be very hard to work through my anger, grief and self-doubt. However, by being strong and getting my life back on track, I needed to survive and potentially help someone else who, for whatever reason, may also be staring down the barrel of their own loaded gun.

All I wanted to do was accept the past as best I could and move on with a positive new attitude, which would defy my emotional upheaval. Firstly, I needed to stop blaming others for the pain I continued to live with. I had to genuinely accept what happened in my past and move on. Ultimately, I needed to take responsibility for myself and my actions. I realized that there was no one else in the world who could act on my behalf to change the person I was. During that time of my life, I was set to embark on yet another new way of thinking. I reached a powerful climax, which brought with it a true belief. That was, any change had to start with me completely understanding and validating myself.

After my parents' death, I believe I found the connection between self-development and self-appraisal. Although similar, I needed to firstly appraise myself to know the objectives and goals which I truly desired from life. Once I evaluated myself, I then had to work toward implementing those changes in order to live again. With that small insight, I also hoped that one day I could inspire others to not give up when they believed there was no way out of a situation. I felt as though I was finally growing into myself as I began to truly accept my differences.

Another important lesson I learned, was to authorize my mind and trust that there were people such as counselors and mental health professionals who were trained and well equipped to deal with my issues, should I need their help.

The reality is, there will always be days where I feel those black clouds of fear, doubt and negativity lingering above me, for one reason or another. However, I knew that I had to remain focused and believe that I *wasn't* a failure. I had to believe I was capable of achieving my dreams and be deserving of the kindness of life.

I knew I was still a work in progress, but that didn't mean I had to stop believing in the power of my own self-worth. I wanted to take stock of all that was futile in my life. I didn't know how long the notion of that life defining moment was going to last, but I certainly had to give it my best shot to make it work.

In the loving memory of my parents, I became determined to prove to myself that I would outlive those tragic circumstances which surrounded me. I wanted to live on, to make this world a better place to live in.

An Unknown Voice of Hope

Returning to Sydney provided me with an opportunity to take that honest and constructive look at my life. I needed an even harder look at some of the choices I'd made throughout my life, which would enable me to finally break free. I realized that some of my decisions which I made were questionable, however I believed I acted with the best knowledge that I had at that time. Although, it wasn't until the passing of my parents, that I was able to see life from that veritable and confronting perspective.

First and foremost I needed to go back to work. To be honest, I wasn't sure if I even had a job to go back to. If I did though, judging from the way our previous phone call ended, I expected the wrath of my Manager to be relentless. I was nervous about his reaction. Not only was he dubious of my less than perfect circumstances, I knew he could potentially make my work environment very difficult for me.

One the day I returned to work, the first couple of hours were just like any other day before I took bereavement leave. Thankfully, the Manager wasn't at work that morning, but I knew I had to face him later that day. It wasn't until after lunch that I was summoned into his office. There was a sullen look of coldness on his face when he asked me again to explain the events which had taken place whilst I was in Melbourne. As I started speaking, I found it very awkward to get my words out without becoming emotional. I struggled to relive those events, which clearly had an impact on the way my words were being delivered.

I began explaining the horrendous situation that was, choking on my every word. As I spoke, I wondered if it was possible to make a complete stranger understand the destructive feelings and emotional desolation that I felt by the death of my two parents. As I continued speaking, the expression on his face didn't waiver at all. His body language was closed, with his arms folded. His demeanor was moody and expressionless, as he avoided eye contact as much as possible. There was a look of disdain in his eyes which made me feel incapacitated, whilst I tried giving him the explanation he requested.

Sitting in that chair, as though I was being interrogated, I broke down in to tears, sobbing profusely. He offered no comfort or consolation. In some way, he appeared to look vindicated. It was as though he took pleasure in what I was saying. Regardless, he seemed to be receiving gratification from the outpouring of my grief. There was nothing I could say to appease him, or to make him understand the depth of my inherent pain. He continued looking at me with a blank stare, until that abrupt moment when he dismissed me from his office. I sat silently, confused, before I realized he hadn't heard a single word of what I said. I found his actions and motives were heartless and calcu-lated.

Aghast and disillusioned, I skulked out of his office. I was stunned that he hadn't extended any words of compassion towards me. I wasn't asking him for sympathy, or even empathy. I just needed him to understand my situation. At the very least, he could have reached out to reassure me that everything would be alright. That wasn't to be, he merely remained cold and aloof. More than anything though, I needed him to know that I wasn't in Melbourne on a lavish holiday, as he assumed previously.

After that encounter, I returned back to my duties. I couldn't concentrate through my sadness, but I wasn't going to give him further satisfaction by going home. I went into the washroom, composed myself and returned back to work. I wouldn't let him have an advantage over me by thinking he could control me. I didn't want to be the brunt of his intimidation tactics, nor was I going to experience any more humiliation from him. I knew I could no longer work for a man who lacked integrity and decency. That was the time I had to make a concrete decision to look for another job.

Deep in my heart, I knew it was going to take some time before I was strong enough to actively unleash my new found independence. Although after witnessing the actions of a person who obviously despised me as much as my Manager did, I wasn't sure if I had the nerve to stand true to my convictions. I realized his distinct lack of humanity was either going to make me or break me. At that time, it could have been easy enough for either option to occur.

The following weeks were nothing more than a living hell at that job. The Manager made it his mission to berate and belittle me at every turn. He made me perform menial tasks such as cleaning the toilets, mopping the floor and where he could, ensured I spent as much time as possible in the garbage room. That 'new' job description was a far cry from the retail job I was initially employed for. Apparently, according to him, that unfair treatment was my punishment. In his mind, I had executed a plan which saw me taking a lovely holiday to Melbourne and enjoying life, without regard for my responsibilities to him or that company.

There was even more fuel to add to that fire. A colleague told me that the Manager wouldn't use my name when he was talking about me to the other staff. To him, I was known as *'the homo'*. That was, albeit second hand information, but judging by his ongoing persecution of me, nothing would have surprised me.

Hearing that vile expression again reminded me of my high school years. Those were years of a time gone by. A time I was never going to return to.

Back in those days though, I was quite naive when it came to workplace law and discrimination, but I knew his actions were way beyond reproach. It never occurred to me there were organizations which dealt with that type of inexcusable behavior. I believe no person should have to endure the despicable treatment of being bullied, in any workplace. If only I knew then, what I know now. Yes, I admit, I'm once again enjoying the delight of returning to that happy escape from reality, just for those few seconds at least.

One morning before work, I recall I woke up to hear a woman on the radio speaking about a situation which she had gone through at her work. She was an anonymous caller who thought it was vital to share her story. I remember thinking that her story sounded similar to mine. As I listened intently, she spoke about how she tried to take her own life, because she could no longer deal with reoccurring negative scenarios and blatant bullying tactics she had received from her Manager.

Her story was extremely sad. I truly felt for her and her situation. The issue of workplace harassment was more common and indeed, more dangerous than I had thought. Although her circumstances didn't surround the death of a loved one, she was still being harassed by an employer who was using the same emotional abuse as I was receiving. I realized there seemed to be more people suffering, sometimes in silence, about working, or even living in adverse conditions. Through her inspiration, her story got me thinking even more about becoming a voice for those who are in need. I wanted nothing more than to hug that woman and assure her that everything was going to be alright. I wanted to reassure her that she could stay strong and that she would survive her circumstance.

That very morning, as I arrived at work, I was again confronted by my Manager. In an abrasive tone, he demanded to see me in his office again. I instantly became tense and afraid. I became concerned about what he wanted to say to me. Knowing what he was like, I couldn't even anticipate the type of repulsive treatment I was going to receive that time around. As I was walking to his office, it was at that very moment when I made the decision to resign, then and there. I simply couldn't take any more of his repugnant mind games.

I gingerly walked in to his office and sat down. With tremendous force, he slammed the door behind me. He started the conversation with the words, '*I'm still waiting for those alleged death certificates...*' In a heartbeat, I became furious and cut him off. I then told *him* to listen to me. In a somewhat forceful and dismissive tone, I managed to perfectly articulate the following words, which led me to my ultimate freedom.

'Your work practices are illegal and should I see fit, I'll take you and this company to court for discrimination and bullying. Furthermore, no person should have to come to work and feel as threatened as I do, every day I walk through those doors. As for my job, I resign effective immediately.'

He slumped back into his chair, shocked, with no words of retaliation. He remained dumbfounded. He could clearly see how angry I was by the irrepressible shaking which had taken over my body. One thing was sure though, I never crossed the line whereby I intimidated him. I was forthright with my statement. I simply needed to have my voice heard. However, I wasn't even sure how I found the courage to speak those words myself. Enough was enough. I wasn't going to let him think he had any power over me whatsoever. I wasn't back in high school, nor was I going to surrender my integrity or dignity to someone as disgusting as him.

There he was, still sitting back in his chair, stunned by what had just taken place. I then took the satisfaction of him watching me walk out of his office and indeed, the store. I was no longer going to be treated like a second class citizen. From my part, there was no door slamming, no vicious attacks or no reprimand. I finally had a sense of victory, for a situation which I thought I couldn't take control over.

I never thought for one second that I had to succumb to that situation. If anything, I saw it as an opportunity to convey that I wasn't going to allow that person to completely strip me of my pride and self-respect. That was the one chance I was given to firmly stand my ground. I certainly wasn't going to let that golden opportunity pass me by. That situation was reminiscent to that one chance which I took all of those years earlier, back in the locker room, except without committing any acts of physical violence. I believed it was that same flight or flight mode which allowed me to take control.

Once I returned to my apartment later that day, I weighed up my options. For a brief moment I contemplated taking my case to an organization which could assist me to seek justice. Although, I think that Manager learned his lesson. I sincerely doubted that he would ever treat any other staff members like that again. I believed I was one of the lucky ones to have escaped a demoralizing situation relatively unscathed. I still felt a little bewildered, but I had all the triumph I needed. No amount of monetary gain was going to give me the same liberation that I already felt. It certainly wouldn't have brought my parents back to life either. That success was a milestone. I hoped one of many more to come, in the fond memory of my parents.

Personally, I saw that situation as a silent win. It was a win which I felt had rightfully validated me as the man I was becoming. Throughout that brief meeting with my Manager in his office, I could have very easily become aggressive or even physical. I wanted to remain calm, as I knew by doing so, he would have no recourse to make any further allegations toward me. It wasn't in my character to provoke aggression. Besides, I certainly wasn't going to let him revel in the satisfaction of my defeat.

I never allowed my ego to become involved when taking back the power he thought he had over me. Therefore, I knew he couldn't hurt me anymore. I simply put an end to a situation which may have potentially cost me my life, if his bullying and character assassination had continued. I knew all too well, people like him, only assist with putting the final nail in a bullied person's coffin. It's generally those types of repulsive people who prey on the timid. Those predators are spineless, they take pleasure in fighting with people who are unable to defend themselves from shameless bullying attacks.

There was also another consolation to that situation, one which warmed my soul. I knew in my heart of hearts I would have made my father extremely proud of my ability to deal with that situation. I was becoming closer to understanding the value of being a man and standing true to my principles, without confusing assertiveness with aggression. In that instant, I felt a tear drop run down my cheek. I was overcome with an intense sense of pride for the way in which I handled myself.

As for the lady I heard speaking on the radio that morning, I often wonder what became of her. She will never realize how her positive words affected me. In some ways, I felt as though I owed her my life. She inspired me to make the changes which I needed to escape becoming another statistic of workplace bullying, or even a statistic towards the increasing suicide rate. That unknown lady gave me something that not even my closest friends could have at that time, a sense of absolute deliverance.

I find it intriguing when the events of one person's life entwine in to another person's. I really began to understand the meaning of that mantra, *'a reason, a season, a lifetime'*, even more. I genuinely believed the lady on the radio was speaking directly to me that morning. I believe she reached out and offered me all that she could. She instilled a reason, and then offered me a season.

It's a terrible shame that I'll never know who that lady was, or if she managed to live on and inspire others with her words. My hope is that she too, is a survivor and living an enchanted life.

The older I become, the more I understand that people actually *do* enter our lives for just a simple reason. This may be to help us, or to show us something new. Some other people come in to our lives for a season. This may be for an unknown, but limited period of time, or at least until they deliver their message. However, if we're truly fortunate, special people come into our lives who will stay with us for a lifetime.

The Three D's
(Dating, Drag & Darlinghurst)

The realization that I needed to find another job had quickly set in. I explained to my housemate about what had happened at work. He was understanding and incredibly proud of me. He offered to pay my share of the rent, bills and utilities until I found a new job, but that wasn't my style. I needed to independently contribute to our household. More importantly for me, I needed to make a name for myself and break away from the uncertainty which the past few weeks had brought. I needed to remain focused on new opportunities and productive enough to make them become a reality.

It was during that period, my life then did another 360 degree turn. It wasn't long before I found myself again waiting tables, back on the cafe circuit. I was not only back at 'The Californian', but back to living my life on Darlinghurst's vibrant *'Golden Mile'*. Although I wasn't living to the extent I had been previously. I was content to be working back at 'The Californian', as I was undergoing a major transitional period. I needed the flexibility to look for my true passion in life. I was earning enough money from that job to survive, which meant I was not only able to pay my rent, but also afford the odd luxury or night out if I felt the urge to splurge.

It was also during that time, I again reflected greatly on my past achievements, It was common knowledge that there weren't actually too many to speak of, however, there were several stand out moments which I continued to draw strength from. That gave me the assurance to keep working towards finally planning a life of fulfillment, which until that point, was still really only a dream life.

One of my most life defining moments, which continued to be reoccurring, was that of my trusted alter ego, 'Angela'. *She* was the one who provided me with my first proper taste of true acceptance and freedom. The night *she* came to life was a definite stand out for me. I believe I could call upon *her*, through my inner strength, when I was confronted by those trying times. With all the new changes to my way of thinking, as well as dealing with the pain I endured, it was time to revive that side of my personality. It was time I started truly living and enjoying life again. I wanted to reconnect with all I loved doing beforehand.

Whilst I had already been out to the Sydney gay clubs in drag many times previously, at that time, I wanted an overhaul which would redefine my drag image and capture the person, who I was becoming. I didn't feel as though I truly embodied the essence of 'Angela Channing' any longer. I was once happy to be that forward, upfront, somewhat loud mouth character, but *her* time had expired. My personality and demeanor had vastly changed from those days gone by, so I knew it was the best time to update my alter ego too.

Along with taking the 'character' out of my drag, it was a time to also express myself in a new, more glamorous way. That had to be done in a way which would praise all sides of the new person I was. I needed to find a point of difference from the other fabulous drag queens who were also around at that time. I wanted to stand head and shoulders above the others to seize the imagination of all those who watched in awe.

I didn't want to rush the planning of my drag reinvention though. In fact, it took several weeks before I even found the right hairpiece to compliment my features. I purchased a magnificent glazed auburn tress, which would become the centerpiece of my new look. I then found the right couture to suit my diva from within. I searched high and low until I found a pair of five inch stiletto high heels, which would match my newly purchased, stunning red rhinestone encrusted dress. To complete that look, the outfit was accompanied with the most fabulous diamante accessories, which allowed me to sparkle, on even the darkest Sydney night.

Whilst reconstructing my new look, I also gave great consideration to finding another drag name which would not only represent, but also symbolize the person under the drag. Sometimes, choosing a memorable name can be one of the most difficult parts of drag. I believe every drag queen, myself included, wants to be remembered by *her* look, but just as importantly, *she* wants to be known by *her* name. There were, and still are, so many incredible drag names being used, by amazingly well known Sydney drag queens such as 'Portia Turbo', 'Mitzi MacIntosh', 'Polly Petrie', and within more recent years, 'Tora Hymen', 'Prada Clutch' and 'Penny Traition', just to name a few.

Although, for me, I needed to find a particular name which people would associate with my unique individuality and statuesque identity. I wanted a drag name which would also remain timeless. Whilst racking my brain for that mysterious name, I hadn't realized, but staring me in the face that whole time was a name which embodied the very person I was. That new name had suddenly became very obvious.

Being a two hundred and twenty-six centimeter tall beauty, what else would I be called, none other than, 'Skye High.' As quickly as that name came to me, it became official. I had a brand new name which was synonymous with having legs to heaven and a personality to match. Instantly, I knew I was going to be *that* drag queen who literally stood head and shoulders above all others. I was ready to once again unleash the diva from within on an unsuspecting Sydney gay scene.

With a dramatic change to my appearance, there came a brand

new shining confidence, which could light up even the darkest smoke-filled room in any nightclub. Unlike it was previously, that new confidence was a genuine self-belief. From that initial night out as 'Skye High', many other sensational nights also followed. It wasn't long after that I became a regular at an array of Sydney gay clubs and hotels. During that time, I once again had the opportunity to meet more of the most amazing people who, like in Melbourne, offered to assist me with anything I needed to improve myself. I yet again, had experienced that same euphoric rush of super stardom as I did when 'Angela' had first presented herself at *The Peel*'.

Different to previous occasions, I realized that dressing in drag didn't need to change the person who I was on the inside. 'Skye High' became another dimension of my already existing attributes. *She* is simply an extension of myself, the boy who lives under the make-up. *She* is a genuine, 100% true representation of who I am and all I stand for. That reincarnation meant there was no act or no illusion behind *her* striking facade. I managed to find a harmonious balance between the parallels of two realities. That meant, I no longer needed to hide myself away. I was able to be myself, regardless of how I may outwardly appear.

At no time did I ever think that drag was a way of dealing with the loss of my parents, nor did I use dressing up as a way of masking the pain for their deaths either. Rather, at that time, it only helped me to further gain control of my sometimes unpredictable and ever-changing emotions for the short term. Which in turn, became a way to retrieve my inner confidence and start rebuilding the trust, which I had sadly lost in humanity. I soon realized I had the ability to use *her* identity, along with my beliefs, to start becoming a voice for those who also couldn't speak out from their own pain. That reason alone, would have made my parents very proud.

I sincerely believe that any person who has been subjected to mistreatment or bullying wants to have their voice, not only heard, but understood. I think a shared story can be used as an almighty tool to educate others on the affects of anti-social behaviors. The power of a survivor's voice can resonate, which will make those who haven't found their own voice yet, more hopeful. That is what drag did and continues to allow me to do. There's no greater sense of personal and professional satisfaction to be able to reach out and offer support to someone, who in return, knows that I have a genuine understanding of what it's like to walk in their shoes.

I realized that in life, offering salvation can be one of the greatest gifts that we can give to anyone. We, as people are really no different from each other. However, one of our primary differences is the way we sometimes view and deal with the circumstances that we're faced with. Having said that, one of our biggest common denominators is our ability to love, as well as receive that same love in return. The power of unconditional love is as miraculous, as it is almighty.

Later that night, I found myself in a broody mood. I was thinking about everything which had taken place in my life since leaving high school the first time. It was evident that I was a very different person to the one I was, or even thought I'd become at that time. It was those very thoughts then had me again thinking about my own lack of love life. I was beginning to think I'd never find that pure intimacy which I saw others sharing. I too, still wanted to share my life with a man who would love me as much as I loved him.

Whilst I pondered on that love question again, I became overwhelmed as there seemed to be so many different options to finding a partner, not all which were suitable for what I was looking for though. After doing some more research, it was obvious that the way forward with life, revolved around the wonders of technology. If anything, I thought that concept only limited my options to find what I wanted most, a 'real life' relationship. Therefore, I never gave much consideration to that new modern age of internet dating.

It wasn't until one night after returning home from dinner with friends, I decided to pick up a copy of the local gay newspaper. After sifting through the pages, I came to the classifieds. As I skipped over the adverts for massage and escorts, I found a small section right at the back. It was for those who wanted to meet other people, whether it be for sex or a relationship. That prompted me to get back to the old fashioned basics of putting pen to paper. It was then, I wrote my very own personal column advertisement. I knew what I was looking for and indeed, what I *wasn't* looking for. With that knowledge, it was easier to narrow my search to target those I wanted to reply to my advert. Or so I wanted to believe!

The advert I wrote was simple, articulate and to the point. It had to be anyway, as there was a limit to the number of words I could use before I had to pay for a larger advert. Besides that, I didn't want to waste anyone's time with too many fluffy and unnecessary words. I thought the best writing approach was to be short, sharp and say nothing about sex. I certainly didn't want my time wasted by people who just wanted a quick fuck. I was bored with that, as I'd been there and done that before.

The following week, I was so excited to see my small advertisement had been published. Luckily, it was in the center of the page, which meant it was easy to see. The advert read,

'Handsome DTE GWM with GSOH seeks possible LTR with like-minded other. Genuine and looking for same' (which translates to, handsome down to earth, gay white male with good sense of humor, seeks possible long term relationship with like-minded other. Genuine and looking for same).

Whilst *I* thought my advert was going to stand out from the others on the page because of the ideal position, unfortunately it didn't. That same week, it appeared that every other single gay man in Sydney must have had the same idea. There were countless other adverts, which were just as similar and generic as mine. I wasn't sure why the universe seemed to be working against me. After all, I had been a very good boy, that week! Nevertheless, if I didn't try my luck with that advert, I would never know what may have been. Of course, there was also the possibility I wasn't going to receive any replies. It was just going to be a waiting game.

As a hopeless romantic, there was something kind of 'old school' about getting to know a person by way of sending a letter. I think it was because the process actually prolonged the anticipation of exploring a new person, in a different, but very exciting way. I thought that perhaps if I was lucky, maybe those who replied may also enclose a photograph of themselves too. I lived in hope that the postman would deliver my mail in a gigantic mailbag for weeks to come, however, I knew the reality was going to be slightly different though.

Unlike this day and age, social interaction and dating was very different back in those days. Without sounding like my father, *but back in my day,* there was no 'Grindr', 'Scruff' or 'Hornet' applications to download for that rapid buzz of instant gratification. Back then, there were only other internet options for 'dating'. Those required you to use an actual computer, not a handheld mobile device. I recall browsing such websites as 'WellHung.Net' and 'ManChat'. I should also point out, it seems as though the definition of 'speed dating' was slightly different back then, to what it is now. Not to mention, the only 'Tina' I knew, had the surname, Turner.

A week had passed since my advert was published. I wasn't sure how long it was going to take to get replies, but I continued to wait. However, I didn't have to wait as long as I thought. It was that following faithful Friday afternoon after work, to my surprise, I arrived home to see three letters in my mail box waiting for me. Once I realized they weren't utility bills, I was so unbelievably excited by the unknown possibilities of what might have been. I couldn't wait to eagerly get inside and see who had replied. In my mind, there was an array of different thoughts buzzing around my head about those men, such as, *Was he tall? Was he short? Did he work? Was he looking for love? Where did he live?*

I quickly collected the letters and ran up the stairs to my apartment. Once inside, I poured myself a glass of 'Cab Sauv Merlot' and positioned myself comfortably on the couch. I was practically bursting at the seams to open those letters. The prospect of finding love could easily be within my reach. I was more exhilarated than I had been for many months prior. I wasn't sure if I was going to find that *one* person who would sweep me off my feet and end up living happily ever after with. However, I still believed there was *one* person who was looking for something more substantial than what seemed to be on offer at the gay bars.

With every letter I furiously opened, I found myself becoming more intrigued by what those potential suitors had written. It appeared I wasn't alone in my pursuit for love, nor did those replies mention anything about wanting a quick fuck. There were actually other people in Sydney, who wanted to settle down and find true love also. My only slight disappointment was that not all of them had photos to accompany their letters. Although in all fairness, they didn't know what I looked like either. At that moment, it seemed as though I was about to begin a journey which would lead me into the uncharted territory, that was the true definition of blind dating.

Throughout that night, one glass of wine led to another. It didn't take long before I found the courage from within that almost empty bottle of 'Cab Sauv Merlot', to start exploring the possibilities of the dating game. As that night progressed, I called and spoke with all three men who had replied to my advert. Before I knew it, I arranged to meet those three different men, over three consecutive nights. The conversations we all shared over the phone seemed free flowing, which I thought was a good start. The more I spoke to them, the more intrigued I became to know who they actually were. I couldn't wait to meet those anonymous men, who all had me spellbound by their voices and their personalities.

All three candidates seemed quite unique in their own right. I admired the effort each of them had taken with writing their letters. Each letter brought to life a three dimensional picture of that person, albeit the reality was they were still very much one dimensional at that time. I also found it a liberating experience to share stories over the phone, with people who I'd never met before. In many ways, it was easier to open up and be myself, without feeling judged. Yet, not dissimilar to many other occasions throughout my life, I had no doubt the empty bottle of wine may have assisted with that too.

Nevertheless, I couldn't help but continue to wonder what those men would actually be like when we met face to face. I hoped they were as genuine as what they led me to believe. I assumed that was just one of the pitfalls of blind dating. However, that really didn't deter me. I was still very interested in meeting. Of course, I was also a little apprehensive about the whole concept of blind dating. But I was aware that I needed to take all the precautions needed, such as meeting in a public area to ensure I was safe, which I did. I definitely didn't want to find myself in any situations that were risky or exposed me to harm.

It was later the following week, I began my tirade of triple dating discoveries. Without going in to the explicit details of each date, only because nothing really special happened that I could write about. I can tell you though, I wasn't even fortunate enough to be given a good-night kiss from *any* of them! I know, right? I was just as surprised by that as you are right at this very minute! With a gigantic sigh, I soon realized that maybe chivalry really was dead!

Now, what I will say about them, is that all three of those guys were charming in their own right. Each date was somewhat the same. They all involved meeting at either a bar or coffee shop, where we spoke about a myriad of meaningless different things. Unfortunately though, there were no supernatural sparks which rocked my universe. From what I could ascertain, that feeling was very mutual also. That was one aspect of blind dating which I couldn't control. Nevertheless, as I mentioned earlier, if I didn't try, I'd never have known what may have been waiting for me.

I'm an avid believer that rejection isn't a personal criticism. My philosophy is that I'm not attracted to all people, therefore, I know that not all people are attracted to me either. That's just a simple fact of life. It took me a while to realize that philosophy, however once I did, my ego didn't take too much of a beating.

It just meant I needed to keep looking until I found that person who thought I was as attractive, as what I thought he was. Even though I wasn't having much luck in the love department, I was still meeting different people. Besides, that was essentially what I needed to further assist dealing with the loss of my parents.

To this day, I believe each of those men came in to my life for a reason. Whilst they may not have known it, even in the short amount of time I spent with each of them, they offered me the opportunity to share my story. That alone, assisted with my recovery process which in turn, led me to finding a more comfortable place, both spiritually and emotionally. I'm grateful for them sharing their stories too. It allowed me take a small piece of their courage and strength, which I have kept with me along my journey.

It was the week after, I received two other replies. Those would be the last two letters I ever received from that advert. I was again excited by the notion of at least making a new connection with someone. However, I resigned myself to the belief that if I didn't find that *one* person, it wasn't going to be the end of the world.

Enthusiastically, I opened the first of those two letters. As I started reading his scripted words, I soon discovered he lived in London and was only looking for a pen pal. Whilst I had no issue with that, I replied with a thank you letter and explained that I was only looking to meet local people. Surprisingly, he was gracious enough to write back to say he understood and wished me well for the future.

Upon opening the final letter, my interest was immediately captured. Enclosed inside the beautifully hand written envelope, was a wonderful hand scribed letter. That letter was different to the others. It was detailed, well thought out and tastefully written. It was obvious, that the man behind the letter was an intelligent and sensitive person. He'd even taken the time to enclose a photograph of himself.

Looking back at me from that picture was a handsome, reasonably masculine looking man, with an incredibly cheeky grin. By all accounts, he too, was also looking for love. Without hesitation, I decided to call the telephone number he provided. I had no idea what to expect, or what I was about to get myself into.

The Art of Learning to Love

With a nervous energy rippling through my body, I started to dial the telephone number. After a few tense seconds of the phone ringing, I was almost going to hang up. The anticipation was becoming to significant to ignore. Just as I was ready to give up, an unsuspecting person answered with a pensive, *'Hello.'* It was too late. I had to say something. I took a deep breath and introduced myself as the person from that gay newspaper advert he replied to. There was a brief pause. I realized I should have been more articulate with the details, in case he replied to many adverts.

A few silent seconds passed. Then, in a cheerful tone, he said, *'Oh, hi, how's it going?'* I could tell he was caught off guard. The voice on the other end of the phone line sounded like what I had expected from his letter. He appeared to be a slightly shy and somewhat reserved man. The tone of his voice implied he was excited, but also very cautious and very nervous. Within the first few minutes of our conversation, he expressed that he'd never replied to an advert from the paper before. He then went on to say that I was the only person he did reply to, so he wasn't too sure about the process. To me, that explained why he seemed a little anxious.

Coincidentally, he had recently moved from Melbourne to Sydney. During that initial telephone call, we discovered we had more in common than once living in Melbourne. Surprisingly, I soon learned that we lived within close proximity to one another whilst I lived in St Kilda, but for some unknown reason, our paths never crossed at that time. Apart from speaking of our old stomping ground, the entire conversation we had flowed smoothly. We spoke about many things that night, such as music, theater and favorite movies. He also indicated that he was a huge fan of Science Fiction.

To be honest, that was a totally foreign concept to me. After all, I thought *'Spock'* was the Captain of 'Voyager', from the 'Star Trek' series. It wasn't until he indignantly informed me that, *'Mr. Spock'*, was actually the First Officer and the Science Officer on the original Starship Enterprise. It quickly became very obvious that we had different tastes, but I really liked that. I was instantly drawn to his personality.

Whilst talking to him that night, I continued to look at the photograph he enclosed. It was a simple picture of him sitting at his work desk, smiling widely. There appeared to be loving tenderness from within his eyes. I could still see that cheekiness emanating from his bright smile though. Yet, I certainly didn't believe he was as innocent as he may have looked. The more we spoke, the more intrigued I became. His personality seemed a little 'left of center', with a slight quirkiness about him. I remained somewhat intrigued. The more he spoke, the further affirmed my attraction became. I knew I wanted to meet that man, face to face.

I didn't want to come across too eager though, but I hoped that he wanted to meet me too. I knew there was no guarantee he was going to find me attractive, however, I thought he may also be drawn to my personality. If nothing more was going to come from our timely connection, at least I thought we could have a lasting friendship. We continued to talk and laugh for many hours. Although, I was a little disappointed when our telephone call had to come to an end. Unfortunately, he had to go to work. Due to the rapport we were building, I took a chance and gave him my telephone number. I extended the offer for him to call, at any time.

Several days passed by and I hadn't heard back from that mystery man. I was beginning to think I wasn't going to hear from him again. I was a little upset because I thought that phone call we shared had gone so well. I then started replaying our conversation over in my mind, just to reassure myself that I hadn't said anything that may have scared him off. If anything, I thought I left a good impression. I couldn't understand why he wouldn't have called me back already. After all, I thought I was a good catch!

Later that night, just as I was about to give up hope for ever hearing from him again, he finally called. I was so relieved to hear from him. Of course, I tried to remain nonchalant on the phone. I didn't want him to think I was totally desperate. However, I was just very happy he called. He apologized for not contacting me sooner, but said he was busy with work. Although I'd heard *those* type of excuses before and even used them myself, I had no option but to believe him. Besides, I didn't consider that he'd given me any reason to doubt him, so I accepted his apology.

Once the air was cleared, we continued the 'getting to know you game' of questions and answers. I found his candor to be refreshing. He was extremely open to all the questions I asked, which made it easier for me to do the same in return. Each of his answers was direct and to the point. Don't get me wrong, we also shared many laughs as well. As the telephone call continued, I did wonder though, if that man was in fact, too good to be true. He seemed to tick all of the right boxes, but then again, most 'catfish' generally do.

For one reason or another, we actually never met face to face straight away. I thought that was strange. The other guys who replied to my advert would have been keen to meet the same night I spoke to them, if I was agreeable. That man was different though. Whilst there was always a 'legitimate' excuse, I began to think maybe he didn't want anything more than a phone friend. Perhaps he was a married man. I started to sense something wasn't right. I found myself over analyzing every word he said. I only hoped that he was being honest. I didn't want to have my hopes dashed by the realization that he was fabricating his sincerity.

Whilst I was happy enough not to hurry into a relationship just for the sake of having one, I really wanted to meet the man, behind the voice, behind the telephone. I became more curious. I wanted to know what he was hiding. I could feel my own paranoia taking over. If he was hiding something, what was the point of replying to my advert? I started to over think all the worst possible scenarios. More importantly, if he really *did* want to meet, the anticipation of not knowing if I was going to meet his expectations made me even more on edge. The 'not knowing' started to eat away at me. I didn't want to prolong our meeting, if there was going to be no point to it in the first place. As much as I continued asking to meet, my requests were only followed by more endless excuses. Looking back now, he must have thought I was a complete stalker.

It was during one of our more meaningful phone conversations later that week, he asked if I had ever used the computer chat program ICQ. ICQ, which is an acronym for *'I seek you'*, is an instant messenger application which was widely used throughout the 1990's as a preferred one on one chat medium. Still used today, ICQ has a distinctive message tone for incoming messages, which makes it an identifiable chat program to many who use it. In an age before there was 'Facebook', this program was one of the most popular for Internet chat. By today's standards, ICQ is similar to that of 'Viber' and 'WhatsApp Messenger'.

Whilst I'd heard of that chat program before, I was a novice when it came to technology back then. I hadn't had much exposure to different computer applications. It seemed daunting to move in to the age of cyber dating. To me, cyber dating was just another expression for cyber sex, with a quick chat beforehand. To be honest, I didn't really see the point to it. Besides, I wanted to meet a real man, in the real world. I didn't believe the computer was going to provide the interaction I was hoping to have with him. Yet, he kept asking.

I found it bizarre he was so determined to use that chat program, as opposed to just wanting to meet face to face. Although, after a few days of cohesion, he convinced me to try ICQ. With some guidance from him over the telephone, I managed to finally download that program. However, I still couldn't stop thinking about why he didn't want to meet though. Perhaps he was just really shy. Perhaps he was more curious to know who he was chatting to first, before taking a chance on meeting. Then I wondered, *'Was he hoping for a cyber 'try before buy' moment?'*

To not prolong the agony any further, as soon as I set up a ICQ username, I decided within the first few minutes of our online chat to upload a picture of myself. I thought it was time to put us both out of our respective misery and let him see who he was talking to. I held my breath as I clicked the upload button. That was a terrifying experience. My mind was again filled with endless *'what ifs'*. It seemed to be the longest period of time before I received his reply. By which time, more negative thoughts consumed my mind. What if I wasn't his type? What if he didn't think I was attractive at all? What if he blocked me?

Finally, the notification of a new message which I seemed to wait an eternity for, had arrived. It's funny how five minutes can seem like a lifetime when you're waiting for something you want. My hands were literally shaking with anticipation to read his message. That long awaited message read, *'Wow, you're really handsome.'* I re-read his message several times, just to make sure I read it correctly, then, I let out the biggest sigh of relief. I was so happy to have received his kind reply, I couldn't wipe the smile off my face. That was definitely a 'high five' moment. Slightly embarrassed though, I thanked him. From that moment forward, I felt more comfortable with opening up and sharing the *real* me with him.

His message gave me the confidence boost I needed. Not only did he think I was handsome, I thought our connection could become the start of something I waited many years to discover. As far as I was concerned, it was a win-win situation. It was shortly after that, we exchanged even more pictures of ourselves. I was lucky there was a newsstand next to my apartment, which at that time, had recently introduced a scanning service for documents and photographs. I took full advantage of that service and filled an entire floppy disk with newly scanned pictures which I could send to him. I thought the technology back in those days was truly amazing.

By that time, our chats had progressed from every few days, to being several times a day, either on the telephone or over ICQ. However, due to our busy work schedules, I accepted that it would still be a matter of weeks before either of us could make the time to take our online friendship in to the real world. At first, I still thought he was only making excuses not to meet. However, I soon appreciated that he had a demanding job which didn't, at that time, allow for much time for a social life. With that knowledge, I became more content with knowing he did actually want to meet me too. That wonderful day when we would finally meet, was just going to be about the right timing for both of us.

Surprising though, the wait wasn't as long as I had anticipated. Several days later, out of nowhere, he asked if I was available to meet him that night, which was a Saturday. I couldn't believe what I heard. The time had eventually come for us to finally meet. I couldn't contain my excitement, apprehension and happiness, which was all rolled in to one. Strangely enough, he suggested we meet at 7:30pm at one of my old drag stomping grounds, *'The Taxi Club'*. To be honest, it was going to feel a little surreal entering a club which I had only been to before dressed in drag, which he was unaware of. Although as far as I was concerned, that was a time for new experiences and new beginnings. Besides, I wasn't going to pass up the golden opportunity to meet the man who had me at, *'hello'*.

For that entire day, the lead up to that night was intense, to say the least. My mind was flooded by thoughts and questions. Although, in a moment of weakness, my mind quickly became overshadowed with doubt. The reality of that situation had hit home, hard. What if he was actually one of those people who lied about who he was, or worse, what if he didn't show up? I recalled our conversations over and over again. There was nothing to pinpoint his motives weren't genuine though. I had to believe that he was different to the thoughts which preoccupied my mind. I only hoped, more than anything else in the world, that he was the man who he claimed to be.

After a few minutes of irrational thoughts, my philosophy changed. It again became one of 'que sera sera'. With only a few short hours before meeting him, I didn't want to become an emotional wreck and risk making a fool out of myself. I had to calm myself and trust my instincts. I knew meeting him was a chance I had to take, regardless of the outcome. At least I was meeting in a public place, so if I needed to escape it would have been easy enough. Yet, the more I thought about it, the more I didn't feel as though I needed to worry about meeting him. He seemed genuine and trustworthy enough. Although, famous last words, I guess!

With the time it took me to prepare for that night, it was like I was actually going out in drag. The only difference being, I wasn't undergoing the three hour make-up application. I spent that entire afternoon trying to find the perfect outfit to wear. I knew I couldn't go wrong with a pair of black Levi 501s, a white T-shirt and black denim jacket. In my eyes, presentation was everything. It all had to be perfect. Even with the limited time I had, I even managed to book in to my local hair salon to have my hair trimmed, just to ensure I looked like that initial picture I sent to him, days earlier.

The few butterflies in my stomach started to feel more like there was a butterfly enclosure inside me, I was trembling from the inside out. I still couldn't wipe the smile from my face though. The more I thought about meeting him, the less inclined I was to sit still for any longer than two minutes. My nerves got the better of me. I even lost track of how many times I checked, then re-checked my hair which by the way, hadn't moved at all. But for good measure, I continued spraying more hairspray, just so my hair couldn't move. I couldn't help but feel as though I was a sweet sixteen year old girl, who was about to go on her very first date with a cute boy. I wanted to scream with delight, I became *that* hysterical.

Before I knew it, the time had come to confront another possible life defining moment. One which had the potential to again, change the course of my life. It was time to leave my apartment and enjoy the countless feelings which I had indulged in for that entire afternoon. Although I only lived ten minutes away from 'The Taxi Club', I left home at 6:45pm. On my way, I decided to stop at another nearby bar. I thought if I had a quick drink before I arrived, it may help settle my out of control nerves. By that time, I couldn't believe how incredibly nervous I actually was. Yet, those were good nerves which I thoroughly enjoyed feeling. For a moment though, they could have easily become quite the opposite.

At 7:20pm, I was standing outside 'The Taxi Club'. I kept telling myself that I had to take that leap of faith. I thought if nothing else, the power of positive affirmation was going to assist my shaky legs to climb that steep staircase. I knew it was a 'now or never' moment to make that event become a reality. With short, shallow breaths, I slowly started climbing those stairs. My palms were beginning to sweat. With every breath I took, I felt as though I was on the verge of nervous collapse. I eventually reached the top step, where I stood composing myself for a few seconds. With one last deep breath, I entered the club. The last words of encouragement I said to myself before entering, was a line from my all-time favorite movie, 'Pretty Woman'. Over and over, I repeated the words, 'Work it baby, work it, own it.' Those very words gave me the boost I needed to brace myself for whatever was about to happen.

Once I turned the corner, I stood in the doorway. My eyes scoured the room, looking intently at all the different faces. I tried to find that mysterious man, for what seemed like hours. I sincerely hoped that our connection was going to be no different than it had been previously, albeit over the telephone or computer. I continued searching, as my wandering eyes were darting all around the room. I was then immediately stopped in my tracks. There, only a few feet away, I noticed his bright smile beaming in my direction. He was sitting directly in front me at a small round table, which was close to the bar. He was surrounded by his two friends, who I knew would be there also.

In what appeared to be like a scene from a 'Mills and Boon' story, our eyes immediately locked as I walked towards him. It was as though there was nobody else in the room, just he and I. The incredible nerves I felt earlier had suddenly subsided. I felt completely at ease with the situation and indeed, my surrounds. My reaction to meeting that man can only be compared to catching up with an old friend, who I hadn't seen for many years. That feeling brought with it a warm familiarity, which reminded me of the closeness of my family, while we were living at that double story house in the country, many years ago.

Once I reached the table, he extended his hand to offer a welcoming, but firm handshake. That was then accompanied by a friendly kiss on the cheek. I was subsequently introduced to his friends. They too seemed like very lovely people. They welcomed me in to their group with witty banter, telling me that

I was, *'a bit of alright'*. It was obvious that his friends had a few drinks already that night. They were harmless enough though. Being the gentleman, my date asked if I'd like a drink, to which I accepted his offer. While he was at the bar, his friends and I continued to make pleasant small talk. After a few minutes at the bar, my date returns with my drink.

It was in that moment, as he was walking back, our eyes met again. Whilst our eyes were again locked on one another, in a slow motion kind of way, he went to place my drink on the table, but instead, he misjudged where the table actually was. All of a sudden, I ended up wearing a full glass of Southern Comfort and Coke. He accidentally spilled my drink, which completely covered me from chest to toe. I sat stunned, as well as saturated. I looked as though I'd been caught in a rain storm of black liquid, smelling like the Southern Comfort distillery. He couldn't apologize enough. I thought he was going to cry due to his extreme embarrassment. He couldn't stop trying to make amends for that unfortunate, but funny, situation. Once I cleaned myself up, we spent that entire night laughing, talking and getting to know more about one other.

There was no doubt in my mind that the person sitting in front of me, was the same person on the phone and ICQ. Although, to this day, he still claims that he wasn't drunk when he spilled the drink over me. In some way, I guess that's open to interpretation, I believe more so his own. To be honest though, I couldn't think of a better way to make a first impression. It was possibly the best way of breaking the ice, for both of us. I wouldn't want to change any of that night, even if I could.

Throughout the duration of our time together that night, apart from feeling as though I had too much to drink, I felt as though that meeting could have been the beginning of something new. Although I had no idea of the path it would lead us to, we both seemed willing to explore the possibilities. I certainly don't believe either of us thought it was love at first sight, but there was an electric connection, which we both felt. With a new friendship blossoming, we continued to drink ourselves in to the early hours of the next morning.

The very next day, late that afternoon, he called to thank me for a very memorable night. He and I both agreed, it would be one that we'd never forget. It wasn't long after, there were other dates which followed. Although as far as I can recall, I didn't end up wearing another drink. I did however, enjoy spending time with him and doing all the things that I'd dreamed of doing with someone I was interested in.

We shared dinners at restaurants, cocktails at bars, movies at the cinema and nights curled up in front of the television. He and I would continue to date for many months before our relationship would take on more significance. In those early days, I wasn't sure where our relationship was heading. In actual fact, due to an extreme feeling of uncertainty, I wasn't sure whether I even wanted take our relationship to the next level.

I admit to a certain degree, perhaps I was more in love, with the idea of being in love. Dare I say it, I felt it was almost a scenario of, 'do I *really* want a relationship, now that I know I can have one?' I became afraid of commitment. I began to doubt myself again. I wasn't sure if I could actually give myself to anyone. Maybe I really did enjoy the 'thrill of the chase' more than what I gave myself credit for. The idea of living out that dream of finding 'Mr. Right', was now retreating further to the back of my mind. It felt as though it had also become even further out of my grasp, due to my own insecurities.

Don't get me wrong, I knew I liked that man very much. He was warm and caring, with a sense of humor not dissimilar to mine. However after everything I'd been through emotionally, I didn't want to hurt anyone, especially him. I was afraid of taking the chance of finding happiness, only to have it taken away from me again. It appeared as though I was still holding onto one irrational fear which I so desperately wanted to let go of. I thought I was going to lose those I loved the most. The more I over analyzed it, I realized I had many doubts about that very notion of commitment. I also knew none of those insecurities had anything to do with how wonderfully that man treated me. In my mind, I was going back on that road to self-destruction.

I often tried to find fault with whatever he did or said, which often resulted in a difference of opinion. I made fictitious situations in my mind, become reality. I, not so slowly, started to drive a gigantic wedge between him and me. As much as I wanted to be happy and in love, that inner voice of unworthiness, which plagued me many years earlier, seemed to be retaliating against my future happiness. Throughout the initial stages of that new relationship, I seemed determined to destroy whatever good was coming my way. As time went by, again and again, I would push him away for getting too close. I would then swallow my pride and assure him, time after time, that I did want him in my life. He was just as confused by my mixed signals, as I was by sending them.

That dangerous inner voice spoke loud and clear. It was trying to stop me from obtaining the very thing that I spent years searching for. Because of that, my head and my heart were in conflict. Those senseless uncertainties were back to bring me down. I didn't want to surrender to my head, but I didn't know if I could control those thoughts. I wasn't sure which would be strong enough, or even loud enough to survive the battle. That struggle seemed to be a duel to the death, between my head and my heart. It seemed as though when anything good came in to my life, the darkness of my own uncertainty followed closely behind. I never knew when it was going to stop, or indeed, if it ever was. I felt I'd been led in to a false sense of security. I was again, on that same tiresome roller coaster of emotions.

Those feelings would give me a small taste of the freedom to be happy, then in a heartbeat, would be quickly snatched away again by an intense feeling of insecurity which I couldn't control.

My mind was jetting around in circles. Just when I thought I had put the demons from the past behind me once and for all, they reappeared stronger and feistier than ever. I was torn between the idealistic relationship which I could have and the scary reality of living a sad life of loneliness with no one to love. I was again so incredibly insecure. I wondered, *'Had that been karma for the mistreatment of my ex-girlfriend?'*

Those same dangerous voices from my past were relentless, albeit in my head, those words were articulated so distinctly that I didn't want to believe they weren't real. It was as though I was hearing those words from a close friend. It was easier to let them take over. After all, they wouldn't accept I was deserving of the happiness which I had been so close to enjoying. Because of that, there was only one question which I kept returning to, *'How was I going to stop letting those doubts come between me and my immediate and future happiness?'*

I wanted to break free from that harmful repetitive cycle which could have had the potential to eventually break me forever. I needed a way to embrace those moments of strength which helped me deal with situations of the past. I knew there had to be a way of getting to my inner strength, without firstly suffering those feelings of psychological weakness and emotional incapacitation. I needed a way to empower myself so I could take control. I spent hours contemplating how I could again move forward and let go of those monstrous voices from my past. That exercise became an extreme battle of mind over matter.

I can only explain my actions to that of perhaps having a dissociative identity disorder, or as it was once referred to, a multiple personality disorder. There appeared to be many different 'personalities' inside my mind, which all wanted something different. One personality wanted to hold that man close to me forever, but another side wanted to cut him loose, after I tortured him emotionally. Then, there was another who just wanted to give up and bury my head in the sand. I knew that mindset would eventually crush me, along with any possibility for having a long term relationship with him. Once again, I inadvertently relinquished all control over my emotions. That type of emotional behavior forced me to erratically change from feeling empowered, to feeling emotionally disabled, to eventually feeling nothing at all.

During that time, my actions were self-centered, but I never once believed they were calculated or self-motivated. From a young age, having to live a difficult life which was turned upside down on so many different levels, made me become a victim of myself. As much as I wanted to continue blaming those from my past, they were no longer a part of my present or my future. I realized it was me, who was to blame for crippling any chance of my own future happiness. Without even realizing it, I continued to damage myself with the same behaviors as I had once received. I continued doing that alone, without the help of those who once degraded me. That type of behavioral regression had an enormous affect on almost every part of my life. Up until that point, I thought I had become liberated. I thought I was living true to my own values. Yet, I was wrong, again.

It wasn't until I met that man I realized I had still been living a sheltered, non-transparent life. I still only wanted people to see the good in me. I put up a facade so people believed I was someone very different to the actual person I was not only hiding from, but was continually running away from. I always knew that deep inside myself I was a decent person. I just didn't realize I needed to stop lying to myself.

I took refuge in denial, which was a habit I realized was harder to break than I imagined. I thought that if I could banish the problems in my mind, they wouldn't be able to hurt me. I soon realized that whilst those thoughts may not have hurt anyone else, they were damaging the one person I needed to rely on the most, me. I needed to stop emotionally harming myself, if

I was ever going to truly set myself free from those I wanted to continue blaming for my downfall.

Whilst all seemed lost, I still considered myself lucky to have found a person who offered to walk through life with me. However, I certainly never realized that starting a new relationship could be one of the most intimidating feelings in the world. For me, that was an extremely genuine journey. One that confronted my every belief, in which I needed to undertake for my own lessons of self-discovery.

I found that I could no longer hide behind the misrepresentation of my own creation, but rather, try to piece together the puzzle which was literally broken into many different pieces. I needed to start with one piece at a time to find the joining pieces, which would interlock perfectly with my life and hopefully reveal a beautiful picture.

Although, little did I know at that time, there was something else I needed to deal with before starting that jigsaw puzzle which had become my life. It wasn't until I decided to take a weekend vacation to Melbourne with that man, I encountered yet another setback. That blow would be one of my most challenging and life defining moments, since the death of my parents.

A Material Loss = A Spiritual Gain

It had been a wonderful weekend break away from my reality, back in my old home town of Melbourne. However, it was again time to return to Sydney and truly take control of my life. During that weekend away I discovered I could reconnect with myself and finally start legitimately taking charge of the negativity that surrounded me. I felt more spiritually revitalized than I had for many months. That weekend away was just what I needed to gain further insight in to how my life was actually traveling.

Whilst I was in Melbourne, which was the first time I'd been back since the passing of my parents, I took the opportunity to visit their final resting place. That in itself was a deep spiritual cleansing, more than I could have ever asked for. I not only got to say my final goodbyes, but I managed to make peace with the internal conflict of emotions which I thought ultimately destroyed my parents' lives. On the day I was visiting the cemetery, I felt as though I had been granted a surreal sense of humility and credence from beyond their graves. That was a feeling I cannot put in to words. I can only describe it as an intense reincarnation of my soul.

Throughout that entire weekend, I also found that I did have the power to more clearly analyze myself from an outsider's perspective. It had taken great self-command to be able to clear my mind and step away from my own bias and opinions. At that point in life, I thought I was one of those people who didn't really care *that* much about what others thought of me. Whilst I was able to brush off snide or hate inspired comments and not show too much concern, I soon discovered I was very wrong. In fact, I more than cared about the opinions of others. I still remained totally consumed by those unjust perceptions they had of me.

Once I started to partially let go of seeking acceptance from others, I could at last start understanding who I was, once and for all. It was an alarming prospect to know that I had the ability to say goodbye to certain characteristics of who I actually thought I was, considering I'd lived most of my life to meet the expectations of others. I no longer needed to hold on to that scared little boy who believed all the bad he was once told. I also realized that I couldn't make all people happy, all the time, nor should I have to. That was a ground breaking moment for me to make. Along with that, I also believe the visit to my parent's grave site and indeed, their sense of spiritual forgiveness, assisted me with coming to terms with the extreme guilt I carried around for many years.

As I reflected, I could never really define what type of 'approval' I'd actually sought from others, apart from the acceptance of my sexuality. It was obvious that my personality had become so multifaceted, almost chameleon like, that I could adapt to *their* ideals and become what *they* wanted. I was nothing more than a puppet on a string. I soon realized that living a life to appease other people wasn't actually living the life I needed, nor wanted to share with anyone else. If I couldn't love myself and find peace within, how did I expect to fully give my soul to a person and expect to receive their love in return? I realized that *inner strength* which I spoke of earlier, was inside me all the time. I just didn't understand how to channel the negative thoughts that bombarded me, from seeing the other side of what my issues were.

I continued to blame the wrong people for my failings. I allowed the fears of my past to take over and control how I dealt with situations. The problem was that I didn't actually deal with anything, except for ways to control my own demise the best way I could. I continually set myself up by believing I was going to fail, even before I started. Fear was an emotion which crippled my personality and my ability to live the life I wanted. I closed myself off from truly exploring positive ways of living and genuinely taking chances on new experiences. In some ways, I had been no better than *those* who allow difference to isolate them, therefore creating their own fear when they don't understand a person or situation.

Another harsh realization for me to digest was something I mentioned earlier, the fact I was living in denial. That was a deep seated sense of denial which had brought along a feeling of oppression. Many times throughout my life I thought I had truly dealt with situations and feelings. However, usually without notice, those same emotions would only later come back. Time after time they slowly devoured the once outgoing spirit I was born with. I really had been blinded by my own personal insecurity and inability to deal with situations. I continually pretended to deal with emotions in a way that I thought was productive. That wasn't the case. In actual fact, I learned that my reactive nature was probably one of the most damaging and soul destroying traits I had.

Throughout those adverse circumstances from my school years and in to my teenage years, my trust in people had become nonexistent. That was further highlighted by the knowledge I had been followed by a person who was unknown to me, whilst living with my parents. I never actually realized how much of an impact that had on my life. Slowly, I then began to understand just how detrimental it had been for me to build lasting relationships.

There were so many unknown variables which I had to work through during those years. More importantly, I needed to continue working on my inner self, if I was ever going to truly have that sacred peace from within. I remained a work in progress for some time. For the entire time I was away I couldn't wait to get back to Sydney. I believed I had something more productive to work towards. I wanted to set the wheels in motion towards becoming free from my old emotional baggage, which I knew had held me back for long enough.

On the day my partner and I arrived back in Sydney, we returned to my apartment building before going out to lunch. As we approached my front door, I was overcome with a cold shiver, which rapidly dominated my body for a couple of seconds. For some reason, I instantly became cautious. I wasn't sure what that feeling represented, or even why I had even felt it. Given my past experiences with 'paranormal' sensations, I didn't know how to interpret it. However, I tried not to think too much of it as we continued to proceed to the front door of my apartment.

As I tried to unlock the front door, strangely, it was tightly jammed closed. Yet, with one hard push, it released until the door quickly opened. Without giving that much consideration to my faulty door, we continued laughing about our weekend away as we walked in to the small hallway just inside my apartment. It was then I realized the homecoming I expected, wasn't quite the homecoming I had walked into. The raucous laughter which was being shared seconds earlier, came to an abrupt end. I stood frozen in my tracks. My body became as cold as ice. I was paralyzed. We both stood at the entrance of my apartment in complete silence, stunned and rigid.

In disbelief, without a sound, we looked around my apartment in a state of shock. All we could see were marks on the floor where my furniture *had* been. Everything in each room, except my bedroom, had gone. My first instinct was to immediately call the police to report a burglary. On closer investigation though, I noticed a letter which was sitting on the kitchen bench. That letter was addressed to me. It appeared by the writing on the envelope, it had been left by my housemate. I was still confused about what had taken place, but I desperately needed to find out what had occurred over that weekend.

I anxiously opened that ominous letter. Reading through the words, which I wasn't actually convinced were written by my housemate as initially thought. Those words looked as though they were written by a young child. Regardless of whose writing it was, I remained at a complete loss. It appeared my housemate decided to move out while I was away. More than that, he decided to take every item of furniture which once decorated our beautiful home. The only reason given, was that he *had* to move out. There was no justification or explanation offered for his abrupt departure, or indeed, for taking everything from our apartment. I was at an absolute failure to understand what had gone on, but just as importantly, I wanted to know why that situation had happened.

I considered him to be my best friend in the entire world. He and I shared over ten years of friendship, laughter and sorrow. I struggled to grasp why he had not only left a note to explain his actions, but why he had stolen the entire life which we had built together. Regardless of his motives, I felt betrayed. Without hesitation, I immediately contacted the police. To my surprise, they informed me there was nothing that could be done, as he was a tenant and had the right to move out. Their hands were tied. Hearing those words only made that unfeasible situation even more impossible to deal with. To say I was angry, hurt and upset, was an underestimation of the true emotions which had reached boiling point inside me.

I resented the fact that there was absolutely nothing that I do to stop that injustice, which had already occurred. It's not as though I had been robbed by a stranger, which may have made that situation more tolerable. Although what I couldn't comprehend, was knowing that it was my best friend who had stolen the life we shared. That alone, made it inconceivable to deal with. I continued with wanting to know why my housemate left in that unexpected fashion. I needed to understand the thought process behind his sudden disappearance. I also needed to know why he wanted to hurt me so badly.

During that time, I could feel myself regressing back to *that* person, who at one time would only want to close everyone and everything out of his life again. There was no doubt about it though, my emotions were running high and I could have easily shut down completely and given up. I desperately wanted to remain strong and take control of that situation, but it was extremely difficult to keep my composure. My world felt as though it was slowly crumbling down around me again. Whilst I understood that incident was a circumstance beyond my control, that notion still didn't make it any easier to digest.

I turned to speak to my partner, but became so chocked up with emotion. I was gutted by sadness and livid with anger. There was nothing I could do to make that situation right. I just knew I needed to find answers. In the solitude of my empty apartment, my partner looked in to my eyes and gently pulled me towards him. He clenched me with such force, I became restrained by his grip. After a few minutes of hollow silence, he released me from his tight loving embrace. He then whispered the words, *'Be strong, I'm here for you and I'll protect you.'* It was hearing those very words which caused me to break down and cry until there were no tears left. In the hours that followed, my anger subsided. I was then left with an overwhelming feeling of desolation, defeat and sadness, all brought on by a situation which seemed to have no meaning behind it.

To this very day, I have never seen or had any further contact with my former housemate. I will never truly understand why he needed to betray and hurt me in such a degrading manner. We shared a strong friendship which endured many years. I never expected that to happen, nor did I ever expect our friendship to ever come to an end. All I had been left with was an empty feeling of loneliness. There was a void in my life, which he had thoughtlessly created. His selfishness had wiped all of the incredible memories from my mind, which I once held in such high regard. Unfortunately, those trusted years of friendship suddenly amounted to absolutely nothing.

Whilst I have my suspicions as to why he had left the way he did, however, it's only speculation. I had started to discover that life could offer me something better than what I thought it ever could. Perhaps he saw my new partner as a threat and thought that our friendship was going to become redundant. I doubt that to be the case though. I never excluded him from my happiness. I believe his sudden departure was due to him too, finding something in his life which appealed to him. Sadly, he became heavily involved within the Sydney drug scene, which had taken over his life several months earlier. As heartbreaking as it was to see him slowly slipping away from his own reality, he made his choices.

When I discovered his new found way of life, I reached out to him and pleaded with him to reconsider those choices. Alas, the power of the drug scene was too strong for my words to penetrate the wall which he had so quickly erected around him. I believe he gave in to a way of life which he perhaps thought brought more happiness than the years of friendship we once shared.

That period, was in itself, another defining moment in my life. It was circumstances brought on by other people, which became the catalyst for me to become more determined than ever to resolve the issues, which haunted me for many years prior. I found the strength from within, to deal with indirect occurrences which greatly impacted my life. I realized that I needed to break free from bad choices and old habits. Under the cloud of unforgiving sadness which was, I saw that as the perfect opportunity to do so.

If I allow my mind to indulge back in to that happy escape from reality, that situation possibly had one of the best conclusions that I could have asked for. Don't get me wrong, I was extremely devastated beyond words by what had taken place, but as I tried to worked through that, I found a new confidence to deal with unfavorable circumstances. From that day forward, I knew it was to be the first day of the rest of my life. I made an immediate decision to start making the changes necessary for me to become an independent man. I had not only been stripped of my material possessions, but also my pride and dignity. My journey now, was to discover the significance of reclaiming my integrity. More importantly, I wanted to reclaim my own value to be validated within society.

Throughout life, there was no hiding from the fact with every upside in my life, there was an even greater and sometimes more dramatic downside. I had to work out a way to stop that extreme downward spinning cycle that my life continued to take. I didn't want to be back on that out of control rollercoaster ever again. First and foremost, I needed to genuinely validate myself. I made another conscious affirmation that from that moment onward, I would stop second guessing myself and legitimately brush off the negative thoughts which I believed once held me back. I was taking one step closer to being able to start living for each and every moment that came along.

Whilst the first step is never the easiest, it is one of the most rewarding. I knew by starting at the root cause of my problems, it would be a long climb to get to the top. However, I believed the time was right for me to take on and hopefully win that challenge. At that time, I also engaged with a professional counselor who understood how I was feeling. He greatly assisted me with working through ill-managed emotions, which had been left untouched from various times within my life. Whilst he never gave the answers I sought, he directed me to a positive place of empowerment with his wise words.

He had the ability to take me back in time, to places I was reluctant to return. Through his gentle and soothing words of encouragement, I managed to regress as far back as my childhood years. It then became clearer to understand how previous circumstances reinforced the unrighteous decisions which had affected me later in life. I concentrated on one aspect of my life, one small step at a time. I used each step as a 'rite of passage' to work towards the provision of a productive and fulfilling life. With sheer determination, courage and the support of close friends, I embarked on the long process of *finally* dealing with the decline which I had allowed certain aspects of my life to become.

That was a process which involved an intense investigation of who I was. I invaded my every thought, to ensure I wasn't going to leave any uncared for emotions behind, which could later come back and poison my mind. I stripped my soul bare and dissected every inch of my life. That was the time to say goodbye to feelings and baggage which were redundant. It wasn't easy to relive the past events and it took me in to some very dark places emotionally. Although, those past places were not as bad, compared to the life which I had actually once been living. The more I genuinely stopped taking notice of what people said and thought, the stronger I became.

I knew there would always be people around who would try to bring me down and continue talking about me behind me back, sadly that's just a heartbreaking element of human nature. Although, it didn't take long for me to realize that whilst people were talking *behind* me, they'd never find their own courage to be *ahead* of me. Whilst some people who were around me at that time had their opinions changed because they educated themselves, I learned that I couldn't control the thoughts of other people and how they perceive me. The one aspect I could control however, was how I let their words and actions affect me.

Another one of my favorite sayings is, *'When you definitively know who I am, better than I know myself, I'll then consider giving you the right to judge me'.* By all accounts, most people will never know me as well as I know myself. Therefore, their judgment towards me or my life only leaves an invalid impression. Unfortunately, some people will only know me as the preconceived image which they have manifested in their own mind. Even though that image may not be 100% correct, perhaps they will never have their minds changed, no matter what I do or what I say. But I accept their opinion is just that, *their own* opinion.

During that time of new discovery, of course there were setbacks. That was mainly because my mind was so engrained with past fear and failures. After all, as they say, *'Rome wasn't built in a day'*. However to combat that, I continued to use positive affirmations, such as looking in to the mirror everyday telling myself that I *was* worthy of a productive life and that I *would* one day go on to inspire people to never give up *their* fight.

By taking control of my thoughts and actions, the more positive my outlook on life became and still does continue to become. As I mentioned earlier, the mind really is a very powerful tool. It *can* be trained to accept new challenges and acknowledge alternative ways of thinking. With those changes I made, plus the wisdom I learned, both of those elements would further assist with what was about to happen next.

The Bittersweet Reunification

After many years of intense soul searching, my new found life was well under way. I began to see things from a new and more positive point of view. That was a perspective which I really never knew existed before, but it was something I always secretly dreamed of. The notion I could achieve greatness in my life had slowly begun to settle in. I could almost taste it. Although it wasn't all peaches and cream, I was still more content and satisfied than I had been for many years earlier.

One of the most identifying characteristics about having to change those bad habits, was understanding that I truly needed to be more grateful of new experiences. I realized that although I was still learning the life skills needed to succeed, I also needed to take the time to genuinely appreciate all of the smaller things that life had to offer too. Armed with the knowledge that life didn't always need to be all about the 'big picture', seemed to help reshape my priorities, which allowed me to gain an improved mental attitude. I had to believe that whether those new experiences were big or small, I simply had to enjoy them all.

At that time, I was happy enough with the positive direction which my life seemed to be taking nonetheless. Although completely unaware to me, there was about to be an unexpected telephone call which would again, change my entire world forever. The news I was about to receive could have potentially sent me back to that emotionally unstable place, where I had already spent too much time previously. That was a place where I had no desire to return.

It was unfortunate that since the death of my parents, it became evident I would never recover the same sibling relationship which I yearned to have, from those cherished years during my youth. Although throughout the years that went by, I was fortunate to regain a partial relationship with my sister. However, our relationship generally only involved speaking a number of times on the telephone and occasionally catching up for a coffee. The relationship I had with her was vastly different from the connection that my brother and I shared. Sadly, he and I remained to have no contact whatsoever after our parent's funerals.

Any chance I thought I might have been given to recapture that close knit bond with my siblings, seemed as though it was nothing more than a dream. Yet, that dream was about to become further out of my reach than I had ever imagined. Once again, the unpredictability of life had stepped in to play a hand that, for whatever the reason or purpose behind it was, seemed quiet inexplicable, even to this current day.

That warm sunny day that was, soon became dark and overshadowed. I received an unexpected telephone call from my sister. She was once again, the bearer of bad news. She called to say that our brother had sadly, passed away. Although my brother and I had been estranged for many years, I was overcome with a deep, philosophical sense of mournfulness. I had not only lost another family member, but I lost the one male role model who guided and cared for me throughout my younger years, while our father was out making a name for himself. My brother had been my first best friend in life. He was the person I aspired to be like. Sadly, he had left this world to go to the afterlife as well.

Hearing that news from my sister, literally took my breath away. I also felt a sense of sorrow for her, who again, was left to deliver news which was far from ideal. I struggled to come to terms with the death of my brother, as I never imagined I would lose one of my siblings so early in their life. The hope that he and I could one day find common ground to reconnect, became a reality which was never going to happen. I realized I was never going to be able to make amends with him. There would never be another opportunity to express my gratitude to him for being one of the few people who I looked up to the most. It became obvious that I left my unsaid words go to long before having them heard. Unfortunately, I don't even think he knew how much of a positive influence he was, throughout my early years.

Since the passing of our parents, I knew he struggled to come to terms with their death, especially the death of our mother. As the oldest child, he had an incredibly strong bond with our mom, one that didn't compare with many others. It was obvious throughout my entire life that he loved her very deeply. I believe the daily fight he lived whilst trying to accept the death of our mom, became too much for him to deal with. Because of that, the decline of his health untimely took its toll, leading to his premature death.

As I looked back, I believe my brother's wedding day, whilst I was in primary school, was one of the happiest days of his life. That day was a celebration which cemented a milestone within our family. It wasn't long after my brother married, that he and his wife were expecting their first child. That would be the only grandchild to our parents, and in fact, my brother's only child. That too, was another family milestone celebration.

Once my niece was born, I remember the feeling of closeness we all shared. There was an abundance of love which surrounded our family, even from me, who endured those circumstances of my school days. At that time, I seemed to be able to block out the anguish I was experiencing for short periods, because a beautiful baby girl had joined our family. Even at my young age of fourteen years old, I felt there was a connection with her, unlike any other that I had ever known before. Unfortunately though, it was only a matter of years after her birth that the choices I made would separate our family. That meant that I would never be able to share her wondrous experiences as she grew up.

The last contact I had with my niece was when she was only two years old. I always treasured the feeling of excitement when my brother, his wife and my niece would come to our family home and visit. All I knew then, was that I wanted to be the best Uncle she would ever have. I wished that she too, would one day look up to me, in the same way as she did with her own dad. Even though my niece was only very young at that time, after all that transpired between my family and me, I hoped that she would always remember me as her Uncle and value the moments we had already shared, for the rest of her life.

As I was still living interstate, I once again traveled back to Melbourne for my brother's funeral. At that time though, I was fortunate to be able to afford a return air ticket to make the journey. Once I arrived back in my hometown, the early hours of that day brought back many wonderful memories. Some of those which I thought were lost forever. I fondly recalled the way in which my brother often included me his life. Whether we were driving around in his car, going to the shops, making model motorbikes, or even the simple pleasure of him sitting beside me when I was young, watching 'Sesame Street' on television. He always made me feel wanted.

During the heartfelt sadness of that moment, I then took great comfort in the fact that both my mother and father would be waiting for my brother, to guide his spirit, as it soared above the clouds on the way to his sacred resting place. I hoped they would lead him to his new journey and care for him in the spirit world.

On the day of his funeral, I arrived at the Chapel. Coincidentally, his funeral service was also held at the same Chapel as where my parents' service was conducted. I recall it being an emotionally bittersweet day. Being back in that environment evoked a gamut of fierce emotions from my last visit there. Those were vast and uncontrolled feelings, which began destroying me from the moment I arrived. I became inundated with feelings of despair, sadness and rage. More surprisingly though, I was also consoled by random feelings of peace and harmony, which I tried to hold on to for as long as I could, before that sensation of unforgiving pain inevitably took over again.

Yet, that day also stirred other emotions too, ones that weren't brought on by the unpleasantness of returning to unhappy memories of that Chapel. Those other emotions were a combination of feelings, of both delight and anxiousness. That was the day I was about to become reacquainted with another family member. It was to be the first time in over twenty-three years, that I was going to be reunited with my niece.

Over the years that went by, I would often think about her and indeed, how her life had turned out. I realized there seemed to be so much that I missed out on. I not only wondered how she lived the day to day moments throughout her life, but I also thought about all of the 'first' experiences she would have had, whilst growing up. I hoped to one day hear all about her journey. More importantly, I was also interested to know if she remembered the first two years of her life, when she and I made those wonderful memories together. I then became more than a little curious to know what she knew of me and my 'checkered' past.

I remember all of the emotions from that day, as though it happened in more recent times. I was frightened by her possible reaction towards me. I didn't know what to expect. I felt disappointed with myself for not being an active part of her life. I never realized the detrimental extent of my actions, which were brought on by my past events. My thought process behind those actions didn't quiet seem to be justified any longer. Because of that, I began to think just how much I really didn't know anything about that young lady, whose life I missed, by not being around. To see her standing tall, especially on a day which was far from perfect, my heart filled with love and pride though. She is my flesh and blood and sadly, I had let her down by not being the Uncle she deserved to have in her life.

That fear-provoking moment of seeing her again had arrived. That was about to become my moment of truth. I stepped out of the car and nervously started to walk towards the Chapel. My niece had her back to me as she welcomed the mourners. I quietly stood back for a few minutes, to observe that beautiful young lady, who seemed so composed. In that instant, she turned around and our eyes met for the very first time in over two decades. My heart skipped a beat. I was incredibly tense and overcome by my own sense of trepidation. Before I knew it, she was standing directly in front of me. There was no need for words. There was only a long earnest embrace, which was way too many years overdue.

She took a step back. I still wasn't sure what was going through her mind. With tears in our eyes, we stood in the silence of that moment, looking in to each other's glazed and tearful eyes. As I continued to look deep in to the windows of her soul, I could feel her insurmountable pain, which was ravaging her. Beyond that though, there was also a look of unconditional love which I felt beaming back toward me. I only hoped that she too, could see the same reflection in my eyes. With another long embrace, the distance that was once between us, became insignificant. It was as though we'd only seen one another days earlier.

Whilst I was deeply upset by the unexpected passing of my brother, I was also appreciative for that moment of unparalleled connection which my niece and I shared. It was unfortunate, that due to extremely tragic circumstances, I had become reunited with my family. That overwhelming event was one which I never expected to experience. I wanted nothing more than to hold my niece as close as I could and never let her go. I wanted to protect her from the pain she was feeling over the death of her dad. I knew I had to be strong, not only for her, but also for my brother's wife, who was clearly devastated by the loss of her husband. That entire mournful day remained about their grief, not about how our family took different directions, or even why it had occurred.

That was also a day I needed my niece to know that I was there to support and love her. Regardless of how many years I'd missed of her growing up, I needed her to understand that I would become an integral part of her life. That became my time to make up for those lost years which once stood between us. I was going to become the Uncle I wanted her to not only be proud of, but remember for all of the right reasons.

As I had expected, my brother's funeral service was a tremendously painful experience for my niece to endure. She always had a very close relationship with her father. She was, and will always continue to be, 'daddy's little girl', no matter how old she is. I could only empathize with her, as I too, knew what it was like to lose a parent at such a young age. Through my own experience, I encouraged her not to give in to the pain which seemed unrelenting. I wanted to be a beacon of bright light, which would guide her through that unbearable time. I'm also sure her father wouldn't want her to become a victim of her own grief, only to lose her way in life, just as he had regrettably done.

There was also another aspect which made that day even harder for her to deal with. She soon realized the distinct similarities between her father and I. Those were the similar mannerisms and features that my brother and I had always shared, such as our eyes and smile, along with a 'knowing' look that we'd give when we knew something wasn't right. To be honest, neither my brother or I had a very good poker face, so trying to hide our facial expressions was at times, very difficult.

I found it intriguing for my niece to discover those similarities. I don't believe she actually knew just how similar her father and I looked, until that day when I was standing directly in front of her. There still seems to be many times when she looks in to my eyes, only to believe she is seeing her father looking back. In one form or another, I consider that gives her comfort though. I feel honored she can see her father in me, considering he was the man I wanted to grow up to be like. As far as our looks are concerned, I can only thank our wonderful mother for providing us both with her magnificent genetic code.

The day of my brother's funeral became a day which I now often look back upon and celebrate. Certainly not because of his death, but for the bittersweet reunification of my family. It was a terrible shame that it took the death of another family member to bring me closer to bridging the gap between having no family to walk through life with, and being able to make wonderful memories with a family, even more so, with the daughter of my beloved brother.

To this day, I don't have many unresolved regrets in my life. Although, I remain a little disappointed that I missed out on the opportunity of watching that innocent two year old girl grow in to the beautiful lady she has become today, all because of the poor choices I had made earlier in my life.

However, the good fortune now, is that we both live in Melbourne and I can be the Uncle she deserves to have. Because of that, I am truly thankful for the close relationship that she and I share. Our connection is one that continues to be unique to any other relationship that either of us currently have, or will perhaps ever have, throughout our lifetime. We will continue to remain forever united by that eternal bond, family.

Live the Life You Love

Over the years, it's been transparently obvious that my life has taken me down a path which consisted of numerous different twists and turns, for many different reasons. One aspect that has always remained the same though, has been my ability to conquer the most devastating of situations and occurrences. Somehow, by managing to find whatever inner strength I had at those times, I knew that I had to overcome those in tolerable events. I knew that I had to live on, to become a survivor.

As I look back now, I can see there was no wrath quite as grand as my own self-delusion. I thought I had been conditioned to a lifelong sentence of negative mind control from other people, to believe that I was useless. However, more often than not, taking on their negativity was more due to my own control, as opposed to those who I wanted to continue blaming. I realized that it was me who relinquished my spirit to some of those people from my past. That in turn, only allowed others to also take away my power, which they heartlessly used to their advantage to control my every thought. In that heavenly world of hindsight, perhaps I should have used their negative energy to defend my self-worth and successfully prosper from it, on my own terms.

I do believe we all have the ability to rise above adversity, to succeed at whatever we put our minds to. I know from firsthand experience that it is possible to overcome some of the most extreme circumstances that life can test us with. I also know there is nothing *more* important than trying to make our dreams become a reality. What's even *less* important, is believing, or being led to believe that we'll fail or that there is no way of survival. There is no reason to allow that treacherous voice of negativity to hold you back. To be honest, if I can block out those voices and conquer a life which was buried under adversity, trust me when I say, anyone can do it. The reality is, there *are* people who are willing to share their stories, their strength and their knowledge, which will not only help with that master plan for survival, but will assist with achieving the dreams and the personal goals which every person deserves to have fulfilled.

These days, I don't need to look far to find the positive affirmations which remind me that life really is worth living. I am my own living proof. I no longer allow the pessimistic views of other people to dictate my future. I *have* taken control of my independence. I am now living the life I was born to, without the battle scars from the past. I am a survivor, to not only those who wanted to destroy me, but to all the evils which once surrounded me. I also understand that I'm not a lone survivor. Without even knowing it, we encounter people every day who have lived through their own courageous fight to become a living testimony. They too, show that it's possible to survive and go on to live a fruitful life of bliss.

Throughout the latter part of my life, I learned that if I was unable to receive the answers I needed from one person, I continued searching, until I found that one person who could help me. Yet, most of those answers were inside me all the time. Although, sometimes it still takes another person to point them out.

Then again, it was also important for me to realize that I wasted a lot of time seeking answers to questions which could never be explained. Those included questions such as, 'Why me?', but more importantly, those questions which surrounded the passing of my family members. There are situations that happen, which sometimes have no apparent meaning. I believe this is because some circumstances, simply just happen. For me, it was at times better to find a decisive solution, rather than an empty explanation. I find this very philosophy extremely helpful, especially when dealing with a variety of different people.

There's an old saying, *'Haters gonna hate'*, although through my experiences, even those with hearts full of hate, can still find the ability to show compassion to those who reach out for help. Generally speaking, once those so-called 'haters' are willing to conquer their own fears, will they then, be able to genuinely extend their hand of friendship. It's important to remember, people *can* have their opinions changed. Whilst I may not always be able to initially explain why people think the way they do, I can only try to find the solution, which may help to change their perceived point of view.

As human beings, I believe we are all collectively responsible to educate each other, that fear is commonly caused by something we don't understand. It is the entity of the unknown in which fear thrives on. That was an affirmation which I needed those very people who despised me to understand. I only began to realize that myself, when I was at my lowest point in life. By speaking the hardest words through my own fear, I unlocked the truth, which finally set me free. Luckily, it is never too late for people to have their views changed by way of education. By teaching that fear is not an acceptable reason to hate, these people may gain a greater understanding that their concerns are simply brought on by the one aspect that should unite us, our differences.

As I mentioned earlier, education in the classroom is vital, but I believe there is nothing more valuable than the lessons we learn, as we walk through life together. One of the first steps to a better way of education, is to break down the stereotypes and misconceptions which societies have made 'standard belief'. This rule applies to many different aspects, not only those who are same-sex attracted or gender diverse, but any group that society deems as a minority. Perhaps if more community leaders became further informed of the aforementioned 'unknown', they too, could send a strong message to their followers, that acceptance and tolerance are both integral ingredients for unconditional love and understanding. I'm sure we'd all agree that the message of love, speaks louder than that of hate.

To be honest, I believe it's not only those who hold power within the community who need to have a greater under-standing of diversity. We *all* need to be more aware, which in turn, assists us to recognize the individual differences from one other's journey. Only then, do we have the proper insight on how to break down those stereotypes and misconceptions. Along with that, people do need be held accountable for their actions if we wish to achieve a positive outcome. By working together, with whatever recourses we have available to us within our cities, our towns and our communities, we do have the ability to reduce the heinous acts of bullying, anti-social behavior and hate crimes which continue to dominate, throughout the entire world. Subsequently, less people would suffer emotionally, or worse, succumb to their own demise.

The reality is such, that depression, anxiety and stress which is brought on by bullying or challenging circumstances are all very real medical conditions. These can lead anyone in to an emotional state of turmoil, which is not only painful to deal with, but can be soul destroying. The symptoms and cause of these emotions must not be overlooked, nor should they be swept under the carpet and ignored. Human pride should not be a reason or excuse to discount these feelings either. By no means are these feelings, or that 'clouded' state of mind, a sign of weakness or imperfection to anyone's character.

I think what's also extremely important, is that we look after each other by proactively taking the time out from our busy lives to ask those around us, if they are in fact, okay. A few simple words can make the biggest difference to a person who's needing to express themselves. A secret life which is hidden, or buried under upheaval or sorrow, is not the life you, I, or anyone deserves to be living. I sincerely encourage everyone to look deep within their heart and soul, to find the person who they were genuinely born to be, then live true to that very person.

Together, we should admire our own unique qualities and attributes. No matter how 'different' we think we are to one other. Those 'different' *qualities* are what make us stand apart from each other. It is also those *attributes* which others admire about us. Sometimes, *ourselves* are a true reflection of what other people aspire to be, regardless if they are ready to admit it just yet.

I, for one, don't want to live in the shadows again, nor do I want to blend in to the stereotypical impression of what society believes my life should be like. I will no longer live to the expectations of who or what other people think I should be, or who or what they want me to be. Whilst I always embrace new people who come in to my life, I will only welcome those who don't expect me to become a person who I'm not. As far as I'm aware, until proven otherwise, I only get one chance to live this life. I don't want this opportunity to be wasted by living amongst people who only want to change who I am.

Over the years, I honestly do believe most people who have come in to my life, have either entered for a *reason, a season or a lifetime*. For whatever that period of time may have been, I wholeheartedly thank each and every one of them for opening my mind to new experiences and showing me that there are other, more positive ways to live. Without most of them even knowing it, they offered me hope, strength and the salvation which I needed at certain times throughout my life. These are the very people who also challenged my motivation, so that I could become a better person. Without their encouragement, I may still be preoccupied by the darkness of the past, too busy to notice the bright future ahead.

Having said that, I no longer feel the need to divert back to that 'happy escape from reality', at least, certainly not as much as I did. In actual fact, the only reality that *should* matter, is living in the here and now. Of course, there are still occasions where I reflect on past events, but those thoughts don't make me want to change the past. With the wisdom of days gone by, I continue to evolve. Reflection only makes me more positive about living for the future. The past simply inspires me to not be afraid of trying different things or taking on new challenges. It opens my mind, which allows me to embrace even more wonderful unknown possibilities.

Throughout various times along my journey, especially when the road ahead seemed destitute, I always thought I was being rejected from all the good things that life had to offer. Yet, the reality was somewhat different. I now recognize that I was actually being redirected to something even more amazing. Although, perhaps with the path it may have taken, I wasn't always able to see the goodness ahead, until I reached that destination.

There will always be those occasions where I wonder if I'll take the right path in the future. However, with the knowledge and foresight I have now, I can only hope that will be sufficient to guide me in to making the right choices. I realize more than most people, just how unpredictable life can sometimes be. For that reason, I acknowledge that life can still take me on an unbearable course. Nevertheless, I now understand that an unfavorable outcome doesn't need to be a lifelong conviction of adversity, pain and frustration.

The ability to break free from that adverse way of life, which is not fulfilling, is possible, but not always easy. My life today, is very different to that of what my previous *existence* was like from all of those years ago. Yes, of course there are still challenging and defining moments, but as my mom would always say, '*Those things that don't kill us, only make us stronger.*' I'm fortunate to have been able to overcome those odds. My past didn't kill me and I'm only stronger for living those experiences.

Above all, I now understand that I have many of life's gifts to be grateful for, both big and small. This includes having a small group of very close friends who appreciate my inner qualities. They ask for nothing in return, except for my friendship and loyalty, which is given tenfold in return. Some of these people don't live in the same city as I do, nor do I see them as much as I would like, but whether they're near or far, our camaraderie and our mutual memories mean more to me than they will ever realize. We all share an honest relationship, which I wouldn't change for anything in the world. They have all endlessly encouraged my endeavors and continue to support whatever crazy antics I sometimes find myself becoming involved with.

In addition, I'm extremely thankful to the man I met through that advertisement I placed in the gay newspaper, all of those years ago. As you're aware, he and I *did* start a relationship, which was at times, very challenging for us both. Although, I still believe it was more difficult for him, because of my unrelenting insecurities. Having said that, I learned a lot about myself, because of him. There are no words that seem adequate to sincerely thank him for his deep compassion and his boundless tenacity. He inspired me at times, which I thought were despairing and hopeless. Without his guidance at that time, I certainly would not be where I am today.

On August 26th 2015, he and I will celebrate our eighteenth year anniversary as a couple. I look back on those early days and truly believe that divine intervention played a leading role, in what has turned out to be the very best years of my entire life. He has been and continues to be, the partner I always dreamed of sharing my life with. We have shared many incredible experiences together, including that fantasy of my youth, traveling to overseas counties.

Over the years, he has also further encouraged my desire to understand more about Science Fiction. I am now proud to admit that I'm a fan of almost every 'Star Trek' series and movie ever made, especially 'Star Trek Voyager'. I only hope that we can continue to learn more from one another and share many more wonderful years together. I cannot thank him enough for being the person he is, but also for the person that I've become, because of him. We are both, truly blessed.

Whether or not you believe same sex couples have the right to marry, I ask that you consider the following. My partner and I have been fortunate enough to share a life that some people only dream of living. I am both honored and humbled to share my life with him. However, our sexual orientation doesn't define the life we share together. It certainly doesn't intrude on other people's lifestyles either. All we ask, is to be given the same overall equality to that of any heterosexual couples, *should* we choose to legally celebrate our union.

If the truth be known, in many respects, we already do live that same life which many heterosexual couples do, excluding the legal equality. We have a built a life together, which is both adoring and committed. We also share our home with our two beautiful cats and our two gorgeous dogs, but no white picket fence, yet! After many years of inner city living, we now choose to live happily in the suburbs. Because of that, we have the best of both worlds by living close enough to the city life, but being far enough away to enjoy the sanctuary of suburbia. In fact, the perception of our lifestyle, from what some people seem to think it is, is a far cry from the real life we actually do lead.

If anything, I understand from firsthand experience, that love *does not* discriminate between sexual preferences, nor does it only allow certain individuals to experience it. I believe love is, and will continue to be, louder and stronger than any political opinion or religious point of view. Love is shared without conditions, boundaries or prejudice. True love between consenting adults should be celebrated, regardless of gender or sexual identity. I only wish other people, particularly those in authority, who haven't yet caught on, both here in Australia and around the world, could understand that very simple concept too.

It has only been within recent times that my life has again, taken on yet another new challenge. However, this is a challenge which has been one of the most uplifting and rewarding to date. My partner and I opened our hearts and our home to the exciting and wondrous world of foster care. By becoming accredited foster parents, we've learned just how much can sometimes be missing in some people's lives, such as the basics of having a proper support network of friends to help these people when they need it most. This is not only relevant to the children that we may have in our care, but to their entire family.

As a matter of fact, one of the biggest *misconceptions* which we continue to hear, is that these children only come in to care because their parents are drug affected or abusive toward their children. Whilst we haven't personally been exposed to any undesirable or explosive family situations, granted, there are those instances, however those type of examples are certainly not always the case. There are many different positive reasons why parents *choose* to place their children in to a range of different foster care programs.

For us to be able to provide a stable, loving and supportive environment for a child, is one of the most extraordinary experiences I could ever describe. Whether we have these children for a night or a weekend, there is so much joy in knowing that we can share new experiences and bring hope in to that child's world, without expectation. At the same time, I too, have learned many things about myself from those children.

I understand more than most, unfortunately, children don't always live up to their parent's expectations throughout life. However, by allowing a child to live up to *their own* expectations, I'm permitting them to form their own individuality. I know all too well, life is not about living to the expectations of others, it's about exceeding our own expectations. Even in the short amount of time we may share with these kids, I hope to encourage them to surpass *their own* expectations also. This will hopefully mean that they will one day go on to achieve the great success they deserve, without holding onto that crippling fear of failure.

I believe all children have the right to grow up to be who they want to become. More importantly, who they were born to be. That same principle also applies to adults. For that to happen though, firstly, we must all be given the right tools and knowledge to make the right decisions in life, without any preconceived bias. If we don't make the right choice to begin with, we need to know that we are supported and encouraged to not give up and keep trying until we become the masters our own destiny.

As much as we love having those foster children stay with us, sadly, my partner and I have both been exposed to some people in society who believe same sex couples shouldn't have the *right* to raise or to look after children. To me this poses many questions, which when asked, usually result in unfounded explanations from *those* who so loudly voice their negative opinion. An example of what we hear, albeit from the minority, is that if same sex couples raise children, there's a chance the child may be exposed to homosexuality and inevitably grow up gay. I'll also point out that it's still believed by that same minority, that my sexual preference is a 'choice' and that I *decided* to live the life of being same sex attracted.

Whilst I can only speak for myself, I *know* I'm not alone when I say that both of my parents were in fact, heterosexual. If it is to be assumed that two people of the same sexual orientation should raise a child to inherit the same sexual preference as their parents, then I must ask the question, *'Why aren't I straight?'* Considering, I was exposed to heterosexuality when I was raised by a loving heterosexual couple for many years.

Once again, only speaking for myself, but I believe that I was born gay. I may not have known I was until later in my childhood, but I never recall a certain day which I *decided* that I would be gay for the rest of my life. I often wonder when *that* defining day was for heterosexual people. Did they too, decide that they were in fact, going to be heterosexual? Was it a conscious decision, or was it the life they were born to live?

Personally, I'm not sure why anyone would willingly decide to *choose* a life which had the potential to leave them open to receiving the incredibly demoralizing elements of hatred, not only from strangers, but also from their immediate family. I don't see any value with anyone making that supposed *choice* of sexual or gender identity. Albeit, people's attitudes *are* slowly changing. People *are* becoming more educated about the different aspects of sexual and gender diversity. Unfortunately though, there still continues to be an unfair negative cognition towards both sexual and gender diverse people, from strangers and their own family members alike. I can't help but wonder, when will society wake up and realize the importance, of *not* making issues out of other peoples' lives, who simply want to be themselves.

Is the fear of that 'unknown' I spoke of earlier, too much for some people to deal with? Why do people become so angry at the thought of those who only want to live true to who they are? Is it perhaps because in the heart of their anger, lives fear and ignorance? Sadly what's also evident, is that it seems effortless for some people to celebrate the tragic death of another human being, who again, only wants to be accepted as themselves, without having to live that anonymous unknown life in the shadows. If only those same ignorant people *chose* to open their mind and understand the value of humanity, they may one day, be able to courageously save someone's life.

The choices that are important are those which will enhance our lives and lead to a greater sense of understanding and contentment, so we can hopefully better ourselves and those around us. I hope to inspire and support others to make positive choices. I choose to have an optimistic outlook on life, along with the encouragement for other people to live the life which makes them happy. No one deserves to feel as though they're not equal to any other human being. Whilst we all have different dreams and desires throughout life, I believe we all need to be validated and celebrated by one another, regardless of our sexual orientation or gender.

Even from those early years where 'Angela' was introduced to the world, twenty-five years on, drag has not only validated many decisions I've made, but still allows me to reach out to people in ways that I would never have believed possible. I am also very fortunate that my sub-figure of drag was accepted by my partner many years ago. Although our home is only big enough for one drag diva, he continues to support and encourage the dragalicious journey, which has been one of personal growth and fulfillment.

Throughout my years of drag, before 'Skye High', there had been many other different incantations of 'Angela'. That was dependent on whether I changed my look, or even my attitude. Whilst some of those other representations never made it in to the real world, it was a learning curve nevertheless. Even today, I use drag as a journey of discovery, one which still continues to be filled with trial and error.

Over the years, the more I grew as a person, the more my alter ego had also grown alongside me. I realized there was no need to continue adopting the character of 'Angela'. *She* had already served *her* purpose. 'Angela' allowed 'Skye High' to come to life which in turn, meant that 'Angela' then became the vehicle which catapulted the combination of my own personality and that new creation to a brand new elevation.

More now than ever before, I truly appreciate how important it is for me to be a true representation of myself. Even with the wigs, high heels and make-up on, I've still been able to remain comfortable within my own skin, whilst taking on a different outward appearance. To be honest, my drag identity and I have a very clear understanding, which is very black and white. Without me, *she* doesn't exist. Consequently, we have become an amalgamated duo which lives in unison with one another.

Some of the drag queens, who I've known over the years, liked to dress to the character they played. Whilst there is certainly nothing wrong with that, I learned that in order for me to continue my personal growth, I considered it was necessary to tailor my alter ego around my own beliefs and my own personality. That was, and will continue to be, a slight point of difference which helps to advance my own personal development. With that insight, it has greatly assisted with becoming the person that I am today, both in and out of drag. I realized I no longer wanted to dress up and become a different person. I only wanted to dress up and take on a different outward impression of myself.

I compare this analogy to when I'm dressing up for a special occasion as a boy. Just because I wear a tailored suit, it doesn't change my personality. It does however, make me look different from just wearing jeans and a sweatshirt. Regardless if I'm in drag or not, I still remain the same person on the inside, with the same beliefs and the same goals. It's only how I construct my look from the outside which makes me appear differently. To be honest, the only real difference between me and *her*, is that *she* can make more of a physical statement, but the words *she* speaks, belong to the boy under the drag. Funnily enough, people tend to respond more openly with *her*, because of *her* overwhelming presence.

Nevertheless, the glorious art form that is drag can bring out an expressive and personal style which only the person wearing it can decide who they are, how they want to look or who they want to be. I personally celebrate all variations of drag and all the different interpretations of how it's delivered. Each and every drag queen brings a unique grace and style to their own individual personality or character. Although one thing is certain, no matter what style of drag the queen is wearing, *she* will have *her* head held high looking fabulous to the extreme, as *she* captivates a crowd from near and far.

I believe there are a variety of reasons why people are not only captivated by, but also drawn to drag queens. For the most part, I think some people are just fascinated by a 'larger than life' personality. Perhaps another reason is because they are either curious about drag themselves, or maybe they just need to escape their own lives and be around a person who can provide humorous entertainment, without the concern of facing rejection from other people. For whatever the reason people tend to gravitate toward drag queens, drag has and will continue to have a well-deserved place, not only within the gay scene, but just as importantly, throughout mainstream society. This aspect of the gay lifestyle should have the same visibility as all of the other colors which make up the LGBT community.

From the very first time, one of my most favorite aspects of drag is having people take the time to speak to me, without pretense or expectation. I continue to be inspired throughout my drag career by people who are drawn to me and recognize that I am easy to talk to. Personally, I appreciate the compliments, comments and sometimes, very in-depth conversations I find myself embroiled in, with an array of many different people. These are the very people who allow me to continue doing what I love to do.

Over the years, I quickly learned that a large part of the territory for being a drag queen is there are occasions whereby people can sometimes see you as a role model, their best friend or even a counselor. Again, I personally see that as a positive affirmation. I enjoy learning and accepting the sometimes varied views of other people. I also enjoy hearing stories of someone's unique journey, which led *them* to where *they* are today. I welcome the opportunity to celebrate *their* success. We should all commend one another for living the journey we have thus far.

After all, many of us have had to walk that same harsh road at some point in our lives, for one reason or another.

Unfortunately though, as much as I have the desire to embrace our differences, I have been exposed to people who have been very unwelcoming towards drag queens. As much as it saddens me to admit, there are even some people, from within my very own gay community, who believe drag queens diminish the masculinity of gay men, or perhaps in some way, degrade the values of the LGBT community. Not only do they have a negative attitude toward the acceptance of drag queens, some of those same people would like nothing more than to see them disappear, or in some extreme cases, be dealt with in a particularly negative fashion.

It's noted that those who display that kind of hatred towards not only drag queens, but also to other people from within the same community as themselves, are becoming the minority. I simply cannot understand the notion that some people, especially those within the LGBT community, have such overt phobias toward other LGBT people. I firmly believe that it's important to embrace sexual and gender diversity in all of its glory, without having a double standard attached. How can any one person seek true acceptance from any other person, when they're not tolerant themselves? The golden rule which needs to be enforced is, that the aspiration for equality and acceptance must be rightfully recognized for all. This rule should be applied to which ever community, society or side of the fence anyone sits on.

Having said that, I understand for some people, acceptance and equality can be seen as a matter of perspective, which may also be subjective. However my question to that is, *'Don't we all want to live in a world whereby everything is equal for everybody, so we can all benefit?'* I never realized that some people still continue to depict a grey area when it comes to the basic fundamentals of human rights. For me, as a gay man *and* as a drag queen, there is nothing greater or more crucial than projecting a positive image of strength and pride, whilst promoting a unified message of parity. Unfortunately though, throughout some of my own experiences, the low level of acceptance and tolerance from society, has at times, been trying.

I appreciate that it has been difficult for many other people too, through hearing their stories. There are, and still continues to be, a countless number of people who have had, or are currently having, their lives callously shattered by inequality and injustice. It's because of that very reason, we must never give up on using our collective voice, so other people don't have to suffer that same fate. What's just as important, is never giving up on ourselves or giving in to the belief that because of an 'alleged' difference, that we can only be offered the entitlements of a second class citizen. I have been there. I truly understand how damaging it is when people disregard or degrade you for being different, or even for thinking outside the societal square.

Once upon a time, throughout my youth and in to my adolescence, I wanted to be fabulous. Whilst there were many times I allowed that notion to slip away, I believe a power from within, or another inexplicable force, kept me going. Now, being fabulous isn't enough. I want to be known as a fabulous public figure who visibly upholds the rights of those who society deem as a minority. I believe even those in a minority can have a much louder voice, than those who claim their collective is holy or just. It is important I continue to surround myself with people who also want to project a bright guiding light, to 'The Land of Fabulousness' and beyond.

Without the support and encouraging wisdom of those who also want to make changes to this world, I may not have found the harmonious balance that I currently have in my life. This balance was where I first became more accepting of the circumstance and diversification of others. This in turn, gave me the liberation to believe I could actually rid myself of the perils from the past. I finally found the road which would set me free. I reached the pinnacle of truly celebrating my own differences, along with the differences of others, with a humble sense of pride.

Throughout years of soul searching and battling internal demons, I realized *'The Road To Fabulousness'* takes on many different variations. Whilst the people I've had enter my life have greatly assisted with my journey so far, not all relationships have been so favorable. However, believe it or not, I still remain thankful to my ex-housemate, who at that time, helped me to discover drag. Regardless of how our friendship ended, his influence and perceptiveness brought out a part of me which may never have otherwise existed.

Since having to emotionally turn my life upside down, the best advice I could give anyone is, if you're confronted by a person who seems different to yourself, it's important to remember that there's no threat involved. It may only be a perception of what *they* believe the difference is. The discovery of a greater education sometimes only needs to start with a simple, *'hello.'* If I had remained closed off to new people who seemed different to me, I would never have enjoyed wonderful new experiences. I also wouldn't have appreciated the similarities which we shared, and still do continue to share.

I now understand that when we step back from our own life and see how other people live, whilst there may be dramatic differences, there are also vast similarities which unite us all. We all laugh, we all feel pain, we all bleed, but most of all, we have that all important ability to accept each other and to love one another, without bias.

I don't believe any person is born with a phobia, fear or judgment toward other people. I believe these are all attributes which have been inherited through different environments or circumstances. If you believe that you need to make environmental changes, or even make slight modifications from within, you can. It all starts with the faith that you *can* and *will* make those changes. After all, life *is* short. There's no need to continue wasting precious seconds with not being happy. Start enjoying the wanderlust of the journey, before the final destination is reached.

With the changes I made, 'Angela' has now long gone. 'Skye High' is now on *her* way to becoming that public figure of sovereignty. *She* continues to be inspired by those *she* surrounds *herself* with, but just as importantly, by those who surround me, who continue to instill a sense of humility back in to my life. I am very thankful that 'Skye High' has, and will continue, to provide that positive guiding light to the very person underneath the drag, who gives *her* life, me.

Today, 'Skye High' has become one of Australia's leading drag queens. *She's* been seen presenting on Melbourne's only LGBT television program, along with being a successful media personality, animal activists, human rights campaigner and anti-bullying advocate. *She* has a voice that doesn't speak alone, but rather, articulates in unison with many other voices, who are also just as committed to making the world we live in, a safer and more tolerant place for everybody. With tireless efforts and unwavering support of other likeminded people and organizations which share *her* passion and tenacious attitude, a new and positive way forward is being paved.

There are now numerous avenues, worldwide, for people who struggle with their own diversity, to finally learn how to live the life they love, whilst gaining the acceptance they seek, away from a life of bullying. In cooperation with these various support networks, we all have the ability to stop the 'bystander culture' which has slowly been taking over our societies. By *not* living in silence, we can further encourage our family, our friends, our neighbors and our communities to speak up and put an end to the bullying and acts of degradation, which may even affect someone in your life, who right at this very minute, may be feeling alone and suffering quietly.

I feel as though I have a responsibility, as a part of my journey, to encourage people to live their lives with a sense of new found determination. By doing this, I hope they will one day regain their independence, which will bring them closer to reuniting themselves with their own self-worth. Because of this, 'Skye High' will continue to be an ambassador and speak on behalf of those who experience prejudice and discrimination.

Even though this journey is only a snippet of what my life has been thus far, there have been other situations which I chose not to write about, for many different reasons. The main reason however, is because I not only wanted to highlight some of the most joyous memories I have, but also describe some of the most excruciating memories of my past and how I survived to tell this tale.

Whilst this book wasn't written to be a 'self-help' book for anyone, it is rather, a journey of experiences. One that can be used to empower others who may suffer some of the same realities throughout their lives.

My story serves as a celebration of who I have now become, compared to who I was. I chose to continue making those life changing decisions, which enabled me to create a better quality of life. I now hope to inspire those who read my journey to do the same. This also applies to parents or friends of those affected by adversity, who may need to understand firsthand what it can be like to fight, a sometimes losing battle of acceptance.

If there's one reoccurring theme throughout these pages, I hope it's the demonstration that it is actually possible to break free, away from a life of obscurity. Every dream, every hope and every ambition that we want to see succeed is worth working hard to achieve. Life is short and there are no guarantees, but we must make the most of every opportunity that's presented to us. If we're prepared to take that all important chance on following our heart, our spirit will certainly follow. Therefore, we will positively achieve the greatness we strive for. The result of such, will be a powerful and pure reward. The key that will unlock the door to that success, is to never give up on being true to who you are and what you believe.

My only wish, is that the resilience and bravery throughout these pages will now resonate to help someone else who may need guidance or positive affirmation to be able to justly love the life they live. I trust that throughout my insights, a glimmer of that beautiful shining light of hope can now be seen. If my journey can stop one person harming themselves, or worse, ending their life, because they believe they are alone, or that nobody will understand their story, then I believe my voice has been successful.

If you feel as though you're being bullied or mistreated because you're 'different', or perhaps you just need to reach out for the kindness of another person, make the time to share your story with someone who will listen. It's never too late to find that *one* person who can change you, for *a reason, a season or a lifetime.*

Living in a world of darkness doesn't mean we must surrender, but to survive, we all need to occasionally unleash our very own diva from within. With encouragement and support from other people, you *can* find the courage, to battle your way out of that darkness.

LIVE THE LIFE YOU LOVE – LOVE THE LIFE YOU LIVE

Thank you so much for allowing me to share my story with you.

Do you want to keep up to date with all of the latest Skye High news? If so, check out these sites.

www.misshighskye.com
www.twitter.com/@misshighskye
www.Facebook.com/MissHighSkye

A Reason, A Season, or A Lifetime

People come in to your life for a reason, a season or a lifetime.
When you figure out which one it is,
you will know what to do for each person.

When someone is in your life for a REASON,
it is usually to meet a need you have expressed.
They have come to assist you through a difficulty;
to provide you with guidance and support;
to aid you physically, emotionally or spiritually.
They may seem like a godsend, and they are.
They are there for the reason you need them to be.
Then, without any wrongdoing on your part or at an
inconvenient time,
this person will say or do something to bring the relationship to
an end.
Sometimes they die. Sometimes they walk away.
Sometimes they act up and force you to take a stand.
What we must realize is that our need has been met, our desire
fulfilled; their work is done. The prayer you sent up has been
answered and now it is time to move on.

Some people come in to your life for a SEASON,
because your turn has come to share, grow or learn.
They bring you an experience of peace or make you laugh.
They may teach you something you have never done.
They usually give you an unbelievable amount of joy.

Believe it. It is real. But only for a season.

LIFETIME relationships teach you lifetime lessons;
things you must build upon in order to have a solid emotional
foundation.
Your job is to accept the lesson, love the person,
and put what you have learned to use in all other relationships
and areas of your life.
It is said that love is blind but friendship is clairvoyant.

~ Unknown Author

BOOKS

O is a symbol of the world, of oneness and unity; this eye represents knowledge and insight. We publish titles on general spirituality and living a spiritual life. We aim to inform and help you on your own journey in this life.

Visit our website: http://www.o-books.com

Find us on Facebook:
https://www.facebook.com/OBooks

Follow us on Twitter: @obooks